# THE INSIDER'S GUIDE TO MATCH-FIXING IN FOOTBALL

DECLAN HILL

ISBN 978-0-9918238-4-0



**Publisher** Anne McDermid & Associates Ltd. **Book Design** Daykin & Storey Ltd.

TO THOSE WHO BELIEVE IN THE GAME AND
ARE FIGHTING TO KEEP IT BEAUTIFUL.

# CONTENTS

## PART THREE: THE SYSTEMS OF CORRUPTION

# FOREWORD

The front gate of the Nafplio medium-security prison is one of the new faces of international sport. There is a set of gates embedded in high concrete walls topped with barbed wire. Behind these gates is an empty yard and then another heavier, thicker steel door. The prison is in the Peloponnese area of Greece. It is a region soaked in history. King Agamemnon launched the Trojan War from his fortress 20 miles up the Peloponnesian valley at the back of the prison. There are medieval castles that dot the entire area, along with classical theatres and ancient ruins. When I visited in December 2011, the orange trees were in full bloom. The fruit, like globes of golden light that lit up the trees, were largely unpicked. The economic disaster of the Eurozone crisis had hit and in most cases it was not profitable for the farmers to pick their own crop.

I waited for hours at the front gate while the prison governor contemplated allowing me into the jail. Behind the walls there were, presumably, phone calls going back and forth to Athens, but in front there was a large crowd of families waiting to see their loved ones. They were an international lot. A concerned Greek father whose grave, bearded face made him look like a Platonic philosopher strode up and down the road. Next to him Roma children played happily in the dust. While a family of worried Afghan refugees begged the guards to let them bring in food.

When I was finally allowed into the prison, the crowd had left and it was darkening into a frozen, wet night. I was searched and then let through the first gate. A cold rain swept across the deserted yard. The guard from the inside doors signalled and I walked into the prison.

As the heavy steel door clanged behind me, I was brought into a typically warm Greek welcome. The prison had been built to house a few hundred men, but it was now crammed with twice as many inmates. However, the guards and prisoners had all the usual Greek charm. They shook my hand, offered me coffees and apologized for the long wait. There was a labour action going on inside the prison, the warders were protesting about the conditions and that had played a part in the slowness of allowing me into the prison.

I was escorted past more heavy doors, down a dingy corridor and into a long interrogation room. The walls of the room were discoloured and peeling, there was a table in the middle of the room and across from me sat Achilleas Beos.

In the midst of their national bankruptcy crisis of the summer of 2011, the Greek anti-corruption bureau, aligned with the Secret Service and National Police Force — had moved into Greek football and arrested over sixty players, coaches and sports officials. The scandal dominated their political stage. At the centre of the investigation were three team-owners who were accused of fixing matches, sometimes in connection with Asian match-fixers.

Achilleas Beos was one of those owners. He is a large man, unshaven and untidily dressed: but deeply intelligent and furious for being in an overcrowded, dirty prison without a trial for six months.

I sat down. At that point, he had spoken to no other journalists. We shook hands and he began to speak.

Achilleas Beos is accused of being part of a revolution that is transforming the sports world. It is a network of crime running across countries and continents. If Beos had been the only alleged corruptor in prison for sports related fixing, it would be bad news for the Greek league, but for few other countries. Sadly, however, the Greek investigation is only a very small part in a revolution that is threatening modern sport.

In the last five years, over one-thousand events in dozens of different sports — from top-level soccer games to Olympic badminton matches to international cricket competitions — have been fixed. Hundreds of athletes, coaches, referees and gamblers have been arrested. It is a revolution in sport that reaches from dingy bookmakers on the streets of Asia to some of the largest stadiums in the world.

This book is about that revolution.

This is an academic book. It is about the structure and function of the corruption that threatens sport. It is not about sensational scandals or new revelations of corruption. You will find many hints and details of those stories, but the main purpose of the book is to explain the motives, means and methods of the people inside today's match-fixing.

However, this is an academic book for non-academics. I have tried to write it clearly and simply. I come from a long line of professors going back several generations. The current academic world is swimming through a difficult tide, where it is often felt that the more obscure the language, the deeper the thought. My forefathers would be ashamed if I wrote in that fashion. My great-grandfather taught rhetoric or the ability to explain complicated ideas in simple words. This book is written in his spirit. Hopefully, there are no places in the text that someone, without a specific background in sociology, criminology or statistics cannot understand what is going on.

The first part of the book *The Nuts and Bolts of Corruption* is about definitions and explores the basic questions about this form of sports corruption. In this section, I lay out the reasons of why and how to study the subject properly. Then there is an examination of some basic definitions and concepts that can help give clarity to the phenomenon.

The second part of the book *The People of the Game* is about the people inside the corrupt deals: the players, coaches, referees and corruptors. This section is an examination of their work: how they put together fixes and why they take this action.

The third part of the book *The Systems of Corruption* is about the sports leagues where corruption has become normal rather than exceptional. It explores why those conditions come about and ends with the good news that there is much that can be done to stop this corruption.

The overall thesis of the book is that rational choice (or the idea that people mostly do things for their own self-interest) is one of the prime motivations for corruption. On the other side of the argument are people who claim that corruption is about culture. In their view, most Mexicans are likely to be more honest than most Africans, who in turn are likely to be more honest than most Afghanis.

It is an argument I have heard over many years from many different journalists who interview me to find out how *other* cultures are fixing their sporting events. I have received calls from Belgians, Canadians, Englishmen, Germans, South Koreans, Scandinavians and a whole range of other countries who tell me that their athletes would *never* fix matches and corruption is the problem of what Albert Camus (who along with being a French philosopher was also a very good goalkeeper) would call "the other" or some nameless, morally-challenged foreigner. I think this argument is, for the most part, racist nonsense.

I argue throughout the book that widespread match-fixing in sports does not depend on nationality or culture. Rather, it depends on a set of specific circumstances. Given those circumstances, some people in all countries will become corrupt. Remove those specific circumstances and levels of corruption will decrease.

The book is an attempt to identify what *are* those specific circumstances that lead to widespread corruption. They can be applied to other areas than football. Given similar circumstances, people in different cultures will act in similar ways. For example, one of the factors that helps corruption spread is not paying the workers their salaries. Rip off a group of English football players, and some of them will try to cheat just as surely as Mexican policemen or African customs officials would do. Pay a doctor relatively badly and they will be more likely to accept kickbacks from a dishonest pharmaceutical salesman be it in Afghanistan, Greece or Canada.

Much of this book was written at the University of Oxford at an extraordinary centre for research into corruption studies and what is called "informal governance". This is a fancy term for how organised crime governs an area. For example, I was conducting research in the Mathare slum of Nairobi, Kenya in January 2007. Mathare is a tough place. It is full of many good people living amongst garbage, little proper sewage or other facilities. At the same time the *World Social Forum* — a meeting of international civic charities — was gathering in the city. The then-mayor of Nairobi, Dick Wathika, made a speech where he spoke about the challenges of governing the city of 3.5 million. What is striking is how little of that city the mayor actually governed.

There are two large slums in Nairobi — Mathare and Kibera — they have hundreds-of-thousands of people living in them and are largely no-go zones for government officials. The areas are ruled by a collection of organised crime mobs and mafias. Morally, it may be a dreadful thing that criminals govern so many people, but the question is *how* do they govern these areas? What are the rules and laws of living in a society controlled by organised criminals?

The research centre at Oxford was an attempt to analyse these rules of the mob. My fellow researchers were a fascinating lot. There was Peter Hill, the James Bond of our department. Hill, a Scotsman, is an ex-paratrooper who was one of the world's academic experts on the Yakuza or Japanese mafia. Hill often began his day by practicing with other Karate black belts. He studied the Yamaguchi-gumi clan of the Yakuza and has written one of the definitive books on their structure. Another researcher was Heather Hamill. She is a glamorous redhead with buckets of Northern Irish charm (one of her coffee mugs read, "It is not gossip, but social networking"). Hamill is so ebullient that it would be easy to miss that her doctoral thesis involved interviewing young men who had had their kneecaps shot off by the ultra-violent wing of the Irish Republican Army (IRA) — on some of the less safe streets of Belfast. Federico Varese, whose work on the Vor v zakone or original Russian mafiya, has been extensively used by the great British writer John le Carré.

At the head of this small group was Diego Gambetta. Gambetta is one of the foremost academic experts on issues like the Sicilian mafia or suicide bombers. Together they were an intellectually formidable, but very friendly, group. Afternoon tea breaks, were times of chats about subjects like media manipulation by Belfast street-thugs, the existence of a medieval English martial art that was close to the fighting-style of modern-day football hooligans or how Japanese mobsters have a proclivity for Andean pipe music.

---

Achilleas Beos had been charged by the Greek police with conspiring with an unnamed set of Asian gamblers to fix games of his team. When we spoke, Beos indignantly denied any of these accusations. He claimed he had never worked with Asian fixers. "Who are these Asian people I am supposed to have communicated with?"

When I asked him specifically if he had ever fixed a game. He looked at me, shrugged, and said, "I have done what any owner of a Greek football team would do for his club. You understand? But I have never done anything on the gambling market with Asian bookmakers."

I was not sure if Beos meant that he had fixed games, but not to profit on the gambling market, or merely indulged in a benign form of creative accountancy. When I asked, he shrugged again and stated that he loved his team and would never do anything criminal.

There is no judicially-approved evidence that Beos fixed any matches. He was, finally, released on bail seven months later. At the time of publication, his trial has been delayed as neither he nor his accusers showed up in court, and all charges against him are unproven.

This is the danger for sport: that potentially innocent people and innocent matches will automatically be assumed to be corrupt. That no longer will the fans assume that they have witnessed unbelievable accomplishments, but they will simply not believe in sport anymore. They will give up on football. It will be abandoned as lacking in credibility to be replaced by a sport that has better protected its integrity.

In the years since I began researching this topic, much has changed. At the beginning of the work, it was difficult to get much attention to the rising danger to international sports. Now — world-wide — there are over thirty national police investigations into match-corruption: more than a thousand sports events are alleged to have been fixed and hundreds of players, coaches and officials have been arrested. More seriously, there have been dozens of suspicious deaths and a series of tragic suicides linked to this phenomenon. There is no sign that this tide of corruption is slowing. Rather it may be getting worse. The research for this book was, obviously, at times difficult and dangerous: but I hope it may help to prevent the spread of corruption and preserve sport for our children.

# PART ONE
# NUTS AND BOLTS OF CORRUPTION

# CHAPTER ONE
# WHY STUDY MATCH-FIXING

*Now there is a new danger coming up that almost all countries have been affected by and that is corruption, match-fixing and illegal gambling. This is the new fight we have to confront it.*

*Jacques Rogge, former-President International Olympic Committee (IOC), July 2011*

There is a set of monuments to sports corruption. They are outside the ruins of the ancient Olympic stadium in Greece and were built with the fines levied on athletes and coaches who were caught cheating or fixing at the games. So sports corruption has a long history, back over two thousand years to the original Games of our spiritual forefathers.

However, we of this generation are facing something almost entirely new. It is a new form of match-fixing as if someone has taken fixing and injected it with the steroid of globalisation. It is an utterly modern phenomenon and it will destroy sport, as we know it.

This new form of match-fixing is sweeping through sports. It has destroyed many sports across Asia. It is threatening tennis, cricket, football and a host of other European sports. This wave of corruption is also lapping at the doors of

North American sports. To help understand, and thus prevent more corruption, the study of fixing in sports is one of absolute urgency.

This book is an exploration of that new threat to international sport. We need to be able to understand how this wave of corruption actually functions to be able to protect our sports.

If you are a sports fan, than you know why you should care about this phenomenon.

However, there are also profoundly important, academic reasons to study match-fixing in football. Even if you are a scholar who has absolutely no interest in sports, it is worth your time to read this book. This chapter is for you. Football and sports fans, if you are not interested in academic discussion or statistical analysis — skip the first four chapters. Go ahead! No one will notice, but to criminologists and other academics these first chapters outline the reasons why you should care about the study of corruption in football.

## Why Study Match-Fixing in Football?

First, football is a big business. As an industry it is estimated to be worth around £125 billion a year worldwide. In 2013, just one club — Manchester United in England was valued on the New York Stock Exchange at $2.3 billion dollars; and the television rights for the league that Manchester United plays in — the Premier League — sold for over £5 billion in worldwide television rights. As an employer, football employs millions of people directly and tens of millions indirectly in the international gambling and leisure industries. The betting market on one football event — the World Cup Finals in 2002 — was estimated to be £11 billion (B14). Interest in the final match of the World Cup 2006 was so great that it was watched by 5% of all people who have ever lived.

The sport also has tremendous symbolic power. The British Labour politician Gerry Sutcliffe once declared, "Football is not just an industry. It has more in common with the National Gallery and St. Paul's Cathedral… it is a national treasure." In Barcelona, for example, the city's most visited museum is not the Museu Picasso, but the Barça museum dedicated to the Barcelona Football Club. According to the Fédération International de Football Association (FIFA), the world governing body of the sport, "the extended football family makes up one fifth of the world's population…1,200 million people, including 200 million players". The faces and names of the best players of those 200 million are known throughout the world. In fact, the 1994 World Cup finals were watched by a cumulative television audience of 31 billion people — more than four times the total population of the world.

George Orwell — upon watching the furore generated by the 1945 tour of the United Kingdom by a Soviet football team — described international football as "mimic warfare". There have been actual wars fought over the sport: men die both watching and playing it every year; and women are frequently beaten to death because of it.

As one European sports officials, interviewed for this research stated:

> *People lose their heads over football. They do things for football that you would not believe: they wouldn't do these things in their normal business or for their families or for a woman but for football they will do strange things.*

The interview subject was not just discussing football. He was also discussing the seed of corruption that lies at the heart of this huge industry: match-fixing. In the last five years the professional football leagues of Croatia, Turkey, Belgium, Germany, Italy, Switzerland, Poland, Greece, Israel, Hong Kong, Singapore, Malaysia and at least twenty-seven other countries have all suffered from documented cases of games being fixed. The gambling public has been defrauded of hundreds of millions of pounds and the essential credibility of the sport has — at times — been questioned. Yet, for all the scandals virtually no scholarly work has analysed football match-fixing.

However, in the specific academic field of corruption studies, an examination of football match-fixing is also of immense value

## The School of Corruption

Corruption studies is a loose academic grouping of economists, criminologists and other social studies who attempt to analyse how and why corruption occurs. The field was catalysed by two events in the late-1990s. The first was the speech by the then-World Bank President James D. Wolfensohn, who spoke about the "cancer of corruption" diverting resources from the poor to the rich, distorting public expenditure and deterring foreign investment.

The second was the development by a young German economist — Johann Lambsdorff — of the Corruption Perceptions Index (CPI). The CPI ranks most of the countries in the world by how corrupt they are perceived to be. The CPI is used widely by the prominent anti-corruption group *Transparency International* and, for the first time it gave social scientists some ability to measure a nation's corruption.

There had been a great deal of research on corruption before this time, from the work of the neo-institutional economists and the political scientist Susan Rose-Ackerman, but those two events led to an explosion in the academic literature on corruption.

However, no sooner was the academic ship of corruption studies loaded and began to sail out of the harbour, then it ran aground on a fundamental problem of definition: what exactly *is* corruption?

Corruption exists and has existed in all societies. Yet arriving at a precise definition of what corruption actually consists of, is a problem that has dogged much of the literature on the subject. For example, there is no set of clearly defined rules that demonstrates the difference between a gift and a bribe. The person who started much of the current-day study of the field — Susan Rose-Ackerman — even wrote that a "one size fits all model" of corruption simply does not exist, "but must be applied with a sensitive appreciation of an individual country's conditions".

Her analysis is a continuation of a discussion that was originally developed by French anthropologists like Claude Lévi-Strauss and Marcel Mauss, who examined the question — "what is a gift?" A question asked by anyone who has ever received a dreadful looking tie from their brother-in-law or more pertinently when someone gives you a gift in a business setting, does that mean they want something in return?

There is a further question that makes the study of corruption difficult: where does legitimate survival end and corruption begin? For example the Russian academic, Alena V. Ledeneva and others argue in their work, *Bribery and Blat in Russia: Negotiating Reciprocity from the Middle Ages to the 1990s*, that to outsiders *blat* in Russian society may seem like corruption, but to a native Russian there is a subtle, but important difference:

> *In contrast to bribery, blat is a matter of belonging to a circle. Blat favours are normally provided to svoim (people of the circle, one of us). In such long-term relations, all kinds of favours are possible... (Lovell, Ledeneva, and Rogacheskii 2000, 40)*

My former colleague, Peter Hill the Yakuza expert (and Karate black-belt), continues this theme in his description of Japanese society:

> *Corruption in Japan is notoriously hard to pin down. This is largely due to the deep-rooted culture of gift-giving, reciprocity, and obligation in which all major social occasions are marked by presentations of envelopes filled with cash. On a more subtle level, just as retiring bureaucrats find rewarding employment in the industries they formerly regulated (a process known as amakudari, or "descent from heaven"), it is not unknown for retired police officers to be employed in industries concerned with the sale or distribution of gambling machines. (Hill 2003, 64)*

Academic studies among Nepalese rickshaw-wallahs, Indian land registry users, the Chinese practice of *Guanxi* and Bengali villagers have all reported similar findings. A culturally universal example of corruption is very difficult to find. What may seem like corruption to an outsider is often regarded as part of an appropriate and legitimate survival network by members of the culture. The key is that although the same cultural insiders may deeply dislike corruption, they do not regard their own practices as corrupt.

## The Benefits of Corruption

There is a further argument that dominates the field: isn't corruption good?

Many commentators, particularly after Wolfensohn's speech, agree with John T. Noonan that, "next to tyranny, corruption is the great disease of government". However, other commentators would side with Robert Merton's idea of the hidden benefits to society of some purported criminal activities. Merton viewed corruption as having a hidden advantage in that it enhanced the political machinery of a country by re-balancing the "deficiencies of the official structure," ensuring that more talented people from disadvantaged backgrounds entered into the political system and, perhaps most importantly, it gave a human face to the political apparatus. He quotes one ward boss as saying,

> *I think that there's got to be in every ward somebody that any bloke can come to — no matter what he's done — and get help. Help, you understand; none of your law and justice, but help. (Merton 1967, 75)*

There is also an economic argument for functional corruption. Possibly the most well-known proponent of this claim is the right-wing commentator Samuel P. Huntington, who wrote:

> *The only thing worse than a society with a rigid, over-centralized dishonest bureaucracy, is one with a rigid, over-centralized honest bureaucracy. (Huntington 1968, 386)*

According to this idea it is not greed or "immoral" behaviour that causes corruption but over-weaning government regulation. Huntington's argument, that corruption can actually aid economic development, has been, recently supported by the researchers Jay Choi and Marcel Thum who argue that a "high level entrepreneur" by accessing the "informal economy" can outwit the corrupt official who is trying to rent-seek in the formal economy. There is also another school of commentators who argue that what really matters is whether or not a service actually flows from the corruption.

So with all these questions corruption studies seem stymied. However, there is a way of shedding light on these questions and that is to study match-fixing in football.

## Football: a Social Science Laboratory

In the last thirty years the world has seen an almost-universal phenomenon arise with which to make accurate comparisons about corruption: the spread of football. Franklin Foer writes of the "globalization of the sport" and he is not alone in noticing this trend. There are, however, differing arguments as to why football has spread to so many countries. Some observers, like Richard Giulianotti argue that the sport has been deliberately commodified and sold, like shoes or Coca Cola, as a commercial product. Other commentators, like the investigative journalists Andrew Jennings and Barbara Smit, argue that the very manufacturers of those same commercial products, Adidas and Coca Cola for example, have used football to sell their own products and have deliberately pushed the international growth of the sport as a marketing tool.

Whatever the reasons, the development in the sport has been truly remarkable: in 1974 less than eighty countries had developed the sport's infrastructure enough to have a national football administration, now, forty years later, the number of countries represented in FIFA, 209, is more than those represented in the United Nations.

Every country in the world plays football. Every country in the world follows both the same rules of the sport and is governed, effectively, by the same organization: a national football association under the international rubric of FIFA. And every society in the world regards match-fixing in football as a deviant, corrupt practice.

Football is an extraordinary case with which to study corruption.

One can understand the mechanisms and the motivations of a fixed match without any of the major problems that have plagued the study of corruption. There are no problems defining what constitutes a culturally appropriate gift and what constitutes a bribe. There are no differences in football's governing regulations between societies or cultures. And there is no discussion about whether corruption in football is good or bad. Give a referee or a player from an opposing team money to under-perform and it is regarded as a malignant corruption from Andorra to Zimbabwe. Football corruption is a universal "sociology of smoky hotel rooms" as one of my former colleagues Jay Gershuny once described it.

## Universal Deviancy

Aside from corruption studies, football match-fixing is also one of those rare academic beasts in criminology — a universal deviancy. For non-criminologists this is the equivalent of reporting that I have a found an intellectual Holy Grail. Universal deviancies are not supposed to happen — but match-fixing is one. Here is why.

Criminologists rarely talk about "crimes." Since the days of the great French thinker Émile Durkheim, they have tended to write rather about "deviancy". They do this because "what is a crime" changes depending on the society and the historical era. What was criminal for our grandparents is not necessarily criminal for us, and vice versa.

For example, the fictional detective Sherlock Holmes is described by his author as a crime-fighting genius. However, Arthur Conan-Doyle also describes Holmes as a habitual drug-user: but he did not think of his character injecting cocaine or opium as illegal, rather it was a simple, moral defect brought about by Holmes' boredom with ordinary life.

This was not an unusual view of these substances in 1890s western society. In fact at that time, one of Coca-Cola's chief ingredients was derived from the coca leaf which is the raw material for cocaine. Today, of course, making a drink consisting of cocaine and selling it internationally would make the manufacturer a drug trafficker. It is for this type of fluctuation in what society regards as a "crime" that criminologists now usually prefer the terms "deviant" or "deviancy".

Over the years of human history there are very few practices that have, in one society or another, not been regarded as normal and then deviant and then normal again. Drug taking, slavery and various sexual practices (including, in some very rare circumstances, like the royal dynasties of ancient Egypt, incest) have all been regarded in some eras or in some cultures as normal.

One of the few, almost unique, exceptions is match-fixing.

The idea of match-fixing as a universal deviancy is not simply about football in current times. Match-fixing, regardless of the sport, has always been regarded as a deviant behaviour. Even in cultures that accepted traditions that 21st century western humanity largely regards as abhorrent, like slave owning or paedophilia, match-fixing was a deviant behaviour.

For example, according to the *Lives of the 12 Caesars* by Gaius Suetonius, the match-fixing of chariot races in the early Roman Empire by some of the most powerful figures in world history, the Imperial Emperors, was regarded by both Suetonius and, reportedly, the ordinary people as something shameful. In fact, four hundred years after Suetonius, the riots that nearly brought down one of the Byzantine Emperors were caused, initially, by rumours of match-fixing by the popular Green and Blue chariot racing teams.

The question of *why* so many different societies have regarded the fixing of competitive sporting events as a deviant behaviour is beyond the scope of this particular book, but one theory using George Orwell's view of sports might be that if sports are "mimic warfare" to fix is to become a traitor. Traitors, be they motivated for financial gain or changing ideology, are rarely viewed favourably. The Flavius Josephuses, Benedict Arnolds or Vidkun Quislings may be lucky enough to choose the winning side (or not), but even when they do they usually have to disguise their shift in allegiances in later historical accounts. Whatever the reasons for the near-universal dislike of fixing, it does mean that match-fixing is an excellent subject to study for criminologists.

This book is a deliberate attempt to use the universality of football to explore corruption and see what common elements, regardless of culture, can be identified. I will attempt to answer, with examples from the sport, the following research questions:

- How can we properly define match-fixing?
- Are there different types of fixing in the overall framework of corruption?
- Why do corruptors decide to fix matches?
- How do corruptors get players and referees to fix matches?
- How do players and referees perform those fixes?
- Why do some rich, strong teams bother to bribe poor, weak teams?
- Why are some games fixed, but not others?
- Are players coerced into match-fixing?
- Why do some rich, high-status players participate in corrupt activities?
- Why do some leagues have more match corruption than others?
- Why do some sports leagues collapse from high-levels of corruption?
- How can an honest sports administrator prevent much of this corruption?

Overall, I argue that the answers to these questions are not specific to a culture or a country. In other words, Mexicans are not any more likely to fix a game for some undefined ethnic reason than Africans, Europeans or Asians. What makes people undertake corrupt actions are a series of rational choices, based largely on specific circumstances that are largely independent of culture.
In this chapter, we have examined *why* studying match-fixing in the world's most popular professional subject is a worthy subject. In the next chapter, we will look at *how* it is possible to study such a dangerous and controversial topic.

## Chapter Review

- Match-fixing is threatening modern sport.
- Match-fixing is a subject worthy of academic study, even if you are not interested in sport.
- Match-fixing is a universal deviancy
- It is caused by rational decisions, not culture or ethnic background.

# CHAPTER TWO
# HOW TO STUDY MATCH-FIXING

*We are suffering from a plethora of surmise, conjecture, and hypothesis. The difficulty is to detach the framework of fact — of absolute undeniable fact — from the embellishments of theorists and reporters. Then, having established ourselves upon this sound basis, it is our duty to see what inferences may be drawn and what are the special points upon which the whole mystery turns...*

*(Conan-Doyle, The Adventures of Sherlock Holmes, 1892).*

In 1892, in a first-class compartment of the Paddington Express going south-west towards Dartmoor, Sherlock Holmes and his partner, Doctor Watson, were off to investigate a case of match-fixing: the mysterious disappearance of a racehorse, the Silver Blaze, the favourite in the up-coming Wessex Cup. Arthur Conan-Doyle, the author of these fictional adventures, describes the furore in the newspapers that the mystery had caused, and has Watson ask Holmes how he will solve this case. Holmes' reply is quoted above and it is easy to understand what Conan-Doyle means. As soon as a possible case of match-fixing arises, articles appear in the popular media are full of "surmise, conjecture and hypothesis" about the honesty of football players or referees. This surmise, conjecture and hypothesis is partly because match-fixing is, by its very nature, a difficult subject to study. The act is hard to uncover: fixing a match is a crime committed by a relatively small number of participants trying to defraud a much larger audience. There is no incentive for the participants to confess or publicize their deeds. Unlike drug dealing or prostitution, two forms of deviant behaviour that need to advertise (it is no use being a drug-dealer or a prostitute, if none of your potential customers know where you are), successful long-term match-fixing is built entirely on secrecy.

There was, when I began my work no previously measured data about match-fixing. The purpose of this book is to try to do what Holmes purportedly advises, and gather a framework of fact around the issue and then to see whether it is possible to make inferences from these facts.

## Terminology

Even the phrase match-fixing has a series of synonyms — match-squaring, match-rigging, match-bending, match-throwing, and match-arranging are a few examples. I choose the term match-fixing, and will use it consistently throughout the book, simply because it is the most widely used.

There are also a large number of terms for the people involved in match-fixing: bookies, gangsters, criminals, mobsters, runners, fixers, bettors, bribers. For example, at times there is confusion because a player who is under-performing in a fixed match is called a *fixer*, but the person who may have bribed the player to under-perform is also called a *fixer*. To avoid this problem I will label the people who are actually fixing a match, by bribing or threatening people, as a corruptor.

Diego Gambetta was one of my supervisors. He would analyse my work over hot cups of tea in his study at Nuffield College, Oxford. These sessions were always intense. He would place me in a metaphorical hot seat — an overly soft arm-chair — where I would gradually sink into the cushions, while my spirits sunk even lower as he peppered me with wry comments and questions. His "Map of Corruption" is a useful tool to avoid confusion in naming of people involved in match-fixing. In this case, Gambetta is not proposing, of course, a geographical map, but a kind of intellectual blueprint into the various agents involved in a typical corrupt deal. He describes three agents in any corrupt action:

(T) the truster — is the person that lays their trust in somebody. In the case of match-fixing these are the spectators, league officials or honest gamblers who trust that the players and referees are being honest.

(F) the fiduciary agents — who are responsible for carrying out the action in an honest way, in this case the players and the referees. If they have been bribed I title them *corruptee*.

(C) the *corruptors* — who are trying to get the fiduciary agent (F) to act in a dishonest fashion. Thus anybody who is trying to bribe a player, referee or official to under-perform in a match is called a corruptor, regardless of whether they are connected to a betting ring or organised crime or are simply from another team.

The players, referees or officials who might be induced to underperform are called corruptees. These terms may sound abstract, but they avoid most of the confusion that creeps into the discussion about match-fixing and identify with precision the defining *action* of each type of protagonist.

## Deceptive Mimicry

In order to sneak up on their victims, snakes, crocodiles and other predators often have the ability to disguise themselves as a "normal" part of the landscape. There are similar strategies with corrupt football players and referees.

A reader may ask, but what about the people who do two different things at the same time? What about a player who is pretending to play well but is actually helping to corrupt other members of his team? Or what about a football official who is supposed to be administering the league, but in reality is helping bribe referees? How does one use Gambetta's Map of Corruption to define these more complicated roles?

The answer is in the concept of "deceptive mimicry" where Gambetta writes of people pretending to be honest when they are not. The trick to analysing them is to analyse corrupt and mimicry acts separately. So, in the two examples above, the player and official have ceased in their normal roles and have become corruptors — and should be described as such.

At this point, the terminology may sound more confusing, but as we go through the work in the book, it will become clearer. Let us now turn our attention to *how* I did the research for this book.

## The Disaster of Malaysia and Singapore Football

Much of the primary research for this book was conducted in Asia, particularly Malaysia and Singapore, because both countries have a long history of match-fixing. The most well-known example of football fixing began in 1989, when the Football Association of Malaysia (FAM) and the Football Association of Singaapore (FAS) founded a new, joint professional league. There were sixteen teams, composed of fourteen Malaysian state teams and two teams from the neighbouring countries of Brunei and Singapore.

The league enjoyed considerable financial support for infrastructure from both the Malaysian and Singaporean governments: new, modern stadiums were built. Dunhill Tobacco and other private companies sponsored the league. There was a well-endorsed television contract that ensured that the league was broadcast nationally with a potential viewing audience in the millions. Teams were allowed to import foreign stars to improve the quality of the play. The league became so popular that some matches attracted over 50 thousand people to the stadium.

It became "a complete disaster".

In 1993, Malaysian journalists wrote a series of newspapers articles alleging that the league was home to widespread match-fixing. Purportedly the fixes were arranged by a series of Singapore based corruptors. Fans began to complain loudly during the games that the results were *Kelung*[1] or fixed.

In the summer of 1994, a police investigation began. It is a source of some controversy as to which country launched the official investigation. The Malaysian authorities claim that they initiated the crackdown; while the Singaporean administration claims that it was their Corrupt Practices Investigation Bureau (CPIB) that started the investigation. However, once the separate police actions began they became "the most professional and organised investigation into match-fixing in the history of the game".

Police forces in both countries arrested over one hundred and fifty players, coaches and officials from the league. During the course of the investigation the Royal Malaysian Police publicly announced that they estimated that 90% of the games in the league had been fixed. There were also a series of high-profile trials involving alleged match-fixing players and referees in Singapore. The controversy between the two countries became so great that the Malaysians expelled the Singaporeans from the league, which effectively collapsed in 1995. There were even wider diplomatic problems with both the

---

[1] *Kelung: A Malaysian word for a traditional fishing trap where the fish channeled into swimming in specific lanes to be caught in a series of nets, or figuratively that the game was a theatrical exercise.*

Singaporean and Malaysian governments exchanging angry words about the collapse of the league.

However, for all the controversy and public attention no one has yet tried to establish what precisely occurred in the Malaysian-Singaporean league during those years. No one has investigated what factors led to so many players fixing so many matches. Many of the interviews and research data were gathered in Malaysia and Singapore.

A further point of interest is that the same corruptors who fixed so many matches in Malaysia and Singapore have since 1994 travelled around the world fixing a range of games from Italy to Finland to El Salvador to South Africa. Understanding their methods will give us a valuable perspective on how they work. Particularly as a number of sports leagues across Asia have "collapsed" for similar levels of corruption.

## The Neglected Art of Talking to Criminals

In 1967, the American criminologist Donald Cressey wrote of the difficulties of conducting research into serious or organised crime. One particular challenge that he highlighted was the inability to gain access to, and therefore interview criminals. Almost forty years later, the British criminologist Mike Maguire also wrote of the "neglected art" of actually talking to criminals. Maguire claims that it is comparatively rare for researchers to speak directly to criminals, outside of prison, concerning their motivations and methods.

This was one of the research methods that this book is based upon: interviews with people who were not only inside the professional sub-culture of football but also those who had some direct experience in the deviant sub-culture of match-fixing. There were interviews with football officials and police officers who, purportedly, tried to fight against fixing; journalists who were, purportedly, investigating match-fixing; referees who had been bribed or offered bribes to corrupt games; and players and coaches whose teams, or sections of teams, were fixing games. Most importantly, there were interviews with corruptors who arranged fixed-matches and players who took part in these games. Table 2.1, indicates the range of professions of the interview subjects:

Table 2.1: Interview Subjects by Profession

| *Job Title* | Gambler | Corruptor | Player | Ref | Sports Official | Law E. | Journo | Other |
|---|---|---|---|---|---|---|---|---|
| *Code in Text* | (B1) | (COR1) | (P1) | (R1) | (SO1) | (LE1) | (J1) | (O1) |
| *Total No.* | 23 | 10 | 37 | 6 | 50 | 21 | 24 | 13 |

Total subjects = 184 | Total interviews = 221

In Table 2.1, the first row lists the various professional categories of the interview subjects. Four of the categories are self-explanatory: referees, players, corruptors and journalists. The other four categories consist of the following groups: *gamblers* — any bettors, odd compliers or gambling industry worker from executive to "runners"; *officials* — any league or team administrators, including coaches or managers; *law enforcement* — police officers, secret service personnel or state prosecutors; *others* contains a miscellaneous range of professions.[2]

Most of the interview subjects reported that the topic of match-fixing in football is immensely controversial and that they feared recriminations from

[2] *Including 2 diplomats, 3 businessmen, 2 members of the Malaysian royal family, an academic, a politician and a political dissident.*

either the corruptors or the authorities if they spoke out. Because of the controversial nature of the topic almost all of the interviews were "off the record". Particularly, people who were still serving in the game stressed that if they were to be quoted, either publicly or in such a way as to allow people to guess their identity, they would lose their job or possibly face more severe consequences.

A number of bookies and corruptors were also kind enough to share some of their time and knowledge with me. Their criminal "bona fides" were thoroughly checked, either through law enforcement or criminal sources or by court records, before the interviews to ensure that they were genuine match fixers. For them, the risk was extremely high, as in many jurisdictions organised gambling, let alone fixing matches, is illegal.

Accordingly, the following device is used in the text: proper names are changed and all interview subjects are given a specific code. Table 2.1, row 2, lists this code. Each category has a specific code — Players = P, Referees = R, etc. — and each interview subject is given a number depending on the date of the interview. So, the first player interviewed is P1, the first corruptor COR1, and so on. The few interview subjects who did insist on being on the record are identified both by their last name and their profession: for example, Blatter, SO44, 2008 or Gregg, P23, 2005 & 2013.

The Malaysian and Singaporean interviews were conducted over three trips lasting, in total, six months in 2005 and 2006. There was then another round of interviews conducted in Europe and the United Kingdom with various interview subjects who had dealt either with match-fixing or Asian gambling. A cohort of high-profile players and coaches, who played with top-level clubs and national teams at prestigious international tournaments were also interviewed. The interviews were generally held in a location where the subject felt comfortable talking. These locations varied from the subject's offices to a favourite restaurant or coffee shop. For some of the more sensitive subjects, the interviews were held in a private and secure location, so that the subject would more freely discuss the issue.

There is considerable discussion among social scientists about the best methods of qualitative interviewing. However, the practical issues generally divide along the following themes: access, nature of the interview and recording of interview.

In arranging the interviews, each subject was told that I was a researcher from the University of Oxford interested in studying match-fixing and that the resulting research would be published. They were then invited to a sit down meeting, or, if they preferred, a conversation on the telephone (this was done only if they were not in the immediate geographic location).

There is also considerable discussion about types of interviewing: some researchers prefer "long," "unstructured" interviews; while others prefer "life histories" or a chronological approach. Even the potential controversies about the storage of interviews has been studied. In this case all of the interviews were focused on the subject of match-fixing. This seemed to be the appropriate choice as it was a subject that was under discussion rather than a person's biography or profession. The interviews usually began with general questions about the subject's role and career to date, but as the interviews went on the questions became more focused on the subject of match-fixing and their personal involvement. As for the recording of interviews the preference was always to tape-record for greater accuracy. However, most of the interview subjects displayed a significant reluctance in allowing themselves to be taped. In his work on the Russian Mafiya, Federico Varese had similar problems and remarked, "there is a trade-off between bad memory and evasive answers: tape-recording made subjects extremely uncomfortable, resulting in evasive answers."

There were similar difficulties in this research work, so I often had to rely on note taking at the time of the interview, with a formal typing up of the notes done as quickly as possible after the interview. All interviews were transcribed (the total count is over 250,000 words) and coded using a method described in the next section. Follow up interviews were conducted and relationships were maintained to re-check statements and ensure accuracy of views.

## Confession Databank

I wanted - as Sherlock Holmes (Conan-Doyle) advises - to get the framework of fact. Thus I wanted to find the actual words of the corruptors as they arranged fixes. I compiled a databank of corruptors confessing to fixing. I use the term "confession" loosely. Sometimes the "confessions" are given in newspaper interviews or books; sometimes they are covertly taped conversations or trial transcripts. The key is that the actual text of each item in the databank consists of the actual words of the person who fixed a match or took part in one.

A few examples that we will see later in this book: the recorded telephone conversations of a Russian football club owner in his attempts to fix a match; the covertly taped conversations of the Belgian corruptors of the Semi-Final of the UEFA Cup of 1984; and the judicial confession of the Italian gambling corruptors who attempted to fix Serie A matches in the 1979-80 season.

One of the most useful and pertinent texts were the police confessions of Malaysian and Singaporean footballers from the 1995 investigation. These confessions have never been publicly examined and I was fortunate to be granted access to them by law enforcement sources. They contain a rich material of primary data on how the players rigged matches and tournaments.

Another source of information were the Singapore court transcripts of eleven cases that were tried in court between 1986 and 2000 on match-fixing in football. These too contained a great deal of information that outlined methods, strategies and structures of the gambling syndicates and their relationships with various players, coaches and referees within the game. In total there were over 313,000 words: from 17 different countries and 6 international tournaments, in 10 different languages. All the databank has been completely translated — using at least two different translators for each language, to ensure accuracy — and transcribed.

The confession databank and transcribed interviews consists of over 560,000 words. It is divided into four volumes and coded using the TAMS system. The TAMS system was developed by the sociologist Matthew Weinstein of Kent State University and it allows a researcher to both mine and code their data in a number of ways. The databank and interviews were analysed for any similarities or consistent patterns. Each interview or text was examined to see if it contained examples of 49 sociological codes — values such as trust, internal markets, anomie or coercion. In this way, through both qualitative interviews and text analysis of actual corruptors' words, Maguire's plea for other researchers to speak directly to criminals is answered.

## Databases

Finally, much of the evidence used in the book comes from the creation of several databases.[3] The two principal ones are the Fixed-Match Database (FMDB) and the Fixing/Non-Fixing Players Database (the FPD database).

The FMDB was constructed by finding in newspaper articles, interviews or through the compilation of the confession databank, examples of fixed

---

[3] *The construction of the database owes much to the advice of Johann Lambsdorff of the University of Passau and Marc Carinci of Betcapper.com. The theoretical model comes from the chapter by Michael Biggs in Making Sense of Suicide Missions (Gambetta 2005).*

matches. The database is, currently, comprised of 301 fixed matches in 60 different countries and 55 different leagues or cup play. The FMDB consists of 39 variables. There are 11 information variables: date of match, name of team, league, etc; 22 categorical variables, listing things like "was organised crime involved in the fix?"; "was the home team fixing?"; 2 continuous variables, e.g. total number of goals scored in the game; and 4 ordinal variables, e.g. degree of certainty of the fix.

There were a number of important challenges to overcome in the construction of the FMDB. The most important of these was how did one know that a game had actually been fixed? After all, almost every Saturday there is some compliant from an outraged manager or a disgruntled fan that their team only lost because someone, somewhere had been "got at." So it was necessary to be clear about how certain it was that a game was actually fixed. Accordingly, a variable was developed — *degree of certainty of fix.*

The first, and highest, degree of certainty was if the game had been declared fixed in court or some legal proceedings. The next degree down was if a football association hearing had declared it fixed. The third was if a number of people who had actively participated in the fix confessed to the fix. The fourth was if there had been a law case or police investigation that had been suspended or not continued. The fifth was if an inside participant in the game, say the other team or honest referee, had alleged that other parties were fixing.

The final level, the sixth, consisted of a range of games that were alleged to have been fixed by a source that was not particularly reliable. For example, in the 2002 World Cup Italy lost to South Korea. During the game there were a number of curious refereeing decisions and afterwards thousands of irate Italian fans wrote to FIFA complaining that the match had been fixed. Unfortunately for the fans, they had no hard evidence of a fix, so the match is included in the bottom level of fixes.

Table 2.2, shows the organization of this variable:

| | | |
|---|---|---|
| **1 =** | **Law case with guilty verdict** | **99** |
| **2 =** | **FA case with guilty verdict** | **59** |
| **3 =** | **Confession of participants** | **67** |
| **4 =** | **Law case suspended not enough evidence** | **24** |
| **5 =** | **Allegations by one side, some proof offered** | **15** |
| **6 =** | **Rumour** | **37** |

***Source:*** *Fixed-Match Database 1 (N = 301)*

Because of the lack of reliability of the fixes in the bottom three levels of this variable, a second database, the Fixed-match Database 2 was developed (FMDB-2), where only the games that had a degree of certainty of level 3 and above were analysed. This is the principal database used in this book. For each game in this database there were at least two match-reports: a statistical one, listing times of goals, number of yellow/red cards, substitutions; and an anecdotal report listing any possible missed penalties or own goals that the statistical report may have missed. Any game, where these reports could not be found was excluded from the database (there are 88 games where this information was not available), so there are 137 games in the FMDB-2 database.

The second challenge was to ensure that there was a control group built into the database. Because football games vary so greatly in terms of culture, style and era (there are fewer goals scored in the Spanish league than in the Italian league and much fewer goals scored in contemporary games than in matches 50 years ago) the games in this database were then matched with games from a control group of purportedly honestly-played games of an equivalent culture, playing style and era. For example, in the FMDB-2 database, there are 12 games from the German league in 1971 that were fixed. To match these games, 12 games were randomly selected from a presumably honest league, the Norwegian, of the same year — so the FMDB-2 consists of 137 fixed matches and 130 control matches.

There was another database used as a "control group of the control groups." This control group consists of five European leagues — England/Wales, Scotland, France, Germany and The Netherlands from the 2005-06 season. The two control groups are contrasted (for example, the average number of penalties per game in FMDB-2 is .20 in the 1st control group; the average number of penalties in the second control group is .19 — .24; and, the average number of penalties in some of the fixed games .42) to ensure that the statistical patterns do actually represent a significant trend in the data.

The last point that is important to mention is that in my construction of the database there is no implication that all the fixes that may have occurred in a league are represented. Nor are there comparisons on the rates of fixed matches between various leagues.

## Fixing/Non-Fixing Players Database (FPD)

There is another database — the Fixing/Non-Fixing Players Database (FPD). It is composed of 117 players who either fixed matches or were approached to fix matches. This database has 30 different variables ranging from categorical variables such as, "Was the player coerced into taking part in the fix?" to informational variables such as name, team and date. The key variable in this database is whether a player agreed to take part in the fixed matches or not. There are 93 players listed who when approached agreed to fix a match and twenty-four players who when approached refused.

## Chapter Review

In this chapter, we have examined *how* to study match-fixing. We found the following themes:

- Use only clear, absolute facts.
- The interviews are mostly with people who have direct knowledge of match-fixing.
- To check the interviews, I also compiled a databank of transcripts of corruptors directly discussing their methods. Some of these transcripts are covertly recorded conversations as the corruptors attempt to fix matches.
- In order to get quantitative data (statistics) I also compiled two databases. One of fixed matches, the second of players who had been approached to fix a match. In both cases, I also compiled a control group to give accurate comparisons.

In the next chapter, using these methods we will examine the two basic types of fixing and show that they are clearly and demonstrably different.

# CHAPTER THREE
# ARRANGEMENTS VERSUS GAMBLING

*The Short Man is back. He told me. "I've been trying to get hold of you." He's telling me. "You're going to lose the game..." So two minutes into the game, I pushed the ball into the back of the net. That was the Coventry game.*

*(Grobbelaar, cited in Thomas, 2003, 191).*

The Bruce Grobbelaar trial dominated the British newspaper headlines during the 1990s. Grobbelaar was a professional goalkeeper for the English teams Liverpool and Southampton. He had been covertly videotaped boasting that he had been paid by an Asian gambling syndicate to let in goals. The Hampshire police charged him and the case went to trial in the summer of 1997. It was a complicated judicial process, but Grobbelaar was twice, seemingly, cleared of the charges, until the House of Lords heard his appeal for libel damages in 2002. In their judgement the Law Lords wrote that they believed the veracity of the transcript — an excerpt is quoted above — and that Grobbelaar was actually receiving money from an Asian gambling syndicate to fix matches. What they could not determine was whether he had actually fixed the games.

However, at the heart of this controversial case there was an issue of *definition* of corrupt practices that so confused the judicial process that, according to some of the interview subjects, it came to influence the entire proceedings. Another professional goalkeeper was also on trial for match-fixing in the same case. The crown claimed that this goalkeeper had a corrupt arrangement with a second team that was in danger of relegation. In the final game of the season the goalkeeper was alleged to have deliberately let in a number of goals. His team lost. The second team was not relegated (This second goalkeeper was acquitted of all charges).

Because the types of fixes in which the goalkeepers were allegedly involved were so structurally different — one was purportedly for gambling purposes, the other purportedly arranged to stop one team from being relegated; one was arranged by a group of Asian criminals, the other was purportedly arranged by players and corrupt team officials (although not substantiated in any way) both the judge and members of the jury had difficulty following the cases.

The confusion of the Grobbelaar trial was not an isolated incident. Because of the controversy that surrounds match-fixing the media tends to use deliberately confusing words like: "dark figures," "shadowy characters" or "murky underworld".

However, it is possible to understand this corrupt practice. The first thing that is needed is a precise definition. In this chapter, there is such a definition, and an outline of the two fundamental types of fixing — arrangements and gambling.

## Match-Fixing is Not Cheating

Let us be clear: match-fixing is not cheating. If match-fixing is where one person agrees to help one side lose by putting in less than a 100% effort: then cheating is trying to win with 110% effort, where the person uses unscrupulous means to win.

In many cultures, cheating in sport is actually encouraged. What differs between sporting cultures is *how* someone cheats. For example, in some countries, to fake an injury to get an opponent unfairly sanctioned shows that the cheater is trying to win. The player who does that is considered to be putting in a maximum effort for their team and receives approval.

Here is an example from Chris Taylor's book *The Beautiful Game: A Journey Through Latin American Football* (1998), Mauricio Taricco, was an Argentine defender playing in England. However, Taricco differed from a part of English football culture:

> *I had a problem with an opposing player and he pushed me. And when I got up and he raised his hand to me and I threw myself to the ground... The ref saw me and sent him off. So everyone told me, "You're a cheat" (including his own team-mates and coach). The mentality of the people is different. Here they don't accept that... I can't completely agree with it... In Argentina it's accepted. If you get someone sent off, after the game the coach will see it as a good move. (Taylor 1998, 58-59)*

The implication in this story is that only Argentinean players cheat to win. However, that argument ignores the English game's reputation for violent play. In English football kicking, punching and elbowing opponents are considered masculine, "fair" forms of cheating. One symbolic example of this form of cheating is the popular, and widely purchased, photo of an English player -Vinnie Jones (who later became a film actor renown for his tough-guy roles) — grabbing the testicles of a better player. In an article examining this iconic photo, a writer for the popular football magazine *When Saturday Comes* claims that the photo resonates with the English soul as it shows a hard working, tough man levelling the field against a highly-skilled, "continental" player.

For Canadian ice hockey fans, this discussion is the same as the controversy that constantly swirls around the television commentator Don Cherry and his drunken uncle at the wedding views on European players. The point then is not that the Argentine game is fairer than the English game; or that the Canadian players are more violent, than their dirtier European colleagues. It is that both sporting cultures condone cheating, just different kinds of cheating. Yet neither culture regard match-fixing as anything but deviant.

## Match-fixing Defined

An accurate definition of "match-fixing" is:

> *When a player or referee deliberately underperforms during a sporting contest to ensure that one team loses or draws the match.*

Given this definition, there are two different types of match-fixing in football. These types are:

> *Arranged match-fixing: when corruptors manipulate a football match to ensure that one team wins or draws the match.*

> *Gambling match-fixing: when corruptors manipulate a football match to profit-maximise on the gambling market.*

The difference between arrangements and gambling fixes mirrors a wider distinction in the academic study of corruption and criminology. The American scholar Marshall Clinard argues that there is a difference between crimes committed by professionals within a corporation that benefit the corporation as opposed to those that directly benefit the actors themselves. For example, the actions taken to enrich the value of the organization such as health and safety violations or the flaunting of environmental regulations versus those crimes committed by a specific individual, such as insider trading or stock fraud. Both are criminally deviant acts and in the first category the individual may also benefit from the overall improvement of the welfare of the organization. However, in the second category it is the corrupt individual who benefits, often at the harm of their own organization.

A similar division is seen in James Morton's 1993 examination of police corruption, *Bent Coppers: Survey of Police Corruption*. Morton found that there are two essential types of corrupt acts by policemen, those when a police officer is "Bent for the Job" and those where they are "Bent for Self."

In corrupted football matches, an arrangement fix will directly benefit one particular team — in the same way corporate executives can deliberately ignore environmental regulations to boost the value of their company. While in gambling fixes, a team can be effectively sabotaged by its own players acting for their own profit — in the same way corporate fraud can devalue a company.

## Arrangements

There are several motivations for arrangement match-fixing: however, the most common feature is that they are based on a "tournament incentive". In other words, the fixes occur because if a *particular* team can win a specific game it will bring them a reward based on the competitive structure of the league; either winning a prize — a championship or a cup — or avoiding relegation to a lower division.

There are three types of this "tournament incentive" fix. The simplest is collusion, in which both teams *win* from the match-fixing given the competitive structure. For example there was the alleged "shabby arrangement" by the West German and Austrian teams in the opening rounds of the World Cup tournament of 1982. In this game the reward for the arrangement was that both teams progressed into the next round, so long as a certain score was reached. In the academic literature, Iain McLean examines a similar potential arrangement in a third division match in England.

However, the most frequent type is where one team *wins* from the fix and the other *loses* in the competitive structure. So a corruptor arranges for the opposing team to lose.

There is a further type of arrangement match-fix. These cases are where a particular team is linked with the fortunes of an external political or corporate entity. If the team is successful the external entity benefits by being associated with it — so the game is fixed to ensure that benefit. For example, there was a long history of symbolic links between Real Madrid and General Franco's fascist regime in Spain or Dynamo Moscow and the Soviet KGB and there was also a long history of alleged fixed games for these teams arranged by their powerful supporters.

The rewards for arranged types of fixes vary. In cases of collusion — like the purported West Germany vs. Austria — the reward is an immediate tournament incentive: both teams progress to the next round and no other form of payment is presumably needed. For the cases where one team loses from the fix, forms of reward vary from a direct payment of cash to provision of prostitutes, holidays, cars or shopping trips. There are also examples of the existence of an informal "favour bank" between teams that allows for "payment in kind" at a later date.

## Gambling Fixes

Arrangement fixes rest on one simple principle: the match must be manipulated so that a *particular* team wins or draws. This is not the case for gambling fixes. In gambling fixes, the key motivation for corruptors is profit maximisation. The corruptors do not *care* if Team A or Team B wins, what interests them is how much money can be made from fixing the game.

If a corruptor can gain more money from Team A losing, they will try to make Team A lose. However, if the corruptors can make more money from Team

B losing, they will do the same for Team B. Their interest is strictly on the betting market and at times, if they can control both teams, they will change the direction of the fix in the minutes before the game depending on the odds in the market.

There is also a sub-group of gambling match-fixing called spot-fixing. This is when a player or referee deliberately underperforms specific events during a sporting contest to profit-maximise on the gambling market. However, the overall result of the contest may not be affected by spot-fixing. International cricket matches have suffered repeatedly from this problem. Cricket test matches are sports contests that can last for several days and there is sometimes a lucrative practice by corrupted players of manipulating certain events — where a bowler bowled a ball or the fall of one particular wicket — to gain money on the gambling market. An invitation to participate in spot-fixing is also a good way for corruptors to recruit players, as this excerpt from the "confession" of Hansie Cronje the former captain of the South African national team shows:

> *I realize now that the purpose of the payment was to 'hook' me for the Indian tour. As set out below, on the Indian tour in February and March 2000. I was increasingly pushed to manipulate results, and found that I had got into something from which it was very difficult to get out. (Cronje, 2000)*

In Chapters 7 and 8, "Five Steps to Success" and "Pitching the Fix," respectively, we will see other methods of recruiting athletes to perform fixes. For now, it is enough to know that there are essentially two modes of operation: those based on the ability to make small, but repeated, profits over a long period of time; and "one shot" games, high-gain, short-term profit where corruptors will risk a higher possibility of punishment to garner enormous profits in one match.

It is very difficult to estimate the total number of all fixed football matches or contrast the relative frequency of arrangement fixes versus gambling fixes. Because of the deviant nature of the activity, we can assume, in general, corrupted matches are under-reported. However, because, generally, both teams *win* in arrangement fixes — be it a payment or a tournament incentive — and, therefore have no incentive to inform, we can expect those to be *more* under-reported relative to gambling fixes.

However, can we predict *when* and *how* a certain type of fix is more likely to occur? In the next chapter, three key differences between gambling fixes and arrangement fixes are outlined that may help predict when and how they occur. But the next section is about *who* organizes these different fixes.

## Corruptors

If the distinction between arrangements and gambling fixes is accurate, there should be a clear difference in the databases between who arranges the fixes. Team administrators should corrupt most arrangement fixes whereas gamblers and organised criminals should be the corruptors in most gambling fixes. To test this hypothesis, two statistical tests — a Pearson's Chi-square test and a linear regression — were run on several variables in the database: gambling fix, arrangement fix and corruptor (statistical calculations are attached in Appendix 8.) The results were highly robust (P value was < .05, with an adjusted R square of .742). In ordinary English, what this means is that the premise is correct. The overall results are seen in Figure 3.1:

Figure 3.1: Arrangement Fixes: who are the corruptors?

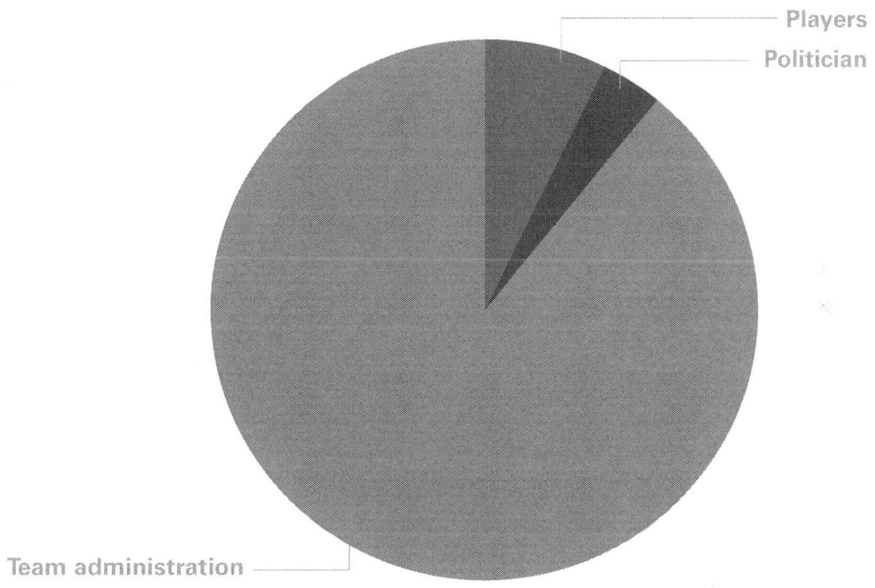


**Source:** *Fixed-Match Database 2 (N = 67)*

Figure 3.1 shows that in arrangement fixes 88.2% of the fixes are initiated by team administrators. There is a small minority of games where the corruptors are the players who claim that they acted on their own violation to fix the game, and that their team management did not know about the fix. In another small section of arranged fixed matches the corruptors are external actors, such as politicians, however, as noted above, this figure is probably an under-representation of this type of fixed matches.

Figure 3.2: Gambling Fixes: the corruptors

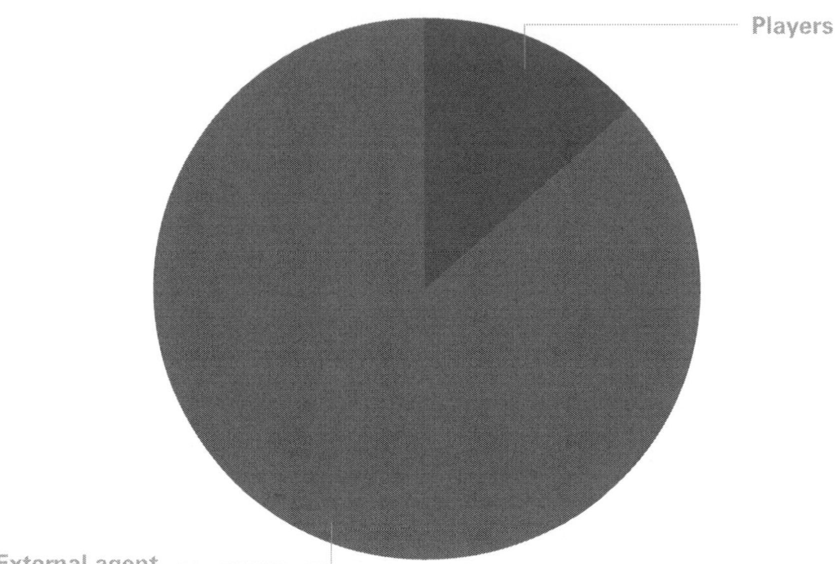


**Source:** *Fixed-Match Database 2 (N = 70)*

However, in gambling fixes the corruptors are a different set of actors. In 86.4% of these fixes, the corruptors are external agents, like gamblers and organised criminals, and the only other set of corruptors are players who on occasion have attempted to defraud the gambling market without using gambling corruptors.

This should be clear: gambling fixes are organised by gamblers; arrangement fixes are organised, mostly, by team officials. However, in the final section of the book, we shall see how the two types have begun to merge, so that if a team official knows that they will lose certain games, they will then seek to profit maximize on the gambling market. For the moment, though this distinction is a useful one, and in the next chapter, we shall see more of ways of determining the type of fix.

## Chapter Review

- Match-fixing is not cheating. Cheating to win is widely accepted and approved of by many fans: fixing is cheating to lose.
- A definition of match-fixing is *when a player or referee deliberately underperforms during a sporting contest to ensure that one team loses or draws the match.*
- There are two types of fixing: arrangements and gambling fixes.
- The corruptors who organize arrangement fixes are team officials or players.
- The corruptors who organize gambling fixes are usually external criminals.

# CHAPTER FOUR
# THRESHOLDS, POWER AND TIMING

*There is the gambling fixing, this is what we see in Malaysia... People are strictly making money out of the deals... Then there is "Sharing and Caring" or "through every pipe a little water must flow". I saw this a lot in the international sports movement. Look, everyone needs to go home with some medal or the government will stop the money... You need the prizes to be shared around, so that everyone goes back with something... Otherwise the sport will gradually die. You cannot be too greedy.*

*Interview, Malaysian sports official, 2005.*

The last chapter was about the definitions of the two fundamental types of sports fixing: arrangements ("Sharing and Caring" — in the words of the Malaysian sports official quoted above) and gambling. It also showed *who* organised the fixes. This chapter outlines three more empirical distinctions between these two types of fixing. Those distinctions are:

- when they occur
- the relationship of power in the fixes (do strong or weak teams fix?)
- the total number of goals that is scored in each type of fix

This chapter is based mostly on statistical analysis of databases. This is known as "quantitative research" by academics. If you are a reader who is not particularly interested in this type of work, then please turn to the next chapter, in that section you will read plenty about the thugs and miscreants who fix matches. From reading the last chapter and the outline above you will understand the essential differences and there is no need to continue in this chapter. We will see each other again on page 62.

If, however, you are interested in this type of statistical analysis but may not have a background in quantitative work, or it may have been a long time since you last examined it, here is a quick review. Again, if you are perfectly familiar with quantitative analysis, please skip this section and pick up on the threshold section below.

## Introduction to Statistics

In every statistical analysis, you need two groups of cases. In this work, these are fixed matches and a control group of non-fixed matches. We contrast these two groups using a set of variables. These variables are literally the factors that may *vary* or *cause* any differences between the two groups.

To use an example, if we wanted to understand why one group of apples were all red, while another group were mostly green: we would establish a set of variables like temperature, genetic type or amount of sunshine. After carefully measuring, we would then contrast the variables with the different groups by a number of different statistical tests. The aim of these tests is to prove the variation is not due to chance.

So using the apple example, you might find that the red apples had received more hours of sunlight than the green apples. The results of the statistical calculation would show above a 95% chance that this difference was due to the sunlight and not a statistical accident. This 95% level is the standard measurement and is called the *confidence level*.

In this chapter we are testing three variables — *when* a match was played during a season, the *relative strength* of the teams and the *timing* of the goals during the match — to see if we can distinguish between honestly played games and fixed games: and also between arrangement fixing and gambling fixing.

## Thresholds

In their paper about underperforming teams in the National Basketball Association (NBA) the American academics, Justin Trogdon and Beck Taylor (2002), claim that as a general trend many teams deliberately underperformed *after* certain key "threshold points" in the season. According to Trogdon and Taylor, these teams may have been deliberately losing because the tournament incentives in the NBA during the time examined actually *rewarded* teams for having lower rankings.

In the NBA there is no promotion or relegation, so no team risked going out of the league if they finished in the bottom. Moreover, the "draft" system actually forced the best new players to sign with the lowest ranked teams. (Each player in the draft is ranked and then the top player goes to the bottom placed team, the second best player to the second worst team, and so on.) So it was in a team's interest to finish as low as possible to get a better recruit for the next season.

The key point to understand in this "race to the bottom" was that no team started the season wanting to finish bottom of the league, rather at a "threshold" point in the season some officials on some teams would make a rational choice decision to start to lose as many games as possible to help get as low a position as possible in the league, and thus get a better draft-pick the next year.

If these "threshold points" exist for underperformance in basketball, is there something similar in match-fixing in football leagues? If they do, we could expect that arranged match-fixes mostly occurred after specific time points in the season, while gambling match-fixes are more or less constant throughout the season.

In the database, there was a variable — *timing of fix in the season* — that gave each part of the season a different value (1 = first quadrant of the season, 2 = second quadrant, 3 = third quadrant, 4 = fourth quadrant, 5 = non-season play, or cups based on a knock out basis, where if one team loses they are out of the tournament). Using the statistical tests — Pearson's Chi-Square and Correlation — I tried to see if there was any correlation between this variable and the types of fixes: gambling or arrangements.

The results were highly significant — P = .0001. This means that there was a less than one-in-a-thousand chance that the result was due to chance. In statistical terms it is described as a *highly significant correlation* meaning that we can accept that there is a statistically significant difference in the timing for different types of fixes. Figure 4.1 shows this difference:

Figure 4.1: Gambling vs. Arrangements: time of season

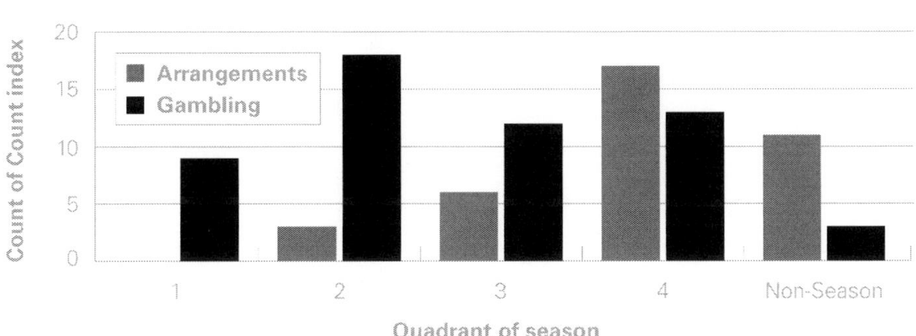


**Source:** *Fixed-Match Database 2 (N = 91)*

In Figure 4.1, the red bars represent gambling fixes; the light-blue bars arrangement fixes. Along the X-axis (bottom of the chart) are the quadrants of the season 1-4, with the fifth category being non-season games. The Y-axis (the vertical measurement) represents the total number of each type of fixed game. It is clear from Figure 4.1 that while gambling fixes, the red bars, are randomly distributed throughout the season, arrangements markedly increase towards the end of the season and in win-loss non-season games.

There are two points to be made from Figure 4.1:

1) No arrangement corruptor *starts* the season corrupting matches. Rather at a point in the season — a corruption threshold — they begin to try to fix matches.

2) This corruption threshold varies from administrator to administrator.

There are a few corruptors who begin trying to corrupt matches even before a season is half over, while others wait for the third and fourth quadrant to corrupt matches. We will see many of the dynamics of team administrators (with all their swearing and violence) as corruptors in the next chapter "To Fix or Not to Fix," but one point should be made now: it is not simply corruptors who have a threshold point to buying games, other actors — the corruptees — often wait for a threshold point to sell their games. It is this point, which teams make arrangements and how, that we will examine in the next section.

## Match-fixing and Power

Most professional football leagues are not dominated by a single team. If they were there would be little public interest. Professional football leagues tend to have three or four "strong" teams who constantly compete for the league championship, while there are another dozen or so weaker teams who may challenge for the smaller prizes of the league. Generally, the teams' strength depends on their relative financial position: rich teams are stronger than poor teams.

Given this framework, a team has two choices. It can *compete* with another team — play the game to the best of their ability — or they can *collude* with the other team — match-fix.

The question we are going to examine in this next section is *which* teams agree to collude with each other? Do weak teams fix together, so they can save their resources when they play strong teams? Do strong teams, who have more resources invested and thus more to lose if they do not win a competition, collude with each other so that each strong team can each win one trophy? Or do strong teams compete with each other but form alliances with weaker teams?

This last scenario seems like it would be the most accurate: strong teams compete with strong teams, strong and weak teams collude. In international relations theory, the political scientist Robert Keohane (among others) advanced the same idea in his discussion of a "hegemonic stability" — weak countries do not group together to form coalitions of smaller powers, rather weak countries form alliances with strong countries; while strong countries do not make alliances with other strong powers, rather they also seek alliances with weaker powers.

## *Key Concept*

*Symmetrical: when two teams are roughly equally strong. Ex: weak vs. weak or strong vs. strong.*

*Asymmetrical: when two teams have a difference in their strength. Ex: weak vs. strong*

If a similar phenomenon existed for *arrangement fixes* in professional football leagues, we would expect to see a plethora of asymmetrical fixes — weak-strong or strong-weak teams — and a few cases of symmetrical fixes between weak-weak or strong-strong teams.

Gambling corruption, on the other hand, would show cases of both symmetrical and asymmetrical fixes.

The following hypotheses is a good starting point to test this idea:

> *If two types of match-fixing — gambling and arrangements — exist, there will be a difference in the symmetry of the fixes. In arrangement fixes, the greater the asymmetry between teams, the more likely the fix. In gambling fixes, symmetry matters far less and there will be gambling fixes regardless of the relative strengths of the teams.*

To test this hypothesis each team was ranked in a specific variable in the database depending on their position in the league table on the date of the match.

1 ) Teams who were in the top five positions in the league were ranked "1."

2 ) Teams in the bottom five positions were ranked "3".

3 ) While teams that occupied the positions between those two ranges were labelled as "2."

The assumption in this variable was that, in general, any team out of the top 5 places is not realistically competing for the championship. In the same way the relegation battle is most severe among the bottom 5 places and there are few tournament incentives or sanctions for any team outside of those places.

Another variable — *symmetry of fix* — was constructed by assigning each game a categorical value. If teams in the same grouping played each other — "1 vs. 1"; " 2 vs. 2"; or "3 vs. 3" — the match was labelled symmetrical. If the match was between teams from different groups — "1 vs. 2"; or "1 vs. 3"; or "2 vs. 3" — then the game was labelled asymmetrical.

I then ran a Pearson's Chi-square test — this is the standard test to measure possible correlation in statistics — to examine the relation between the variables *symmetry of fix* and *type of fix*. The result was highly significant: p = .021. Again, this means that there was a correlation and that the link between the variables was over the threshold of 95% statistical significance or that result was probably not due to chance.

However, an examination of Figure 4.2 shows *why* the result was positive and that this result does not necessarily represent a universal asymmetrical-symmetrical split between arrangements and gambling fixes.

Figure 4.2: Symmetry of Fix vs. Type of Fixing

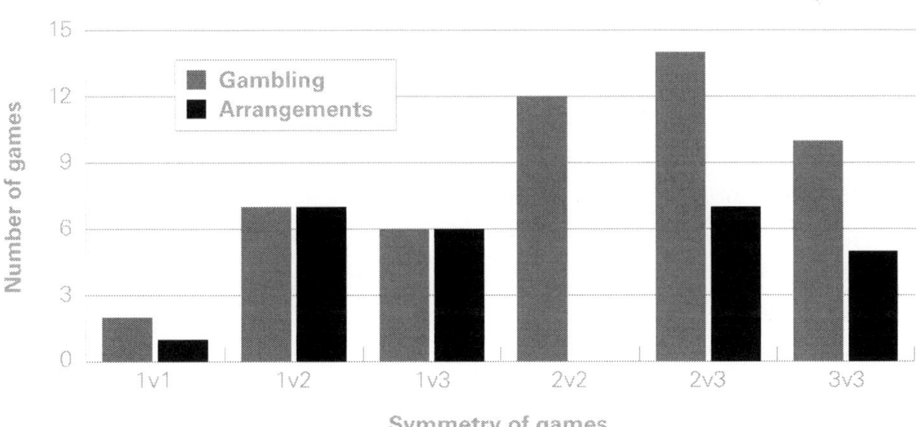


**Source:** *Fixed Match Database 2 (N = 77)*

In Figure 4.2 the red blocks represent arrangement fixes, the light blue blocks gambling fixes. The Y-axis is the total number of games of each type. The X-axis shows the six types of symmetry of the matches — 1 vs. 1, etc. There are three findings that are seen clearly in Figure 4.2.

1 ) Gambling fixes occur across all types of matches — symmetrical or asymmetrical.

2) Arrangement fixes do *not* occur in the symmetrical 2 vs. 2 matches.

3 ) However, arrangement fixes do, occasionally, occur in the symmetrical matches 1 vs. 1 and 3 vs. 3. There is, then, a statistically significant difference in the type of fixes and their rate of symmetrical fixes, but this difference is not seen in all cases.

4 ) As the teams grow weaker, and presumably have fewer resources, the rate of fixing rises.

To explain this result, another factor needs to be considered. I conducted another statistical test with the variables "symmetry of fix," "arrangement fix," "gambling fix," and added the variable "corruptees." In other words, I was interested in *who* was actually fixing, or at least being approached to fix, the games. (Note: this is not corruptors — those who arrange the fixes. We already know that for arrangements the corruptors are usually team administrators, and for gambling fixes the corruptors are usually gamblers.)

The results are shown in Table 4.1:

Table 4.1: Symmetrical Game vs. Corruptee as Player

| | Referee | Player | Total |
|---|---|---|---|
| Symmetrical Fix | 17 (48.5%) | 18 (51.5%) | 35 (100%) |
| Asymmetrical Fix | 11 (13.9%) | 35 (76.0%) | 46 (100%) |

**Source:** *Fixed Match Database (N = 81)*

The results indicate that there is actually no difference between gambling and arrangement fixes, in terms of who is corrupted versus the symmetry of the fix, but there was a positive result for this test ($p < .028$), and it shows an interesting connection. For both gambling and arrangements when there was symmetry of teams in fixed games — weak vs. weak or strong vs. strong — the corruptees were almost equally likely to be players or referees. However, when the matches were asymmetrical — weak vs. strong — the players were three times as likely to be chosen as referees.

The work of Ian Preston and Stefan Szymanski partly explains this result. In their journal article *Cheating in Contests* (2003), they claim that "disparity in desire" is a key reason for match-fixing. Fixing comes about when one team, be it weak or strong, has a far greater *need* to win or draw a match than their opponents.

What their analysis missed is that in the cases when both teams *equally* need to win there are still fixes attempted; it is just that the corruptors in these fixes will try to fix the actors who, purportedly, have no desire to win the game — the referees. Presumably in these games the corruptors tend to corrupt the referees, because it would be more difficult to corrupt the players who wish to win the match.

In arrangement fixes then, the teams are acting like Robert Keohane's analysis of countries in a multi-polar community. They are not entering into alliances with teams that are equally powerful. When attempting to fix games with teams that are stronger or weaker than themselves, teams attempt to make alliances with the opposing team. But when they fix games against teams of equal strength, they fix other actors — the referees — *not* their rivals.

Table 4.2, reviews the differences that we have seen so far between arrangements and gambling fixes.

Table 4.2: Summary of Differences: arrangements and gambling fixes

| | Arrangements | Gambling Fixes |
|---|---|---|
| Corruptors | **Team Administrators 88.2%** | **Gamblers — 86.4%** |
| Timing in Season | **End of season — 75%** | **All parts of season** |
| Symmetry of Fix | **Mostly asymmetrical** | **Gamblers — 86.4%** |
| Corruptees | **In Asymmetrical fixes — Players and team administrators are preferred to referees**<br><br>**Symmetrical Fixes — either referees or players** | **In Asymmetrical fixes — Players and team administrators are preferred to referees**<br><br>**Symmetrical Fixes — either referees or players** |

***Source:*** *Fixed-Match Database 2*

A further discussion of who is corrupted depending on the symmetry of the fixes is presented in Chapter 5. However, there are clear, and statistically significant, differences between the two types of fixes. And we can begin to make predictions if we know *when* the game is fixed about *what type* of fix it is — arrangements or gambling. Knowing the *type* of fix, we can then make predictions as to who fixed the matches and if we know both teams in the fix, we can make accurate predictions as to which agent the corruptors are most likely to approach. But in the final section of this chapter, we see that there is a significant difference in how the fixed games are played depending on the fix.

## Fixing Goals

One night in the fall of 2005, a Singapore team was to play a match against a touring Malaysian team. The odds compilers at Singapore Pools were expecting a quiet evening.[4] The match had not attracted a large amount of interest from the betting public. But suddenly, two hours before the start of the match, the betting "line" began to move wildly. It began to move on a particular score. Not just that one team would win, but that at least nine goals would be scored in the game. This result is very unusual (most football games have total scores of 2 or 3 goals) and as such had odds of roughly 30 to 1. In the next two hours, so many people placed bets on the score going over 9 goals that the betting line crashed. It went from 30 to 1, down to 1.5 to 1; meaning that if a bettor had placed a bet at 6.00 p.m. that both teams would score nine goals combined, for every Singaporean dollar they placed, they would have won 30 dollars back. By the start of the game at 8.00 p.m., the same bet would only have won 1.5 dollars.

Such a change in the betting line is virtually unprecedented in betting markets where an odds movement of 3 or 4 dollars over the course of a week is considered heavy trading. A change of 28 dollars is equivalent to "Black Monday," October 29th, 1929 when the New York stock market crashed. The result of the game? Exactly as the fall in the line predicted — one team won 7-2. Singapore Pools lost several hundred thousand dollars and the game was widely assumed to have been fixed by a set of gambling corruptors who lost

---

[4] *An "odds compiler" is the person who sets "the betting line" for the bookies. The "betting line" is the odds that the bettors will bet on the match. Singapore Pools is the government-run sports gambling company*

control of their information and thus began a "run on the market" (COR1, B2, P8 — all who claimed to have particular knowledge of the alleged fix).

In the 1970s Carlo Petrini was a forward who took part in a number of fixed matches in the Italian Serie A. He claims contrary to the Singapore example, that in arrangement fixes the scores were generally low scoring draws.

Is it possible to find general trends from these two examples? Will gambling fixes, generally, be higher scoring than arrangements? The reason why there may be such a difference in the goals scored is because gambling corruptors are seeking to profit maximize in the gambling market. They often need to manipulate the game not just so that one team wins — the same as an arrangement fix — but also to ensure that a particular *goal spread* is beaten. The gambling market for football in Asia and many parts of the world is based on handicap scoring rather than odds. So if a strong team is to play a weak team, they are assigned a handicap of, for example, 2 goals on the betting market.

Thus if the weak team wins, draws or loses by 2 or less goals, on the gambling market it counts as a win for the weaker team. The stronger team must score 3 or more goals for it to be counted as a win for them on the gambling market. If a gambling corruptor controls the weaker team, they must arrange that the weaker team lose by a larger margin than the *goal spread*.

However, arrangement fixes vary little from regular games because what is important for a corruptor in this type of fix is that a particular team wins or that there is a draw. This is the reason why gambling fixes, on average, would have a larger number of goals scored than either normal games or arrangement fixes.

If gambling corruptors could make more money the more goals that were scored; it would make sense that there would be more goals scored in gambling fixes than arrangement fixes. To test this idea, the hypothesis was:

> *There is a difference in the total number of goals between the two types of fixes with more goals in gambling fixes than in arrangement fixes.* [5]

I constructed a continuous variable — average total goals per game. Figure 4.3 shows a graph of the relative frequency of the average goals per game.

Figure 4.3: Arrangements vs. Gambling Fixes: total goals per game

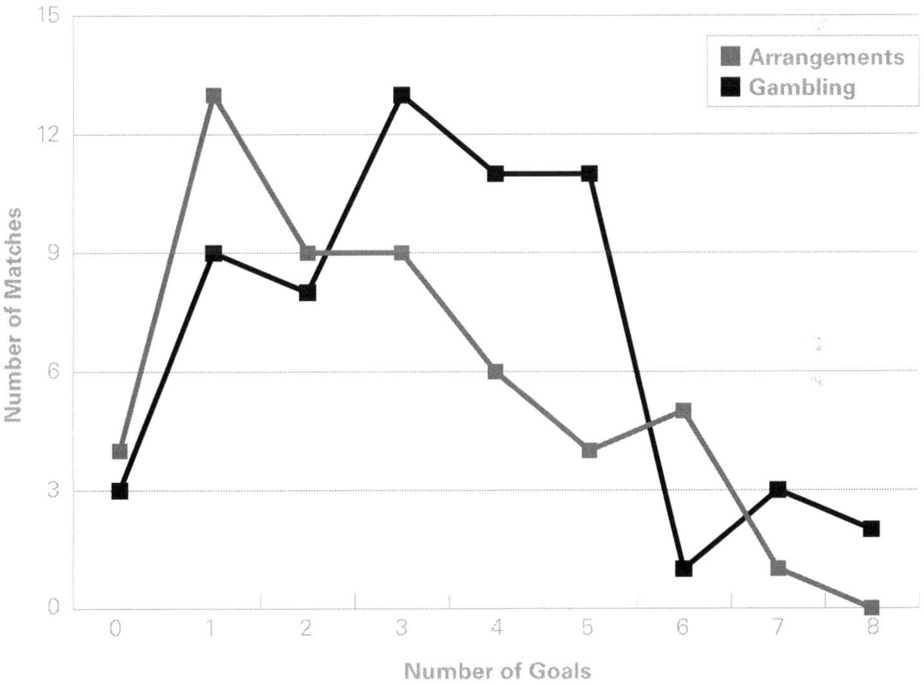

15
12
9
6
3
0
Number of Matches
Arrangements
Gambling
0 1 2 3 4 5 6 7 8
Number of Goals

**Source:** *Fixed-Match Database 2 (N = 111)*

---

[5] *In the original, academic research, this was, of course a null hypothesis. For clarity in this book, all the null hypotheses have been changed.*

The green line represents the number of gambling fixes, the red line arrangement fixes. The Y-axis is the total number of games; the X-axis the total goals scored in a game. At first glance there does seem to be a difference in the two types of fixes shown in Table 4.3: the mean of goals scored in arrangement and gambling fixes is 2.73 and 3.38; the median 2.00 and 3.00. In the control group, the average total number of goals scored in a — presumed — honestly played game is 2.81. Table 4.3, lists the median of both types of fixing and the control groups:

Table 4.3: Arrangements vs. Gambling Fixes: total goals

| Grouping | Average Number of Goals Scored Per Game | Difference from Control Group |
|---|---|---|
| Control Group | **2.81** | **0** |
| Arrangement Fixes | **2.73** | **-.08** |
| Gambling Fixes | **3.38** | **+.57** |

**Source:** *Fixed-Match Database 2 (N = 237)*

There is little difference between arrangements and the control groups, however, there is a difference of .57 between gambling fixes and the control groups and arrangement fixes. However, is this difference statistically significant?

In testing the hypothesis, there was a challenge to overcome: the variable of total number of goals scored per game is non-parametric. In other words, the variable lacks a normal, "bell-curved" distribution because it begins with a high number of games at zero and there are, obviously, no games with negative goals. Thus the distribution curve is cut in half.

Because the data was non-parametric, I ran a Mann-Whitney test — essentially, a Chi Square test for non-parametric numbers — on the following variables: Total Goals, Honestly Played Games, Gambling Fixes and Arrangement Fixes.

The result was a p value of .041, or less than .05%, so there was less than a five in a hundred chance that the difference was due to chance. The hypothesis was proved — there is a statistically significant difference between the average number of goals scored in a gambling fix and a "normal" game and an arrangement fix.

## Conclusion

This first section of the book is about the basics: definitions and introductions to the methodology of the research on sports corruption. We began with a discussion of a high-profile legal trial — the Bruce Grobbelaar case — that involved match-fixing. According to law-enforcement and judicial sources, the progress of the case was handicapped by a confusion of *types* of match-fixing. This confusion is common in both the popular and academic literature. To address this confusion, I presented a definition of match-fixing that stresses its difference from cheating — where players try "too hard" to win a match. In match-fixing, the corruptees are *underperforming* or "not trying hard enough" to win a match. I then show that there are two fundamental types of match-fixing: arrangements and gambling. The definitions are:

> *Arranged match-fixing: when corruptors manipulate a football match to ensure that one team wins or draws the match.*
>
> *Gambling match-fixing: when corruptors manipulate a football match to profit-maximise on the gambling market.*

## Chapter Review

In this chapter, we saw a number of statistically significant differences between these types of fixes:

- Who arranges the fix
- What time of the season they occur in
- Which matches are most likely to be fixed
- Who is likely to participate in the fixes
- The number of goals in a game.

These findings are actually very useful. For example, an honest football league administrator, faced with a possibility of fixing in their league and limited resources, could start to understand the underlying patterns of corruption. If they knew *when* the game is fixed, they could probably tell *what type* of fix it is — arrangements or gambling. Knowing the *type* of fix they could make predictions as to who fixed the matches and knowing both teams in the fix, they can make accurate predictions as to which agent the corruptors are most likely to approach.

This difference in types of fixing — arrangements and gambling — is important and we will return to it a number of times in the book. However, in the next chapter, we shall examine the question of motivation. If fixing is a universal deviancy, regarded across countries, cultures and historical eras as deviant, *why* would anyone fix a game?

# PART TWO
# THE PEOPLE OF THE GAME: CORRUPTORS

# CHAPTER FIVE
# TO FIX OR NOT TO FIX?

*When I was a coach of the XXX under-20s (a national team). I remember a Sheikh walked into our dressing at half-time with a briefcase full of cash — $250,000 U.S. for us to lose the game [to the Sheikh's team]. It was in the qualifying rounds of the Under-20s World Cup and there had been an offer before the game*

*(SO15)*

On the evening of May 19, 1993, Jean-Pierre Bernès and Jean-Jacques Eydelie sat in a hotel room in the northern French town of Valenciennes. They were on the phone speaking to Bernard Tapie. Bernès was the general manager of the Olympique de Marseille football club, Eydelie was one of the players and Tapie the team owner and a sometime-cabinet minister in the French government of the time. The next day Marseille would play Valenciennes FC. On paper it was an easy match for Marseille — they were one of the strongest teams in Europe while Valenciennes was third from the bottom of the French 1st Division. But despite the relative strengths in the teams, Tapie and Bernès decided to fix the match.

The next two chapters will examine how internal corruptors like Jean-

Pierre Bernès, Bernard Tapie, or the Sheikh with his $250,000, arrived at their decisions. It analyses the constraints and incentives that an internal corruptor must consider, in making the choice to fix a match. These are not gambling corruptors working to fix a match for profit. They are people inside the sport — most often the team management — who are considering arranging a match to gain some kind of advantage. In these specific cases the incentives are a place in the Under-20 World Cup or the French league championship.

## High Corruption versus Low Corruption

One academic definition is needed before we begin the analysis. In their work on organised crime, Maurice Kugler and his research colleagues propose a model with two "jurisdictions": high corruption versus low corruption. They write that the effectiveness of punishments varies between these two areas.

In this book, there is a similar distinction: leagues of *high* and *low* corruption. For example, in later chapters we will see that gambling corruptors' methods of approaching potential corruptees depends on whether they are operating in leagues of high or low corruption. However, what do the terms — leagues of *high* and *low* corruption — actually mean?

- All leagues can be presumed to have some, perhaps very small amounts, of fixed games

- A league with low levels of corruption has the occasional arrangement fix towards the end of the season or an isolated gambling fix

- A league with a high degree of corruption has both gambling fixes that occur throughout the season and a high degree of arrangements at the end of the season

## A Decision Tree

In analysing the actions of a potential corruptor, let us use a "decision tree" to illustrate their constraints. It is a useful tool that academics sometimes use to clarify a complicated process. This is not to suggest that at moments of great stress a corruptor sits down with a piece of paper and pencil and draws a similar tree. Some corruptors indicate that the decision is taken so quickly and it is so much part of a "normal" corrupt business environment that they gave it little reflection.

Figure 5.1: Possible Outcomes of Fixing a Game

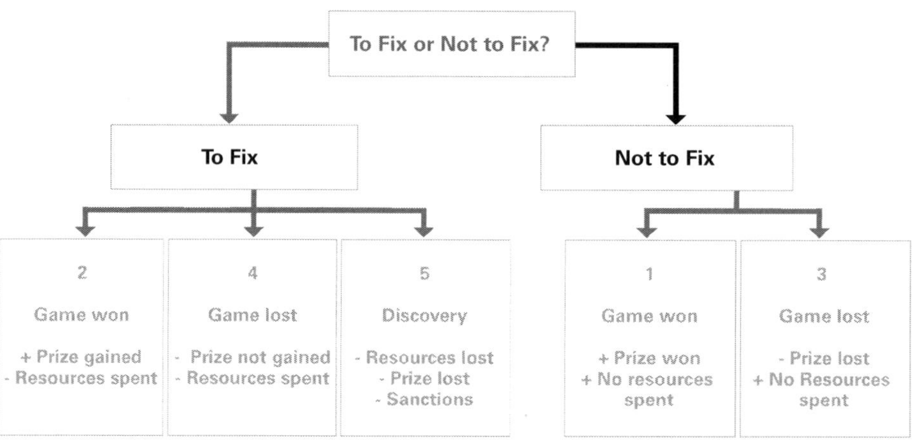


Figure 5.1 shows the possible outcomes to the question — to fix or not to fix? — that an internal corruptor asks before facing a game. The blue squares on the right of the diagram illustrate the outcomes of the decision "not to fix." The yellow squares on the left of the diagram illustrate the outcomes of the decision "to fix the game." At the top of each square is the preference ranking of the outcomes. Figure 5.1 illustrates one important underlying trend for a potential corruptor: the preference is always towards *not* fixing the game.

This trend supports what the American sociologist Howard Becker wrote, "A person commits an offence if the expected utility to him exceeds the utility he could get by using his time and resources at other activities." In ordinary words, Becker is saying that criminals respect their own time and money. They will not spend one-million-dollars to steal ten.

In football terms, this means that if the game can be won honestly, the corruptor does not have to spend additional money or resources to ensure a victory through fixing. If the game is lost honestly, the corruptor loses none of these resources. However, the absolute worst outcome is if a corrupted game is lost — the fix does not succeed — then the corruptor loses both the game, the money spent in attempting the fix *and* face possible sanctions.

So if the preference for a corruptor is always to play the game honestly, why would anyone fix a match? The next section explores that question with an examination of one team in the Russian league.

## To Fix or Not to Fix?

In September 2004, Slavic United was a team in the Russian First Division.[6] The Russian football season runs from March to late October, and by this time in the season it was clear that Slavic was in trouble. They had had a terrible season, winning only 27 points out of a possible 99. If they continued in this fashion, they would be relegated to a lower division. The team manger, Vanya Rubinov, decided to attempt to fix games against two teams, Rangers and Rovers, to try and save his team. Over several weeks, his phone was tapped and his attempts to arrange the matches were recorded. It is unclear who exactly taped the calls, the best guess is that a rogue, presumably football-

---

[6] *Effectively, the second division. All the names of both teams and individuals have been changed.*

loving, section from one of the myriad Russian security agencies like the FSB did the taping and then leaked them to a local news magazine. In September 2004, the magazine published copies of the text.

Another team mentioned in the transcripts confirmed the authenticity of the tapes. Rubinov resigned soon afterwards and the tapes have never been challenged in court. In this chapter, I use excerpts from these transcripts to illustrate the questions that underlay Rubinov's decision to attempt to fix the matches.

In the next chapter, I examine the *challenges* that Vanya Rubinov had to overcome in attempting to fix the matches.[7] Throughout these two chapters, I make reference to Figure 5.2 — a decision tree for an internal corruptor to fix a match — that is found on the opposite page.

## Question 1: **Is the game important enough to fix?**

*Corruptee:* *So I think it is not a problem [fixing the game]. I will find him [another possible corruptee] now and talk to him.*

*Vanya:* *Genya. I'm not asking you. I'm* ***begging*** *you. I need the result. Fuck!* ***Life or death!*** *Fuck! [emphasis added]*

The above quote from Vanya Rubinov illustrates the first key question in the decision of an internal corruptor — is the game important enough to bother fixing? The primary indicator in this question is ***time*** in the season or tournament. If Rubinov can successfully arrange a fixed match then Slavic United's chances of being relegated will be much less. The cost of relegation

---

[7] *My thanks to Paer Gustafsson, Natalia Gorina, Eugene Demchenko, Ekaterinea Korobtseva, Ekaterina Kravchenko, Alisa Voznya and Svetlana Guzeeva for their translation and insight on this case.*

Figure 5.2: To Fix or Not to Fix: decision tree for an internal corruptor

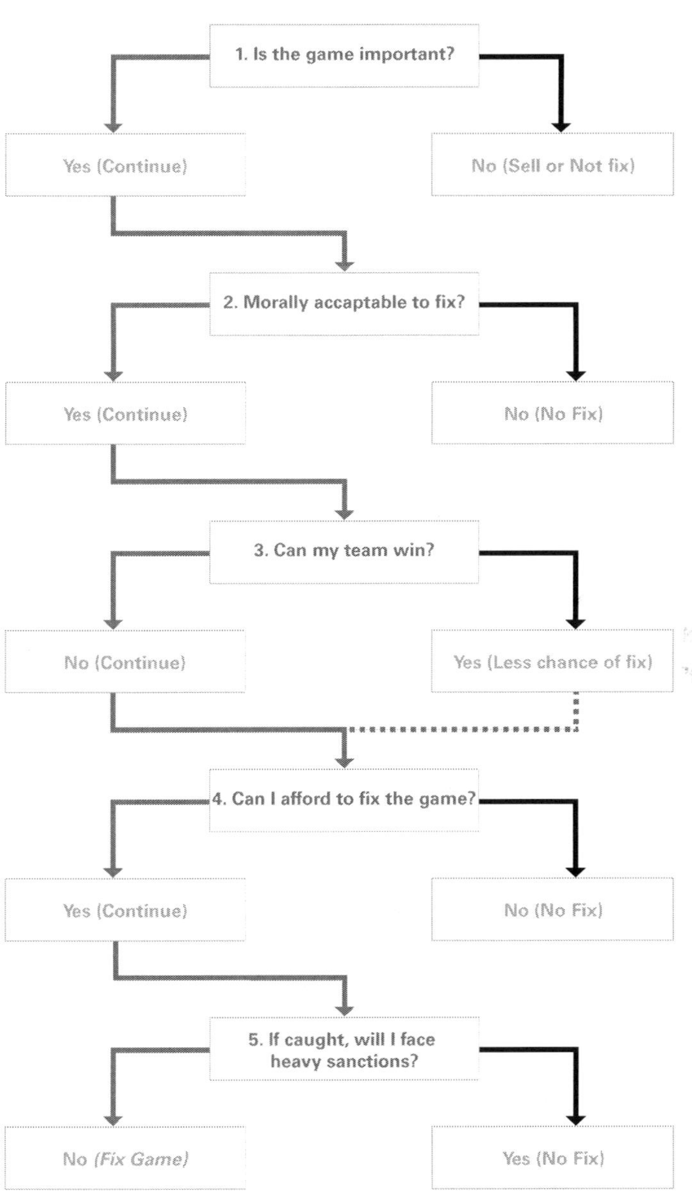

and the subsequent loss of sponsors and television rights is an important consideration for internal corruptors. For example, the difference for an English or Welsh team to play in the Premier League or the Championship (effectively the first and second divisions) is estimated to be £60 million. For Rubinov and Slavic United the figure is lower, but they are still crucial games.

This is a general trend across leagues of varying levels of corruption. We have already seen the statistics supporting this conclusion in Chapter 3. In the qualitative data, crucial games are frequently mentioned by both the interview subjects, and corruptors and corruptees in the confession databank as being the principal motivation for arrangement fixes. A few examples:

> *They had to get a result at XXX to pip YYY for the First Division championship (Laxton et al., 1977).*
>
> *All Everton's League championship and European Cup hopes depended on this May 11 match (Gabbert 1964).*
> *Last week of the season and Rizespor are playing Beşiktaş. Only a win would save them from being relegated (Kilinç 2006).*

There is an important distinction in the discussion of threshold points. Preston and Szymanski write of the "disparity in desire" that signals many fixes. As there is a threshold point for teams to buy games, so there is also a threshold point for teams to *sell* them. The two points are not necessarily the same.

This means that a team may want to fix games relatively early in the season. For example, Luciano Moggi, the corruptor for Italian team Juventus, was attempting to fix games by the second quarter of the season. But other teams may not want to sell points until later in the season, when their own position is guaranteed.

To test the idea that there are both buying and selling threshold points in a season, I ran a statistical analysis on arrangement fixes versus the type of corruptee versus the time of season, for the games in the match-fixing database. The results were highly significant (Pearson's Chi-square value of .038). Figure 5.3 shows the data more clearly.

Figure 5.3: Time of Season vs. Corruptee as Player

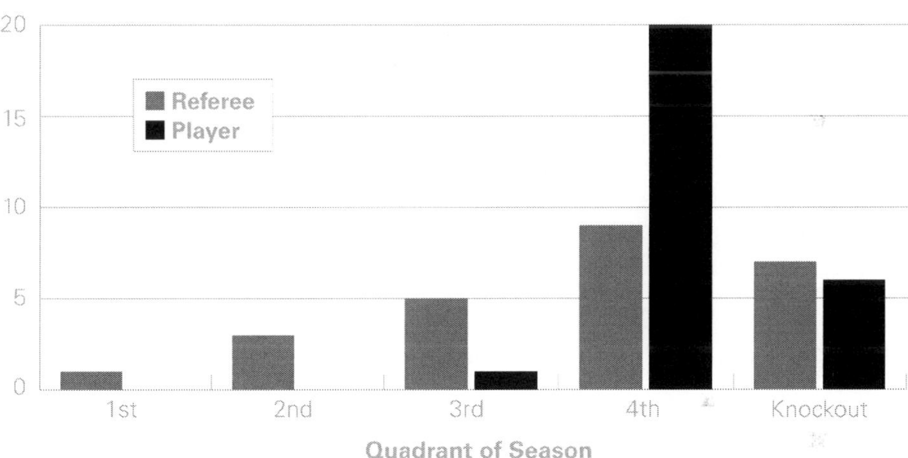


**Source:** *Fixed-Match Database 2 (N = 55)*

In Figure 5.3, we can see that there were no arrangement fixes before the third quadrant of the season that bribed players. The people that the corruptors used before the third quadrant were the referees. However, in the fourth quadrant of the season, as the number of arrangement fixes rises, so also does the number of players prepared to fix games. In other words, neither individual players nor team owners were prepared to sell games to their opponents before the *third* quadrant, and most waited until the fourth quadrant before selling games. Presumably, they did this because they wanted to make sure that they had already gained the maximum necessary points that they needed for their own team's survival in the league.

## Question 2: **Is it ethical to fix a game?**

The next potential constraint is a moral consideration: does the actor's ethical make-up prevent them from corrupting a match? Rubinov and his aides seem completely unbound by any moral considerations. From what we can tell from his telephone conversations, he and his colleagues seem to be entirely self-interested actors. In fact, when one person reportedly does not want to fix a game for ethical reasons, Rubinov's aide is unable to understand what they are talking about and imagines that they must be frightened:

> ***Aide:*** *Hello Vanya, I managed to talk to [the President of the Rovers team] he says that he doesn't want to fucking do anything [fix a match]. Their coach is too principled...So I said to him, "It doesn't matter, your team is already relegated." And he said, "Well, I understand, but we won't fix."* ***I don't get it! Maybe they are chicken?*** *[Emphasis added]*

In his work *Ulysses and the Sirens* Jon Elster writes of the complex interplay between emotions and rationality. Elster argues that morality and altruism are not easy to measure, for they frequently depend on external circumstances like culture and context. In this case there is a similar problem, for there are actually two questions that the possible corruptors ask themselves: Am I moral and is my competition moral? In this case one of Slavic's opponents is presented as being "too principled," even when they are already relegated, to fix a game with Slavic. However, the real consideration for Rubinov is whether another team, a rival of Slavic United for relegation, may fix their games.

The problem at this stage for potential corruptors is that they are relying on imperfect information so the corruptor does not know if another team will fix their match or not. In his discussion of "social dilemma games" Douglas Heckathorn writes of honest actors being like "suckers" in a dishonest environment. In a market where the norm is dishonesty, no one wants to be the honest exception; the risk of being cheated is too high. In fact, there is a moral argument that would state, in a league of high corruption an official *must* fix a game; otherwise they are not performing their duties properly as a team official.

A number of internal corruptors in the database cite this as their reason for fixing matches. Ljubomir Barin is a typical example. Barin was a match-corruptor for the French teams Olympique de Marseille and Girondins de Bordeaux in European Cup matches between 1983 and 1993. He testified that he began to help fix matches after a match that Bordeaux lost 1-0 on a controversial penalty, given by an allegedly corrupt referee:

> *I said to Claude [Bez, the owner of Girondins de Bordeaux], "If you want us to win you've got to make a move, and do something* ***like the others*** *[create an illicit fund to bribe linesman and referees, emphasis added]." He said, "Okay." Afterwards, the referees started falling over themselves to come to Bordeaux (Herve 1995).*

This factor gives rise to "incentive payments," in leagues of high corruption, where some corruptors pay the opponents of their rivals to *play honestly* against their rival's team, and not to accept any potential fix.

CSKA Moscow is one of the top teams in the same Russian league as Slavic United, and their managing director Yevgeny Giner has spoken openly of paying incentive payments to teams so they would not take part in fixed matches that would help CSKA's rivals. This was not merely the complaint of one disaffected club administrator, when he made the announcement of incentive payments Giner was also the President of the Russian League. In this context, Rubinov's decision not to debate the morality of fixing is partly understandable, since to do otherwise may be to fail in his duties as an administrator.

## Question 3: Can my team win honestly?

This question, and the themes that surround it, is vitally important for a potential corruptor. As we saw, all things being equal, even corruptors will want to win games honestly. However, Rubinov had absolutely no confidence in his team's ability to win matches. Rubinov's sentiment was shared by others, as this conversation with a team sponsor, whom Rubinov approached to help with fix, illustrates:

| | |
|---|---|
| *Rubinov:* | *Yes, that is why I'm phoning you. I wanted you to help me with some money, fuck. Because now with the Rangers game coming up, fucking hell, it's needed! There is little hope from the players.* |
| *Team Sponsor:* | *(laughs)* |
| *Rubinov:* | *What the fuck are you laughing about?* |
| *Team Sponsor:* | *About the players.* |
| *Rubinov:* | *But I really wanted to make you a present — a victory.* |
| *Team Sponsor:* | *A victory?!* |
| *Rubinov:* | *Yes, fuck.* |
| *Team Sponsor:* | *But what is needed from me, so they win?* |
| *Rubinov:* | *I need twenty pieces [$20,000 U.S.].* |

| | |
|---|---|
| ***Team Sponsor:*** | *Shit! Twenty pieces? In order to beat Rangers, twenty pieces?* |
| ***Rubinov:*** | *Yes.* |

This laughable ineptitude on the part of Slavic United does not mean that strong teams never fix games against weaker teams. In the example that began this chapter, the French champions, Olympique de Marseille, fixed their game with Valenciennes. One of the questions that perplexed many observers is why Marseille would have *bothered* to fix the game. They were one of the strongest teams in Europe and Valenciennes was near the bottom of the French first division. However, in the Match Fixing Database there are a number of other cases, like the Marseille game, of strong teams fixing games against much weaker teams. Why would internal corruptors go to all this trouble to fix these matches?

The answer is a complicated one. It is partly, as Eydelie would write later, that a culture of fixing had arisen on the Marseille team. The culture had become so embedded that the club officials and some players had grown too confident and cocky and "cheating had become second nature." In part it was also to save their players from injury, since they had another big match the next week.

However, there is also a concept from betting that is useful in understanding what goes on in the minds of corruptors at these moments. At the heart of all wagers is the mathematical idea of probabilities: there is predictable rate of chance that will always occur unless significantly altered in some fashion. For example, tossing a coin 100 times will result, roughly, in 50 heads and 50 tails. Successful professional gamblers and bookmakers use derivations of this idea to either place bets or calculate their odds.

When it comes to a football match those odds can be altered honestly by buying better players or changing coaches. However, within the theory of probabilities is a fundamental concept that drives match-fixing: no matter how strong one team becomes, there is *always* a chance that the weaker team could win the game.[8] If the value of the game is low, a corrupt manager will be willing to risk the chance that his stronger team will win honestly. However, as the value of the game grows the incentive to leave the outcome to chance diminishes on the part of the corruptor. Therefore, in important games corrupt officials will fix matches, even against much weaker teams. For Olympique de Marseille, it was a very important game, win and they could win the entire French League championship, estimated to be worth more than 30 million French Francs. Match-fixing officials are searching for *certainty* in the very uncertain world of soccer games.

An excerpt from Joe McGinniss' book *The Miracle of Castel di Sangro* may be helpful for the reader to understand this concept in practical terms. McGinniss, an American writer, witnessed first-hand an arrangement fix in the last game of the season in the Italian Serie B (second division). The game was between A. S. Bari, a team that could win promotion to the first division (estimated to be worth $10 million) if they won the match and Castel di Sangro, a team that was neither in danger of relegation or promotion. One of the players of Castel di Sangro explained to McGinniss, before the fix, the phenomenon of searching for certainty that high-stake threshold matches brought about:

---

[8] *In the case of a football match between two equal teams, say Team A and Team B, playing in a neutral ground the probabilities of the match are, out of a hundred, 35 — 30 — 35. Or for roughly every three matches, one should be a victory for Team A, one should be a draw and one should be a victory for Team B. For evenly matched games when one team is playing at their own ground the rate changes to 45 — 29 — 26, this is what is called "home advantage" and has been shown to affect both players and referees.*

*My thanks to Alistair Flutter, Joe Saurmaurez-Smith and Professor Allison Gilmore (Department of Mathematics – UCLA) for their insights.*

> *.... a one-to-one draw would be for Bari a bigger calamity... than an earthquake. For a matter of such importance,... not one speck can be left up to chance [emphasis added]. And this year, Joe. I know of Lucchese, and Salernitana [two other Serie B teams] [They] pay for points. They take care of their business last Sunday, when they play Cremonese, from last place. You say* ***senza dubbio*** *[without doubt] they will win. But again there must be* ***no uncertainty*** *[emphasis added]. So they pay and they score four goals...*
> *(McGinniss 1997, 390)*

## Question 4: Can I afford to fix the game?

The next question that corruptors must answer is can they afford to fix the game? A weak team may lose to a strong team and be relegated but the *cost* of fixing the game is so prohibitive that they simply cannot afford fixing the game. For example, many people may want to fix a game against Manchester United — a club valued at $2.3 billion, some of whose players are paid vast sums of money each week to play — but aside from the players would not take part in a fix, the corruptors simply do not have enough money to do so.

This consideration plays a large part in Rubinov's discussions. It is the basis for most of the conversations between various actors. Most of the participants seem to be willing to discuss the possibility of fixing the game, but whether Rubinov can afford their price is the central point of their discussions. In this typical excerpt, he has negotiated a fix with players from the opposing team. However, he does not have enough money to complete the deal and is forced to ask the corruptee with whom he has arranged the deal to give him some more time to get the money:

***Rubinov:*** *It's not ready, I don't have the whole amount.* ***We have to fix. We have no other way*** *[emphasis added]. I have only 35. Fuck. But I am preparing*

| | |
|---|---|
| | *something. I could bring you the rest on Saturday. But at the moment I just don't have anything.* |
| ***Corruptee:*** | *Oh fuck.* |
| ***Rubinov:*** | *We can give you this 35 now. And on Saturday, I will bring you the rest. What the fuck! You understand we only have 35.* |
| ***Corruptee:*** | *And....* |
| ***Rubinov:*** | *Okay, I'll give you 35 [thousand dollars] no problem. And then I will give you the rest on Saturday. Maybe after the game, we will collect something from the tickets and I will give it to you. Fuck. I will bring it Saturday. I have to get at least 3 [thousand dollars] more.* ***I cannot make a mistake here. Maybe we will win anyway. But we may lose and I do need guarantees*** *[emphasis added].* |

As we can see from this excerpt, Rubinov's decision to fix is based on the rational calculation between what he can afford and the need to guarantee the game.

### Question 5: **If I am caught is there a high risk of sanctions?**

The final question that is whether the league or another outside force (the police or the legal system) will impose sanctions on them, if they are caught: There are effectively two parts to this question: will the corruptors be caught? And, secondly, if they are caught, will there be heavy sanctions?

Interestingly, in the Slavic United case Rubinov and his aides do not seem to consider possible sanctions for their corrupt activities. Their attempts to fix the game are genuinely impressive in their thoroughness. They approach almost every conceivable potential corruptee: players, coaches, opposing team administrators and referees. Yet from what we can tell both from the transcripts and subsequent widespread media coverage, none of the internal sports actors revealed their actions to the authorities and no football sanctions were ever taken against him or the Slavic team.

This attitude may reflect a general trend of high corruption in Russian Football. Over the last few years, despite a number of cases of alleged fixing being brought forward by senior coaches, team owners and bettors (and Yevgeny Giner's admission of incentive payments) only one team has actually been punished for fixing. Perhaps Rubinov and his aides made a realistic appraisal of the situation, as despite the publication of the transcripts no action was ever taken against Rubinov or the Slavic club. However, in the next chapter we will see examine why Rubinov's next action is to double-cross the opposing players when he tries to set up a deal with someone else.

## Chapter Review

- Most team officials will prefer not to spend money in bribes to ensure that their team wins.
- There are thresholds times in a season for corruption including when players and teams will start to *sell* games.
- Some teams will try to fix games at any point in a season; their main targets will be referees.
- The five questions are a corruptor asks themselves are:

    i) Is the game important enough to fix?
    ii) Is it ethical to fix a game?
    iii) Can my team win honestly?
    iv) Can I afford to fix the game?
    v) If I am caught is there a high risk of sanctions?

# CHAPTER SIX
# CERTAINTY, FAVOUR BANKS AND GUARANTORS

| | |
|---|---|
| *Fayad:* | *So, how much certainty can you give me today [emphasis added]?* |
| *de Carvalho:* | *Maximum, of course.* |
| *Fayad:* | *What is the certainty? Can you give me that guarantee? [emphasis added] For the love of God, my life is on the line!* |

*Intercepted telephone conversation between Nagib Fayad, and the referee he was bribing, Edílson Pereira de Carvalho. (Rizek, André and Thais Oyama, 2005).*

In the last chapter, we examined the specific case of a Russian corruptor that I call Vanya Rubinov — and analysed *why* he wanted to fix matches. Rubinov's team "Slavic United" were in the last few weeks of the season (names have been changed). They were a dreadful lot, seemingly incapable of winning any match without corruption. Their manager, Rubinov, who was also the corruptor in this case, made a series of frantic telephone calls to club sponsors, potential match officials and competing teams his phone was being covertly recorded. The telephone conversations, subsequently leaked to a local magazine, do not relate his actual decision-making. In the calls, there is no Hamlet moment where he dithers between honesty and corruption. Rather the reader has to infer from the conversations after the decision, why he undertook to fix the matches. In the last chapter, we examined five questions that seemed to be included in his decision. However, there is a great deal of direct material in the transcripts on *how* Rubinov goes about fixing the games. In this chapter, I am going to use this material to show how he overcame the challenges of corrupting the match.

For Rubinov the first challenge is *whom* to approach to fix the game. There are three possible groups of people he can ask to corrupt the match: the referees, the opposing players and the opposing team administration. There are also three questions implicit in Rubinov's decision to choose one of these three groups:

- Can he get access to them?
- Can he trust them?
- Can they actually deliver the fixed match as promised?

In the next chapter, we will see a similar challenge from the perspective of a gambling corruptor. The principal difference between the two is ease of access. Gambling corruptors have to spend a great deal of time and resources seeking access to people inside the sport. Rubinov has none of those problems, he, and his aides, are seemingly able to contact all potential corruptees. So Rubinov and his aides spend considerable time debating *which* actors they should corrupt as the following excerpt illustrates. At this point in the attempted fix, Rubinov has contacted both the referees and players of the opposing team. They are, allegedly, both willing to fix the match, but the players are insisting on being paid $60,000 U.S. Rubinov does not have that kind of money so he telephones a friend and they have the following conversation:

| | |
|---|---|
| *Friend:* | *$60,000?! The players want this?* |
| *Rubinov:* | *Yes.* |
| *Friend:* | *Fuck... Well, just give the referees the $40,000 — if you don't find the rest.* |
| *Rubinov:* | *What else can I do, fuck? Faggots! We can give them [the players] $60000 or $20000. The most important thing is the effect [fixing the game]. Now we will be talking with them and see and maybe we can make a deal. We will give 40, and then bring the 20 later. Fuck! So then there is a guarantee already?* |
| *Friend:* | *Yes, of course, the guarantee is needed [emphasis added].* |
| *Rubinov:* | *Well, fuck. They also have enough. Those fuckers [the players] already have too much. This is the situation.* |
| *Friend:* | *Maybe you fucking give the referees 30 [$30,000] fuck. And say to the players: fuck, if you don't do it for 30, I will give the other 30 to someone else, rather than you fuck!* |

This conversation shows the following dilemma: how much certainty can the corruptors buy and for how much? In other words, which group can give them the best chance for a successful fix: the players who want $60,000 or the cheaper referees?

In the qualitative data — the confession databank and interviews — there is a strong undercurrent that corrupt referees simply cannot guarantee the fix with enough precision to make it worth bribing them. The comments of SO30, a European football official who has investigated a number of fixed matches, are typical:

> *Ha! I had a case a few years ago. The referee had been bribed. So he gave a penalty. And the team missed the penalty! So you know even if you bribe people you are not* ***guaranteed*** *[emphasis added] to win. (SO30)*

The transcripts of the covertly taped calls between Brazilian gambling corruptor Nagib Fayad, and the referee he was bribing, Edílson Pereira de Carvalho, that we saw at the beginning of the chapter, also reveal a similar pattern. In another intercepted telephone conversation, one of Fayad's partners complains of giving money to Edílson — "that S.O.B. of a ref" — after the referee is unable to deliver the correct result in several games. The German referee Robert Hoyzer and his corruptor also had the same problem. The corruptor lost a great deal of money when Hoyzer was, unwittingly, unable to deliver a successful fix.

If this is what the *words* (qualitative data) indicates what do the statistics show? Do referees have a lower rate of success than players in delivering successful fixes?

In my analysis, I defined a "successful fix" as a fixed match that took place, but no one at the time was able to determine if a fix took place; there was no suspension of betting, no negative reaction by the crowd watching the game and no adverse media reports. Table 6.1 shows the result:

Table 6.1: Rate of Successful Fix vs. Corruptee

| Corruptee | Successful Fix | Failed Fix | Rate of Success |
|---|---|---|---|
| Referee | 28 | 8 | 77.8% |
| Players | 54 | 11 | 83.1% |
| Team Administration | 38 | 4 | 90.5% |

**Source:** *Fixed-Match Database 2 (N = 143)*

As Table 6.1 shows, corrupt players and referees have an almost equally good rate of success in delivering the fix. The rate of success of referees is only slightly lower than players. The anecdotal evidence seems to be incorrect: referees have almost as good success rates as players in fixing matches. However, what is immediately noticeable from Table 6.1 is that of all the possible corrupt groups, the team administrators have a higher rate of success than either the referees or players. To corrupt a team owner gives a potential corruptor an almost 12% better chance of success than bribing a referee. Why would corrupting a team owner be more successful than corrupting a player or referees? After all, players and referees are actually on the field and can directly corrupt the match, whereas team administrators are simply watching the game.

The key is the number of players involved in the fix. In a statistical analysis, successful corruption was linked to size of fixing networks: the larger the number of people involved in the fix, the better the chance that the fix would succeed. A logistic regression was performed with "success of fix" as the dependent variable and each increased level of a network as the independent variables. The variable "network" had five distinguishing levels — network of 1, 2-4, 5-7, 8-9, 10-11 (a football team has 11 players on the pitch). Presumably, corrupting another team owner allows the *entire* team to take part in the fix, rather than simply a few players. So as the size of network grew, so the chance of success of the fix grew as Figure 6.1 illustrates:

Figure 6.1: Success of Fix vs. Size of Network

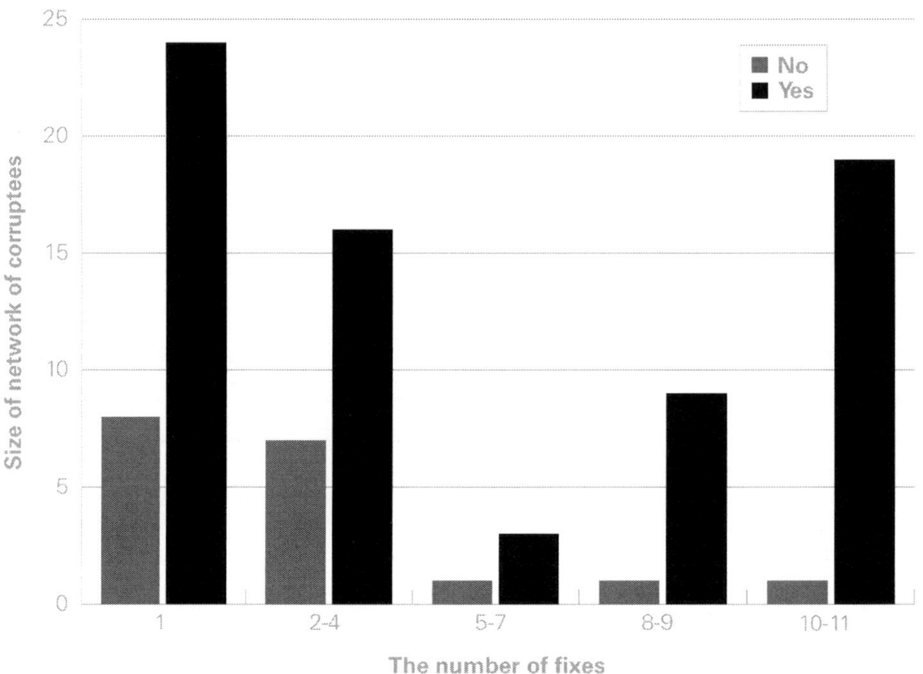


**Source:** *Fixed-Match Database 2 (N = 91)*

After a lot of discussions, Vanya Rubinov decides to arrange a corrupt deal with the team administration. In the following excerpt of the transcripts, Rubinov is speaking to "Sergei," a team administrator of Rangers. He has already negotiated a potential deal with the Rangers players but now he is going to betray them to their club officials:

| | |
|---|---|
| *Rubinov:* | *Okay. I'll tell it to you. Our way. I'm dealing with you. Because some of the players came and offered this [to fix the match] but I'm dealing with you.* |
| *Sergei:* | *Who came?* |
| *Rubinov:* | *Your players.* |
| *Sergei:* | *They contacted you themselves?* |
| *Rubinov:* | *Yes. But it is not to be talked about in a rush. I will tell you their names later, if you want.* |

The underlying question in this excerpt is why does Rubinov bypass the players? There is, as we have seen in Table 6.1, a 7.4% increase in the chance of a successful fix, if he arranges a deal with the club administration. However, it is doubtful if Rubinov knows the precise statistical difference in the success rate of corruptees in fixing football matches! Rather, Rubinov is turning down the deal for other, longer-term reasons.

## Trust, Favour Banks and Guarantors

Rafael La Porta and his academic colleagues wrote an article entitled *Trust in Large Organizations* (1997). Essentially, they argued that trust can be helpful in fighting corruption as it promotes cooperation between bureaucrats and other officials. However, the opposite is also true: corruptors *need* trust. It is equally, if not more important for corrupt people to trust each other. As Johann Lambsdorff writes:

> *Corruption is not a single act between anonymous partners. Rather, it is embedded into a complex relationship. Corruption comprises implicit, informal, and nonbinding agreements that are enforced by*

> *being rooted in long-term business or hierarchical associations. (Lambsdorff 2007, 215)*

In this case, the more times corruptors can successfully fix matches between themselves, the more they trust each other. The more they trust each other, the more matches they can fix. This is the reason why Rubinov chooses to betray the deal that he made with the players and set up a corrupt transaction with the team administration. The money that Rubinov would pay is exactly the same, but if he made a deal with the players, it would simply be a one-shot agreement: done and then forgotten. However, if he makes a deal with the team administration it becomes part of the on-going system that team officials conduct with each other and will not be affected by player turnover.

However, he runs into a problem, soon after the conversation excerpt above, the team administrator — "Sergei" — claims that an administrator from a third club had said that Rubinov had not honoured a corrupt deal in the past. If he wants to continue this corrupt deal he must clear his reputation. Rubinov is furious and phones up the administrator from the third club as the following piece of text illustrates:

| | |
|---|---|
| ***Rubinov:*** | *Grigori, this is Rubinov. Explain to me this fact! Where or when do I not keep my obligations to your club? What are the times that I have let you down?* |
| ***Administrator:*** | *I don't understand.* |
| ***Rubinov:*** | *You are telling "Sergei" [the Rangers administrator] that I won't keep my promises!... He told me that you don't trust me. And that I will end up tricking him. This is* |

*fucking nonsense! Because when I had to, I solved all the problems...*

| | |
|---|---|
| *Administrator:* | *I told him that you and I made a deal [fixed a match] but nothing else!* |

In this excerpt, Rubinov is not simply angry because the deal may go wrong, he needs to re-establish his credibility quickly, otherwise his chances of conducting future match-fixing deals will be negligible. This is not only important because of the present corrupt deal, but because in a league with high corruption, the capacity and reputation, to arrange fixed matches is an important business asset for an administrator to have!

This is a self-reinforcing phenomenon because in a league with high-levels of corruption the honest officials will be at a disadvantage and will, eventually, be forced out — leaving only dishonest, but trustworthy team officials who will construct a corrupt network that serves their own purposes.

Joe McGinniss writes of a similar, favour bank, arrangement among owners in the Italian Serie B. He describes an Italian professional player telling him of these arrangements in the following way:

> *Joe, the truth is... some teams that badly need points pay for them. Others to whom the points mean nothing accept. And it is not always only a matter of money. It can be a favour requested or a favour repaid between the presidents of the Serie. It can be many things. In Italy it is called **il sistema**, and for someone who has not grown up with it, I am sure it can seem very complex. (McGinniss 1999, 385)*

This type of corrupt arrangement is seen in other sports, one interview subject — whose expertise was Olympic sports like weightlifting or boxing

— described the fixes that he had witnessed as "sharing and caring" or "through every pipe a little water must flow." The fixes were arranged to ensure that each national sports federation had at least one medal to boast about in their home country (SO4).

The American economists Duggan and Levitt (2002) also showed this type of match corruption and "favour banks" existed in Japanese Sumo wrestling. Without trust between them, potential corruptors would be unable to perform corrupt actions, so enormous amounts of energy are spent by corruptors maintaining this favour bank to ensure future corrupt deals.

Earlier in the chapter, I wrote of Luciano Moggi, the Italian corruptor for Juventus. Moggi was a master craftsman of a favour bank. The covert tapes of his transactions reveal he not only coerced and bribed people, but far more often he enacted a constant series of favours that were either repaid or withdrawn with a large network of internal sport actors. The following excerpt is typical. It shows Moggi's relationship with Pierluigi Pairetto, the official in charge of appointing referees for the Union of European Football Association (UEFA), the ostensibly neutral organization in charge of running the Champions League. Moggi's Juventus team has a difficult game against the Dutch team Ajax coming up and he has requested an excellent referee for the match, Pairetto phones him:

***Moggi:*** *Hello.*

***Pairetto:*** *Hey, have you forgotten me? I always remember you!*

***Moggi:*** *Oh come on!*

***Pairetto:*** *Hey, I've put in a great referee for the Amsterdam game.*

***Moggi:*** *Who's that then?*

**Pairetto:** *It's Meier [Urs Meier, a Swiss referee].*

**Moggi:** *Well done!*

**Pairetto:** *I only called you to tell you that. See I remember you, even if you these days…*

**Moggi:** *Oh, don't break my balls!* ***You'll see that when I'm back you'll realise that I haven't forgotten you*** *[emphasis added].*

There is absolutely no suggestion that Urs Meier was in any way involved in corruption. Rather, his name was advanced as he was a very good referee. However, a few days later, Moggi arranges for Pairetto to acquire a rare four-door Maserati. Moggi's conversations are full of these "favour" transactions. Here, as another example, he is talking to one of Italy's top football journalists, Fabio Baldas, who ran a television program that critiqued the performance of football referees. Moggi has essentially "fixed" Baldas' show. He has vetted the comments and determined which referees get the most favourable comments or criticism. The conversation ends in the following way:

**Baldas:** *OK… if I need a favour will you do me a favour?*

**Moggi:** *No problem.*

**Baldas:** *You'll call me back soon?*

**Moggi:** *Yup, soon.*

**Baldas:** *Fine, bye.*

Vanya Rubinov is not in the same class as Luciano Moggi. He simply does not have the resources that Moggi did. So midway through his fixing attempts, he runs into a problem. As the academic Susan Rose-Ackerman argues reputation is extremely important in corrupt deals; and Rubinov's credibility has been damaged by rumours of unreliability. Now he must use another common corrupt football practice: a guarantor. In this excerpt he is complaining to a friend about his difficulties in getting the Rangers team administration to accept the fix:

> *You understand that is how it is being talked about. Fuck! I'm saying [to the Rangers officials], "that when asked [to sell a match] I solved the problems. Fuck! I didn't say fuck [nothing]. And I didn't try to pass it to other people. And I didn't tell anyone, and I didn't say, "Give it [the payment] immediately." You understand? And he started telling me stories [about Rubinov's purported unreliability]. And I say, "Borya, wait. If, fuck, you need the guarantees, go to the Chechnyan [another football administrator, who presumably Rubinov has arranged corrupt deals with before] and clear up the situation.*

In a previous excerpt we saw that Vanya Rubinov was attempting to *guarantee the match*; here he needs a third party to *guarantee* his trustworthiness. He needs someone to guarantee that he will pay the bribes that he has promised to pay. After all, if he does not pay — what can the other people do? Go to a judge and complain?

Johann Lambsdorff writes of this problem in general for corrupt people when he says — "corrupt contracts are not legally enforceable". So when there is very little trust between the people: a good football corruptor needs to ensure that the fixed match will go off without a hitch. Rubinov is now entreating his potential corruptees to seek a third party that he names who will do two things: re-establish his reputation and also guarantee the fix. In other words, this third party is forceful enough to work as a quasi-legal system.

Thomas Schelling in his definition of organised crime writes of the crime syndicates striving to establish a "monopoly of violence". In this case, it is clear that there is no single, illegal authority providing this governmental service as a shadow and rival to the main Russian Football Association. Presumably, if one source were able to provide a single guarantor of all fixed-matches in a league, that league would cease to be competitive. However, the practice of guarantors is common in high-corruption football leagues. For example, the Turkish mafia Godfather Sedat Peker has helped guarantee a number of fixes as this excerpt from a covertly-recorded telephone conversation reveals:

> *Corruptor: We did our best for Rizespor. Beşiktaş [two Turkish football teams] people helped too. Sedat Peker* ***managed*** *the issue [emphasis added].*

There is an important distinction to be made here. Said K. Aburish (1985) wrote a superb description of corrupt agents in the oil industry and various other commentators have written extensively about the use of agents in arranging other types of corrupt deals. There has also been a long accepted corrupt practice in football of using agents to gain access to corruptees. However, what Vanya Rubinov is seeking at this point is *not* an agent to gain access to potential corruptees, he already used his aides as this type of agent, but someone more akin to a banker or a financial institution, who can guarantee that he can and will pay. These guarantors use their "good" name that implies the threat of force, to ensure that the corrupt deal goes through. In the corruption literature, commentators often conflate these roles. Figure 6.2 illustrates the difference.

Obviously, at times the same person can play both roles (see Aburish for a good discussion of these roles). Diego Gambetta illustrated a similar circumstance in the organised crime-connected horse-seller in Sicily. The point is that access to the market is not the difficult part, the horse market is well-

Figure 6.2: Agents and Guarantors in Corrupt Deals

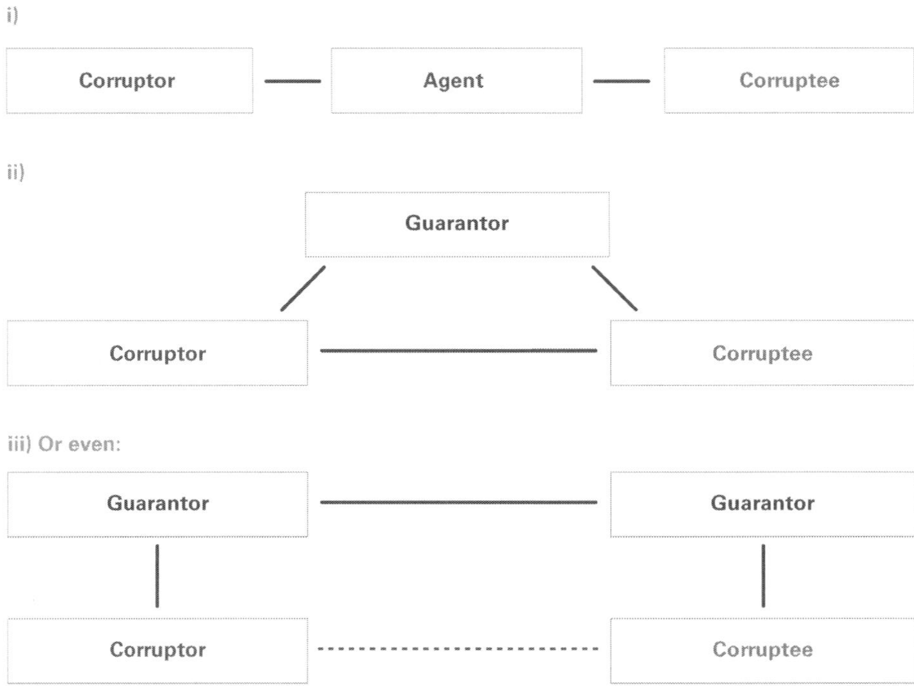


known and inside highly corrupt football leagues, corrupt access is relatively easy to negotiate. It is accepting the bribe and guaranteeing the corrupt deal takes place as planned that is difficult. It is for this reason that the other people demand from Rubinov that he provide them with a guarantor.

The game eventually takes place and Vanya Rubinov's team wins 1-0, the goal being scored in the 11th minute of the game.

In these last two chapters, we have examined how internal corruptors go about fixing football matches. These are not gambling fixes. Rather the decision to fix is based solely on tournament incentives and the corruptors are searching for *guarantees* when fixing a football match. Overall, we can see the difficulties of corrupting a match even in a league of low-enforcement. The corruptor must deal with a whole series of potentially dishonest players, referees and other teams' administrators who may take their bribes but then refuse to perform the fix. The corruptors have to maintain both their "honest" reputations when being corrupt and a network of favour banks. If corruption is difficult for them, what of the difficulties that someone who is from completely outside the sport — like a gambling corruptor — must face in fixing a match? In the next chapter we will see how they overcome similar problems using a successful "five-step" method.

## Chapter Review

- The corruptors are searching for certainty
- The best group to ensure a successful fix is the team management
- In highly-corrupt leagues the corrupt team officials will form "favour-banks" and exchange corrupt deals between themselves
- Even in highly-corrupt leagues — *guarantors* are needed. People, sometimes associated with organised crime, who will guarantee that the fix is carried out successfully and the bribes are paid.

# CHAPTER SEVEN
# FIVE STEPS TO SUCCESS

*But what I do is not a simple job... we have to teach them... Everything we have to teach to the players... Fixed match — not an easy job! So you have to know how to do, how to make. You know lot of things in these fixing matches...*

*(COR3)*

There have been fixes throughout the history of sport: from Imperial Roman chariot races to 18th century cricket games and 19th century professional rowing races. But arguably the most famous fix of the modern era is the story of how criminals working with Arnold Rothstein, the Jewish gambling mobster, corrupted baseball's 1919 World Series. There is an entire cultural industry — books, movies and even a restaurant chain — that are based on the central figure of "Shoeless Joe" Jackson, the star player of the Chicago White Sox who took money to fix the biggest series of games in the sport. The stories around the whole episode are now the stuff of legends: the little boy who looked up at Joe, while he was outside the courthouse, and said, "Say it ain't so, Joe. Just say it ain't so."

This is a touching story but when all the evidence is examined two things are very clear: one, some players on the White Sox did take money to lose the series: and secondly, this kind of fixing was relatively common in the baseball of that time. However, *how* did they go about the fixing? How did Rothstein's thugs and corruptors put into place the largest fraud in the history of modern-sport?

When meeting sports corruptors in the course of the fieldwork, it was often a good way to "break the ice" by asking them about the difficulties of their work. Usually much laughter would answer the question and it would start a series of stories of betrayals by players, suspicious bookmakers or freak sporting accidents. In the next three chapters we will examine all the challenges that the corruptors face. We will see first a case study on how not to organize a fixed match, then a section on the role that networks have in ensuring a successfully fixed match.

In this chapter, I use academic theorists to explain how successful corrupt networks differ from unsuccessful corrupt networks. Then in the next two chapters, we will examine the use of neutral language in "pitching" fixes and then how counterfeit relationships are used to build long-term fixing relationships. However, unlike the last section of the book, in these chapters we are only examining gambling fixes, that is games where the motivation of the fix is to rig the games so as to win bets on the gambling market.

The data shows that all these techniques are used in five distinct and seperate stages to establish a successful sporting fix. These five stages are:

- Access
- Set up
- Calling the fix
- Performance
- Payment

So in the following chapters, I outline each of these five steps to successfully completing a fix. However, let us begin with an example of how *not* to fix a sporting event.

## How Not to Fix a Match

On April 6, 2005 Kenan Erol walked into the Sebatspor football stadium in Eastern Turkey with a bag full of 500 Euro notes. He was going to try to bribe Hakan Olgun the goalkeeper for the Turkish Super League side Akçaabat Sebatspor. Their opponents in the match were Kayserispor. The morning of the match, someone had entered a betting shop in the nearby town of Trabzon and bet over 210,000 Euros with a Turkish betting agency that Sebatspor would lose. Someone wanted Sebatspor to lose the game and was willing to pay a lot of money to make sure that they did. Kenan Erol was their man.

Erol had talked to at least seven other players on the team, but he needed to make sure the goalkeeper, the player who could destroy a team's chances with a couple of mistakes, was on board. Kenan Erol met Hakan Olgun, the goalkeeper, that morning. This is a verbatim transcript of part of their conversation:

***Kenan Erol:*** *I have spoken to all the other players about this fix. The others know about it.*

***Hakan Olgun:*** *What? The whole team knows?*

***Kenan Erol:*** *Don't worry about it!*

***Hakan Olgun:*** *I don't understand. Do you want me just to leave the goal area and "eat" a goal?*

***Kenan Erol:*** *First half you will be ahead 1-0. But Kayseri should win the game. You should let in 2 or 3 goals in the second half.*

***Hakan Olgun:*** ***Can I trust you?*** *[emphasis added]*

| | |
|---|---|
| *Kenan Erol:* | *The money is in the car. Let me show you.* |
| *Hakan Olgun:* | *You mean it is betting? Or do you have an arrangement with the other team? Does our team management know?* |
| *Kenan Erol:* | *If you talk about this to your management you won't get a single lira! I'm trying to do you a favour. These guys are trying to bet 500-600 billion Lira (he shows him the bag with the money inside). There are 200,000 Euro in the bag and there will be more. Just get the score we want.* |
| *Hakan Olgun:* | *Brother! They are all 500 Euro notes. I have never seen that much money in my life! Are you going to give it to me?* |
| *Kenan Erol:* | *When the match is finished, it will be in your pocket.* |
| *Hakan Olgun:* | *I have 130-140 billion Turkish Lira debt. How much will I get?* |
| *Kenan Erol:* | *At least 75 billion Turkish Lira. The rest will go to your friends.* |

The identity of "these guys," who were purportedly willing to bet 500-600 billion Turkish Lira on the game, has never been revealed. When Veli Sezgin, the owner of Sebatspor, heard about the attempts to bribe some of his players, he fitted out the goalkeeper, Hakan Olgun, with a tape recorder to record their conversation. This particular action may have cost Mr. Sezgin, four months later he was ambushed as he walked to his car and shot in a machine gun attack.

The administrative board of the Turkish Football League upon hearing the tape, suspended six players for their alleged role in the fix, gave Hakan Olgun 50,000 Euro as a reward for his coming forward and invited Kenan Erol to explain his actions before their committee. Unsurprisingly, Mr. Erol declared that he was unavailable to meet with the committee.

One thing is clear from the transcript shown above. Kenan Erol is a terrible match-fixer. His bribery attempts were inept and clumsy. His instructions were incompetent and in his conversation he displayed all the finesse of a dodgy used car salesman. If he wanted to, how could he improve his performance?

## Step One — Access

The first problem that confronts a gambling corruptor is how to get access to the players. In the chapter, "To Fix or Not to Fix," I wrote of the challenges facing an internal corruptor. However, a gambling corruptor has a much more difficult job. They are not in the sport. They may not have the necessary connections or entry to the sports world to even begin their corruption. So they have to negotiate access to at least one influential player. This is the first key challenge for them: if a corruptor cannot speak to the players, then they cannot arrange a fix. And like most professional sub-cultures, access into the world of the players is closely guarded not only by the players but also the people close to them. How, then, do corruptors get access to the players?

***Direct contact:*** For long-term corruptors working only in a domestic league, the process is something akin to seduction, they may try to establish a bar or club where all the players will feel comfortable, or they may try to establish themselves in some official capacity at the club. For example, Kenan Erol, the Turkish fixer, ran the food concession at the Sebatspor Stadium.

In international matches and tournaments, however, the constraints are far greater. The players and corruptors may not share the same cultural background or even language, and the time to make the corrupt deal happen is much shorter. In these cases, the corruptors often have to rely on other methods. Several players and corruptors talk about the corruptors manoeuvring so as to share the same hotel corridor. The corruptor would then also sometimes use prostitutes to establish a connection between the players and themselves. Other corruptors, as shown in the excerpt that began this chapter, would pretend to be journalists: they would then request an interview with a player in order to get close to them before they proposed their corrupt deal.

***Runner-arranged contacts:*** The second method of ensuring access to players is for the corruptors to essentially hire that access. In this scenario they employ agents, known as "runners," to ensure access between them and the players. This is a very common practice; because, depending on the levels of trust between corruptor and agent, it is quicker to ensure and protects the corruptor from detection. In the fixing/non-fixing players database, there are one hundred and seventeen players who have been approached for gambling match-fixing, in forty-nine of the cases the corruptors used runners in order to establish access to players.

Examples of this method can be seen in the recent cases of match-fixing in European leagues, where purported corruptors from Chinese gambling syndicates used player-agents to gain access to players. In the Malaysian league where the corruption was, purportedly, better established than in Europe, there existed a series of independent runners who worked for corrupt players on each of the teams. These runners could then be contacted by potential corruptors when they wanted to establish a fix.

In the chapters about fixing in the Russian league, we saw the role of agents as *guarantors*, essentially providing the trust and possible coercion to enable a corrupt deal to take place. In the current example agents are not guarantors; rather their strength is their ability to get access to the corrupt players. Their roles are akin to the middlemen of corrupt oil states that Neil Jacoby and his colleagues as well as the great Palestinian journalist Said K. Aburish write of in their works. This is another difference from the corruptors in arrangements who have access to the players and referees; here the agents are providing that access to the gambling corruptors.

P2 is a former player who was approached a number of times to fix games. He also had team-mates who fixed games. He claims that this type of access agent was key to the operation. They would make friends with players, figure out which players may be susceptible to bribes, and then introduce them to national level bookies.

> *... there were runners. They were ex-players, good friends of the team. Sometimes they would be guys we would meet in a disco. The owner or someone, they would party with us for months. Then maybe say something. These guys were key. They had to be people with access to the players. They had to be people the players would* **trust** *[emphasis added]. It was the same as the cricket fixing. You needed people who could contact the team. They were vital. They had to be people who could come to training sessions or games and matches (P2).*

The common thread between these two methods — direct contact or runner-arranged contact — is that at this initial stage of the corrupt deal, the corruptor is simply seeking to gain access to as wide an assortment of players as possible. Which players are approached to make the corrupt deal and what is said to them is dealt with in the next stage.

## Efficient Corrupt Networks

Before we begin this analysis, a quick review of what we have seen so far in the book. One, all corrupt interchanges have the following actors: A — the corruptor (in this case, the gambling fixer); B — the fiduciary agents or corruptees (in this case, either players or the referee); and possibly, C — an agent who introduces the two actors or guarantees the transaction.

Reality is more complicated. All players are not created equal. Some players have higher "playing capital." A fancy term for saying that they can affect the outcome of a match to a greater degree than their team-mates because they are better players or have a more influential position on the field. There are also some players who may reveal the fix, while others who will refuse to participate but not blow the whistle. How does a corruptor deal with these issues?

The first part of the solution is to remember Gambetta's definition of organised crime as "a successful cluster or a coalition of clusters," not as a network of individuals. But Kenan Erol, the unsuccessful Turkish corruptor, in his attempt to fix a game, treats the players as a collection of individuals. Figure 7.1, shows the network plan that Erol was working with:

Figure 7.1: Fixing Network on Sebatspor — Organised by Kenan Erol

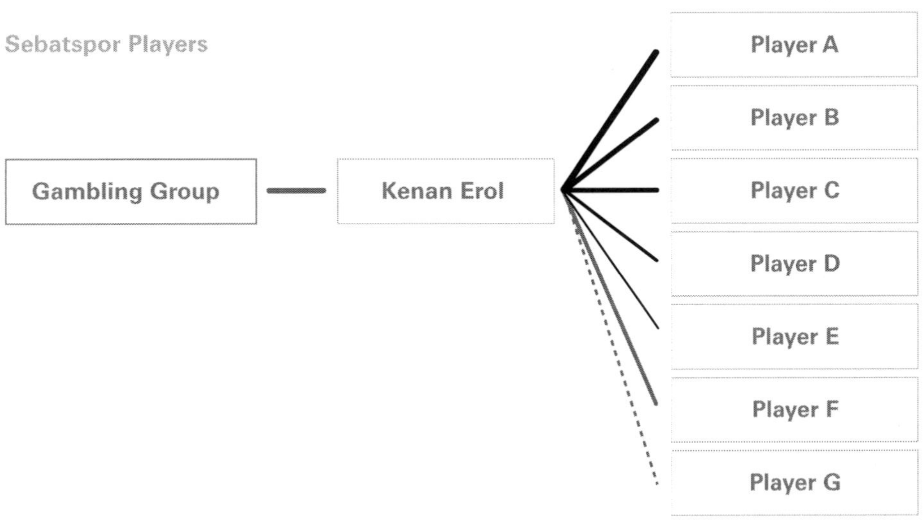

The academic Mark Granovetter wrote of "strong and weak ties" between actors in a network. (He showed that our weak ties are more efficient in finding us employment, than our stronger ones.) In Figure 7.1, we can see the lessening of the strength of the relationships as Erol approaches players until finally the dashed lines (....) indicates a betrayal of trust. Erol's attempts at fixing were discovered precisely for this reason. He had gone to so many players on the Sebatspor team that he eventually stumbled on an honest player who revealed his plan to the owner.

A more effective plan would have been for Erol to charge one player with the responsibility of organizing a fixing network within his own team. The player knows far better than an outsider which player can most affect the game, and more importantly who is likely to be persuaded to fix a match. As one former player said, "The fixing groups generally divide along the cliques in the team. Not by position" (P7). In other words, players in the corrupt network are frequently not chosen because of their playing capital or position but because of their social connections with the corruptor, who then knows about their potential corruptibility. It is this player, who generally does have high playing capital, that becomes the head of the fixing network inside the team. This method is seen frequently in the interviews. One former player referred to this role as "the project manager."

> *What happened with our mob was that there was a ringleader. And the bookie would contact him and say, "You're playing such and such a team, we are desperate for you to lose the game. Here is 50,000, how you distribute is up to you. There is 50,000 for you." So then he would know that there were 5 or 6 corrupt guys on the team and he would go up to five of them and say, "OK here is 4 or 5 thousand for you after the game. I will pay you cash if you help me lose the game." He will pay out 25,000 and keep the rest for himself. (P6)*

Figure 7.2, represents a more efficient network. We can presume that Erol knew at least one of the players well. This player is the bridge who, along with Erol, would link the two clusters.

Figure 7.2: A Suggested Network for Fixing Players on the Sebatspor Team

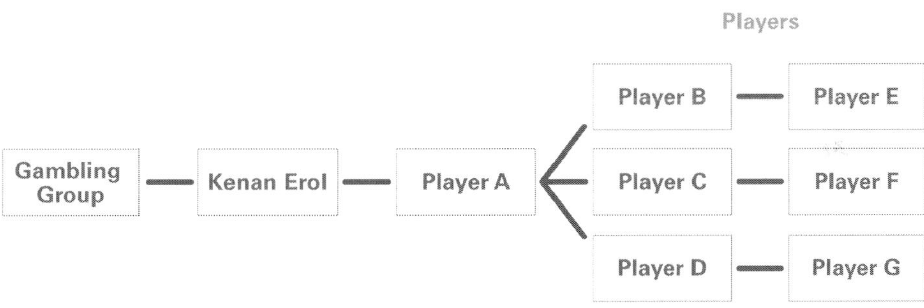


Note in figure 7.2, unlike figure 7.1, all the ties in the network are strong. However, the bridging person (A) has to be a senior player, someone with the authority to influence several of his team-mates. Players E, F and G (in figure 7.2) are far less likely to betray the fix if they feel their team-mates are organizing it rather than an outsider like Kenan Erol. P2 played for one of the top teams in Malaysia that fixed many of its games. He reported that this role was aided by the strict hierarchy that existed inside the team:

> *The [fixing] problem was with the senior players. You have to understand that there was a hierarchy. The senior players were very influential. The coach couldn't even name the starting line up without the senior players saying what was what. These were established international players and if they said something that was it. (P2)*

In 1961, Senator Kefauver established yet another controversial committee of inquiry in the United States Senate. In the 1950s, Kefauver had come to public prominence by heading the first U. S. legislative inquiry into the existence of the La Cosa Nostra (or LCN) mafia (much of the transcripts of the hearings served as source material for the *Godfather* novels). This time, Senator Kefauver began an investigation into price-fixing in the heavy electrical equipment industry. He discovered that price-fixing was, according to one witness, a "way of life" among certain company executives. The American sociologists, Wayne Baker and Robert Faulkner, studying the transcripts of the inquiry almost thirty years later, found that to facilitate illegal business practices, these executives had established a "decentralized network" whose chief benefits were both the ability to promote secrecy and protect members from possible detection.

A similar type of network is seen in successful gambling-motivated match-fixing. The advantage for the corruptor in this type of network is that it prevents information exchange. P3, a former international player, concurs with this assessment when he claims that the junior players actually had no idea who the corruptors were or the size of the entire organization of the corrupt deal.

| | |
|---|---|
| ***Hill:*** | *Did you ever see a corruptor?* |
| ***Player:*** | *No, I never saw one. It was all done by senior players. There was no direct connection between the players and the top bookies... We, the junior players, were told nothing. There was nothing obvious... (P3)* |

In these interviews with players on teams that had been corrupted, we can see clearly the difference between the successful and seemingly long-term corrupt networks in Malaysian football and the network that Kenan Erol had tried to establish at the Sebatspor team in Turkey. The key differences between these two networks is first, strong ties rather than a combination of strong-weak ties: second, the information of who is actually generating the corruption within the network is closely guarded and thus the risk of betrayal is reduced: and finally, we can also see that the trust relationships

— because of the strong personal ties between people in the network — are very important.

In later chapters, how this trust is governed will be examined. However, for now, let us turn ourselves to the following question: if successful corruptors use the internal hierarchies of teams to arrange corrupted matches, how do they first approach the players and referees to fix the games? The next chapter will show the language and strategies used by successful gambling fixers.

## Chapter Review

- There are five stages in setting up a fixed football match:
  - access
  - set up
  - calling the fix
  - performance
  - payment

- In gaining access and setting up a fix; using runners who have strong networks inside the sports world is extremely important

- The structure of the network in establishing these corrupted games is not a pyramid; rather it is a network of strong, close ties.

# CHAPTER EIGHT
# PITCHING THE FIX

*I will tell you a scenario we had, that we ran more than once... We used to hang out in some of the clubs in Manhattan, Brooklyn... And a lot of these basketball players would go to the same clubs... and we got our eye on one or two of the guys. We would wine them and dine them... Finally you set up him for the conversation, because we are friends now. And I say, "Listen, you are a smart guy. I'm your good friend. Let me tell you how you are going to make some money." [Then you pull out the money], put it on the table in front of them, more money then they have ever seen in cash in their life.*

*Michael Franzese, former Mafia Capo/sports corruptor on how to bribe an athlete — interview, September 2011.*

In the last chapter, we saw how the gambling corruptors set up efficient networks and have to work very hard to gain access to players and referees. However, all this work begs one important question — *how* do gambling corruptors actually propose dishonest deals to players and referees? It is not enough for a corruptor simply to be introduced to players. As we saw with

Kenan Erol, the unsuccessful Turkish corruptor, being in the same room does not guarantee a fixed match. What is also important is *how* the corruptor approaches a player or referee.

The data shows that there are two main types of approaches that corruptors use and, ironically, they mirror the two principal business strategies of erotic dancers in North American strip bars. Before we go any further, a note on the research into the profession of erotic dancing. Much of it was produced by traditional male academics doing ethnological research in a "deviant" field. However, more recently, there has been some work produced by feminist scholars who have begun to break the paradigm that many of us were raised with of — women — sex — victims. They began to research how women worked and negotiated their survivals in difficult professions. Their work is very helpful in understanding the strategies of the fixers. As always in the book, the following description is a simplification of a complex and intricate theoretical work.

## The Business Strategies of Erotic Dancers

For those readers who have never been into a North American erotic dance bar, this is how they work. A whole bunch of men go in with lots of money in their pockets to look at semi-naked women. They *think* the whole experience is about sex. They are wrong. The women *know* the whole experience is about getting as much of that money out of the men's pockets as possible. In other words, it is about profit maximisation.

In order to maximize that profit, erotic dancers need to do as many "table dances" as possible during a shift. In a table-dance a dancer will either dance or grind herself against a seated customer for the length of one song. She will receive a set fee for each song. The more songs the customer pays for, the more money a dancer will receive.

The women's task is not easy. Along with customers who are often difficult, and a management who is often exploitative, there is also strong competition between the women themselves for a limited number of clients. Academic researchers discovered that to overcome these difficulties, the dancers generally choose one of two business strategies: there are those who try for fast bucks — quick, direct approaches to as many different customers as possible ("Hi, honey, want to see my tits?") and those who manufacture "counterfeit intimacy" or pseudo-relationships with specific customers ("Hi, sweetie, you look like you had a long day — want me to sit down and be your little girl?") who then spend both more time and money on them. The dancers will not always chose one strategy over the other, rather they will switch between "fast bucks" and "counterfeit intimacy" depending on a variety of circumstances like time of shift, the perceived wealth of the man or the number of customers in the bar compared to the number of other women.

For the readers who may be shocked about the morality of using comparisons with erotic dancers, the literature on corporate fundraising almost exactly mirrors the same strategies that the women have developed. Successful corporate fundraisers are also advised to build pseudo-relationships that while money is the sole objective, it is often discussed as if it were the last thing in mind. So fundraisers are advised to "cultivate" their potential donors over a long period of time. The executives are told to keep databases with the personal likes and dislikes, names of their children and hobbies of the donors, and only after a relationship has been established to ask them for money, as this typical quote illustrates:

> *Remember that you are attempting to establish a life long relationship with this prospect. Remember and acknowledge their anniversaries, birthdays, children's weddings. Do not concentrate solely on their financial investment. (Lange, 2003)*

As with corporate fundraisers, match-fixers also mirror the strategies of erotic dancers. Earlier in the book, we explored the differences between leagues of *high* and *low* corruption: or leagues where there is a strong norm towards corruption and other leagues where corruption is a relatively rare act. This is an important distinction for corruptors, for it changes the way they approach referees and players to fix games.

For example, Asian corruptors in leagues of *high* corruption often use the "fast bucks approach." P8 was a player who agreed to play in fixed matches in the Malaysian-Singaporean League. When asked about the methods of approaches he replied, "Oh no, there was nothing subtle. They would just phone us up at the hotel and propose it over the phone," (P8). In the 1990 World Cup in Italy, the FIFA referees were hidden away in a maximum-security compound used by the Vatican in central Rome. R4 was one of those referees, he reported, "The phone lines were supposed to be confidential and unlisted, but we were receiving phone calls in our rooms from bookies offering us bribes" (R4). In these examples, because there was so much corruption in the league, in the first case; and access was so restricted, in the second case, the corruptors had to use fast, direct approaches.

In leagues of *low* corruption, corruptors face a more difficult job. However, a pitch can, with time or the right agents, be negotiated. It is at this point that the "counterfeit intimacy" method is frequently used.

One example from another sport was described by a U. S. College basketball player in the early nineteen sixties. Art Hicks was black. One day after a white team-mate made yet another racist comment, Hicks decided to fix some games with an organised crime syndicate. He was eventually caught and when he testified he revealed how the corruptors were "experts at human nature":

> *One thing you never heard about the gamblers is how good they were at what they did. They were experts at human nature and that's why so few of the kids they approached ever turned them*

> *down. They catch you at just the right time, when you're vulnerable. They can look at a kid's game and see there ain't no love there... Whatever the problem, they knew how to exploit it. The gambler becomes the most reliable person in your life. He replaces the coach. (Whelan 1992, 141)*

The German football referee Robert Hoyzer was "turned" by a group of Croatian criminals living in Berlin. The referee had been invited to spend time in a café owned by the corruptors. Over time they were able to get him to fix matches for them. Afterwards, he struggled to explain how they were able to do so. He had always regarded himself as very honest and a "well-brought up" person, yet in a relatively short time they were able to persuade him to do something that he never would have considered before:

> *It was an on-going process that I wasn't aware of anymore in the end. It affected me in a way that I stopped noticing things going on around me. I only hung out at this café, at some point it was like my second living-room. I was around all the time. I was there eight days out of the week and was treated by them like a very special person (Kerner, 2005).*

One of the former money launderers for one of the principle groups of the Colombian drug industry's Medellin Cartel — Humberto J. Aguilar — told me of a similar process in enlisting bank officials to help him wash drug money.

> *You join the same club as the bank manger. You know his kid's birthdays. What car he drives. What his wife does. Then you make sure everyone gets a Rolex. Everyone. You remember the tellers' names. You invite them to parties. You make them feel part of the group. Then for the big ask, it feels to them like the same process. Just another part of the relationship (Humberto J. Aguilar, Interview, May 2009).*

A specific example of a match-corruptor who used the counterfeit relationship type approach is the former New York Mafia capo Michael Franzese whose quote began this chapter. Franzese claims to have fixed professional sports matches, including boxing bouts and U. S. college basketball games. Although, Franzese's corruption was in a different sport there are similarities in the corruptor's methods. Franzese claims that at first a corruptor will pretend to be friends with athletes. The idea is to find the *weakness* of players: if it is blondes, they use blondes; if it is drugs, they use drugs; if it is gambling, they use gambling. Whatever it is, the corruptors use it to get a hold over the athlete, and then they try to get them to throw games. In this interview excerpt, he describes some of his methods:

> *You might approach [the athletes] or set them up with a woman. She would get pregnant or pretend to be. That would screw their game up. Or you would get them partying hard the night before the game ... (Franzese, 1999).*

Here a corruptor is *not* trying the direct, fast method; rather the corruptor's actions are more akin to those of a predatory animal stalking its prey. The corruptor gets close to their prey (the sports person) using "counterfeit intimacy," weakens them, or uses their weakness, to propose match-fixing.

## The Language of Bribes

However, for all this discussion about relationship building, how do corruptors actually propose a corrupt deal? What language do they use? Along with the use of counterfeit intimacy, it is the use of neutral language when corruptors propose match-fixes that helps to drive the establishment of corrupt deals in sports.

An example of the use of neutral language from Kenya: in 2007, while driving late at night with friends in Nairobi, our car was stopped by a group of armed policemen. The officer in charge of the group engaged me in a brief, rather tense, conversation and then said, "Sir, it is very cold tonight. Can you spare a few shillings so the boys can have a hot dinner?" He did not state the obvious, that his policemen could have robbed us, nor did he ask directly for a bribe, rather his demand for money was couched in neutral, almost friendly, terms allowing a cover of charity.

The data from both the confession databank and the interviews show that similar techniques are seen in match-fixing where it is rare for corruptors to directly address the issue of bribes and corruption; rather they will speak of "coffee money" or "shopping money." There seems to be two underlying motivations for this use of language: first, it allows a personal language or code to develop between the corruptor and corruptee. This personal language both keeps an uninitiated outsider from completely understanding the conversation. The Pete Rose gambling case in American baseball — although not fixing — had this type of code between the participants. So the amount of money to be placed on each bet was disguised, as was the actual betting as this excerpt from the official Major League Baseball (MLB) report shows:

> *Rose [the baseball player] and Chevashore [the bookmaker] explained the mechanics and language of betting to him [Janszen — who was to act as their go-between]. Chevashore informed him that there were special "key words" that he should use when placing a bet over the phone in the event that the phone was being tapped. Specifically, Chevashore explained that Janszen should never use the word "bet" or ever See Pete Rose when placing a bet for him. Instead, Janszen was directed to say "my friend," and Chevashore would accordingly know that this friend was in fact Pete Rose. With this understanding, the Rose-Chevashore connection was cemented, using Janszen as Rose's runner.*
> *(Office of the Commissioner's Report, Major League Baseball Page 53-54.)*

Along with the protection of secrecy that these special codes give to the potential fixers, it also adds to the intimacy between the two parties, in that they, like lovers, are speaking their own personal language. For example, in the Czech match-fixing cases, the private language between the corruptors and corruptees was so well-developed that after their conviction, the transcripts were presented as a successful play in Prague. One of corruptors liked fishing, so they used the names of fish and fishing terms — "carp" meant a bribe — as a device to disguise their illicit payments.

Perhaps more importantly, the use of neutral language also allows a sensitive player or referee, taking a bribe for the first-time, to be able to rationalize their acceptance of the money. In early chapters, I wrote of the cognitive dissonance that existed in many of the Malaysian-Singaporean interview subjects who had helped the corruptors in some way. They claimed and spoke as if they were utterly honest and non-corrupt people, yet when admitting to acts of their own corruption had constructed a rational defence for their actions. There are similar examples in the literature on corruption. Said K. Aburish (1985), in his excellent and colourful analysis of corruption by oil companies in the Arabian Peninsula, writes of the gift presentations and formal ceremonies that accompany most bribes there which allows both the corruptor, corruptee and agents to colour the transaction in a different light. Robin Warner (1996) in his book *Bungs, Bribes and Bad Language: Some Strategies of Portuguese and Spanish Conspiratorial Talk* gives similar examples of these personal codes of corruption.

A football administrator in Malaysia describes a similar pattern where the corruptors would use language that would allow the players not to "feel criminal in their thinking... they [the corruptors] would call it coffee money [the bribe money]". This process demonstrates some of the aspects of Edwin Sutherland's ideas of "differential association". Sutherland, an American criminologist, advanced the idea that people perform deviant acts when they are surrounded by people doing similar deviant acts. We shall examine Sutherland's work in later chapters, but essentially it is the academic framework of your mother's advice, "Don't hang around with Jimmy. He is a bad influence." So burglars teach burglary, fraudsters teach fraud and prostitutes teach prostitution. Later disciples of Sutherland's ideas pointed out that this "transmission" of deviancy is helped if the language of invitation is couched in neutral terms. So it would be rare for a burglar, for example, to explicitly say they are going to rob a house, rather an invitation to a young initiate would be put out there for "a job" or a "bit of fun".

## How to Set Up a Fixed Game

The following excerpt is a good example of *how* to set up a fixed match in a league of high corruption. It is a "direct, fast-bucks" approach; however, the corruptor tries to ensure that there are high-levels of trust. Presumably, the corruptor felt comfortable using this strategy rather than one of establishing counterfeit intimacy, as by the early 1990s, corruption was well-established in the Malaysian league. One of the chief corruptors of the league — in this excerpt named "Chieu" — was something of "an expert in human nature". He created one of the networks of corruption throughout the league, and made a great deal of money. In this excerpt, from a previously unpublished Royal Malaysian Police confession, Chieu has already established a relationship with "David" — a top Malaysian player — who then introduces him to two other players — Ali and Rahil — on his team to help set up a match-fixing ring.[9]

***David:*** *This is our friend Chieu.*

***Chieu:*** *I am Chieu. (Ali and Rahil shake hands with him)... I have come here to talk to you. I will try to help you reach the final of the Malaysian Cup. Okay, I'll make it*

[9] *All names have been changed.*

| | |
|---|---|
| | *simple! First, I help your team in 5 games. I will pay you 15,000 RM for winning each game. After winning those five, you will have to lose or draw the game. I will pay you 25,000 RM to draw a game, and to lose a game 40,000 RM.* |
| ***David:*** | *Don't worry! The Boss (Chieu) will help us out.* |
| ***Chieu:*** | *Okay, easy to talk. I control your coach. I brought in your two foreigners. I paid the transfer fees for them, not the state FA.* |
| ***Rahil:*** | *I will think it over fast.* |
| ***Chieu:*** | *(Gives him an envelope full of cash) This is the FA Cup money.* |
| ***David:*** | *Don't worry. Chieu will help.*<br>*(Malaysian Police Confession: no. 6, 3)* |

This excerpt shows the difference between Chieu and the far less subtle, Kenan Erol. For a start, Chieu does not show up alone to the meeting. Rather he uses a player to introduce him to other players. This action immediately helps to establish his credibility. David, a prominent player (he had recently won a prestigious award), twice vows for Chieu's trustworthiness.

Chieu also shakes hands with the players. He shows himself to be from a similar working class background thanks to the Malay vernacular he uses[10] and is friendly and direct with the players. This is in contrast with the attitude

---

[10] *This was stressed a number of times by the translator, although it is, obviously, not apparent in the English version.*

of many club owners who tended to treat their players in a class-conscious manner. Often players are expected to kiss the hands of the owners when they met them.[11] Chieu, on the other hand, is friendly, courteous and, he claims, has the same owners on his payroll already. Even if this later claim is untrue, it still poses a risk in the player's head, making them fearful of going to management. Again this is in direct contrast to Kenan Erol, who when asked if he controlled the management responded with a weak threat against the player, showing instantly that he was an outsider with little power. So in a few sentences, Chieu has managed to both be ingratiating and to isolate the players from their management.

David C. Whelan in his thesis *Organised Crime, Sports Gambling and Role Conflict: Victimization and Point Shaving in College Basketball* claims that in the corruption scandals of American college basketball, at the beginning of their relationship corruptors pay "win bonuses" to players, encouraging them to play as well as they can. Players regard the win bonuses as relatively benign: they will win and thereby keep the loyalty to their teams, but they still get the financial rewards of fixing matches. However, these payments were often what Whelan calls "gateway crimes" which brought the players into the corruptor's net without them being aware of it. In this case, however, the players are told up-front that they will be later called upon to lose games on-demand.

Chieu uses Whelan's "gateway crime" approach. He claims that if the players cooperate with him, they will not only get money for winning the next five games but that he will also help them reach the final of the Malaysian Cup. Then, he gives the players money for a game they had won several weeks ago. This is an important step. For as soon as the players accept the money,

---

[11] *This is the customary way of greeting Malaysian Royalty — of whom there are a great deal as the country is a conglomeration of several indigenous Kingdoms — many of these people own or run football teams.*

they have de facto, accepted Chieu's offer of a long-term relationship. For the acceptance of the corruptors money by the players, no matter what the motivation, signals the closing of the deal and the end of the possible innocence of the players. A Singaporean police officer supports this view in an interview, "But you know if they take the money once, it is over. They can never turn back because the gamblers will say, 'If you don't do it. We will let people know that you took the money.'"

Susan Rose-Ackerman declares this strategy to be "reputational hostage taking" or the threat of exposure. Another corruptor, in a later interview, claimed to use a method similar to Chieu's:

> *As soon as [the players] take the money. They have to do what I say. I don't do this thing where I show them the money and say, "This is yours if you do the match." No, I give them the money. I say, "This is coffee money. Take it. But don't cross me. Or I will get you." (COR6)*

In this excerpt, the corruptor is not only showing the importance of a player accepting the money, but also demonstrating the significant change in attitude, from friendliness to menace, that drives the next stage of match-fixing. This shift in attitude may seem strange to a reader, after all a corruptor has spent considerable time getting close to players and referees and then suddenly they are threatening them. In the next chapter, we will see exactly why this shift occurs and why it is of vital importance in the next stage of the fixing.

## Chapter Review

- The business strategies of erotic dancers or corporate fund-raisers are useful in understanding the tactics of match corruptors.
- There are, in general, two strategies; fast, direct approaches (leagues of high corruption or limited access) and "counterfeit intimacy" (leagues of low corruption).
- The language of corruption in the pitch is as neutral as possible. Then once the bribe has been accepted, the participants will often use a personal code.
- "Win bonuses" are often used by corruptors as "gateway crimes' to entrap the players and referees into longer-term fixing.

# CHAPTER NINE
# CALLING THE FIX

*The bookmakers' reward? Easy pickings from bets they themselves laid on the thrown matches. One of the greatest problems in "rigging" matches for betting coups is to get enough money staked on the "bent" games to make it worthwhile... Suspicion is quickly aroused when bookie "A" rings up bookie "B" to hedge a bet and finds that bookie "B" has already taken large bets on the self-same matches and is himself trying to lay off part of the money. Very soon, the match riggers find that it is impossible to get any more money on...*

*Michael Gabbert and Peter Campling. "How Two Bookies Cashed in on Fixed' Matches." The People May 3, 1964.*

In the last chapter we saw the different strategies that corruptors use to successfully propose corrupt deals. In essence, they work like erotic dancers or corporate fundraisers and use two methods: "fast bucks", where corruptors propose the fixes with very little establishing relationships and "counterfeit intimacy", where corruptors spend time finding out about the corruptees and establishing relationship. In both methods, the corruptors will often attempt to use neutral language or "gateway crimes" which allows the corruptee to justify the bribe in moral terms. However, once a player agrees to work for the corruptor a significant change in the relationship can occur. It becomes less friendly and more businesslike, even threatening. The next section explains why this change frequently happens.

## Calling the Fix

In 1806, English cricket was rife with match-fixing. William Beldham was a prominent cricketer of that era who was approached by corruptors to throw games for them. He claims that he refused saying, "You never buy the same man but once:... No, sir, a man was a slave when once he sold to these folk." Two hundred years ago Beldham was describing the attitude change that affects the relationship between the players and the corruptors once the players have taken the money. It is the same transformation that a contemporary footballer speaks of when he said, "The problem is once you have done it once, the bookies have you by the balls... you were in their arms for life." Michael Franzese, the New York mafia corruptor, claimed the same thing in his description of his relations with corrupt players, "You don't treat the gamblers as friends... you're more friendly with the guys that don't throw games."

Why would the dynamics of this relationship change so dramatically, particularly after the corruptor has spent so much effort in getting access to the players and then setting up the match-fix by using neutral language and counterfeit intimacy? It is because it is in this stage that the corruptor's greatest chance of loss or profit can occur. Gambling match-fixing differs from arrangement fixes. In arrangement fixing the ultimate goal is to fix the result of the game. In gambling, the ultimate goal of fixing is profit-maximisation, so there are actually two fixes going on: the fixing of the game and the fixing of the gambling market.

To fix the market the corruptor has to find out the spread of the betting market, place the bet that will ensure the greatest profit and then ensure that the players deliver the result. So the corruptor has to make completely sure that the players will follow instructions to the absolute letter. Failure to do so ensures an enormous loss of money on the corruptor's part. The stage of establishing a relationship with the player is over, now it is business.

Before we begin looking at specific strategies of fixing the gambling market, a note about how this market actually functions. The gambling market is in some ways similar to the stock market. Each sporting event, be it a Formula 1 car race, an international cricket match or a football match has specific odds attached to it. So let us say that there is a football match between two teams: the Rovers and the Rangers. The Rangers are a weaker team whose best player has recently suffered a major injury. The bookmakers will say that when the Rangers play the Rovers, they are 3 to 1 to beat them. Meaning for each pound a punter places on the Rangers to win, they will get three back if they win. If the punter decides that they think the stronger teams — the Rovers — will win the odds will be something like 1 to 2 for the Rovers. This means that for every 2 pounds placed on the Rovers to win, the punter will get back one if they win. The difference in the odds is the profit for the bookmaker. There are lots of terms for this percentage difference, American mobsters call it the "vig" or the "juice", but essentially it is how a bookmaker ensures their profits after balancing the odds to ensure that about 50% of the money is being placed on the Rovers and 50% of the money is placed on the Rangers to win.

There are some slight technical differences depending on whether you bet with a North American, Asian, European or British bookmaker. For example, non-British bookmakers use different ways of expressing the odds (1.5 to 1.2 rather than 3 to 1 or 1 to 2), and they often use "a spread" to encourage more gambling. A spread in the above case would be to say that Rovers has to win by two or more goals for the game to be counted as "a win" in the gambling market. Thus, if the game is tied, or Rangers only loses by one goal, then on the gambling market it counts as a Rangers victory. All these terms may sound complicated to readers who do not have a background in sports bets, but essentially these are simply differences in expressing the odds or the statistical probability of a victory by one team or another. These statistics are popularly called "the line". The line in sports betting is roughly equivalent to a company's share price. Just as all publicly traded companies have a share price, so too do all sports events that are being bet have a line.

The corruptor's problem is that if they have successfully bribed the athletes of one team to lose, they want to bet a lot of money against that team winning. The more money they can bet against that team, the more money they can win. This is called fixing the gambling market. And, like defrauding the stock market, there are a number of logistical challenges that confront the corruptor. First, the corruptor has to know what odds the gambling market is giving on the game. That is reasonably simple, but then the corruptor has to be able to get a sufficient quantity of money on to the market to make the fix worthwhile. If the corruptor puts in too much money on their specific team to lose, "the line" will change dramatically and the bookmakers will begin to realize that there is something wrong. If the corruptor is not able to put enough money on the game, it makes the fix not worth doing and the bribes paid to the players or referees are wasted. The corruptor also has to disguise the fact that he is placing the bets or his rival corruptors will be aware of the fix. The successful gambling corruptor has to avoid all these problems, and the challenges can be as difficult as fixing the actual game.

To make matters worse for the gambling corruptors, in the last few years, a new potential challenge has also arisen to hinder their work. A number of betting companies and football associations have announced the formation of "early warning systems". These systems are specifically established to monitor odds of all the games to see if there is any unusual activity or too much movement in the line. In fact, the obstacles facing a gambling corruptor are now so great, the gambling monitoring purported to be so precise, that according to the public statements of some of the executives of "early warning systems", fixing is now impossible.

If this is true, how can gambling corruptors possibly overcome all these different challenges? Well, first off, as difficult as arranging a gambling fix may be, the statements that the "early warning systems" have made fixing impossible are patent nonsense. The evidence from a number of European police investigations is clear that there are lots of fixes occurring. These investigations actually tapped the gambling corruptors' phones and their conversations show that hundreds of games were fixed over a number of years even while these "early warning systems" were in operation. The public statements of the systems infallibility are mostly made to reassure a nervous public, as some of the same executives privately admit.

An additional aid to their work is that many of the very people who are purported to be in charge of ensuring that the sport is uncorrupted have a vested interest in *not* reporting any fixing. In Chapter 17, we see that the data indicates that relatively few scandals are uncovered by the actual administrators of the league. This general lack of action by the officials presumably is because it may reflect badly upon the "product" of the sport that they are promoting.

Another factor that aids the corruptors is that, like the stock market, the gambling market can change for perfectly innocent reasons. In the same way the share price of General Motors may rise with the news of a successful earnings report, or fall with the dismissal of a popular executive; so too can "the odds line" on a game change because a star player is injured or the weather conditions favour one team over the other. Thus there are lots of rises and falls of the odds line that have absolutely nothing to do with fixing.

One real-life example, of a semi-professional team in southern England, shows the difficulty of monitoring the gambling line. A few years ago, one team lost a match by a lopsided score. The bookmakers were worried because, on paper, it was a match that the losing team should have easily won. Worse, there had been heavy betting against the team winning the match the morning of the game. Even worse, almost all the heavy bets had come from the town where the team was located. A fix was immediately suspected and the bookmakers began an informal inquiry.

Almost immediately the investigators discovered what had happened. The team had gone to a wedding reception the night before the match. Most of the team had become so drunk they were severely hung-over when due to play the game. Many bettors in the town had gotten to know of the player's post-drunken state and had quickly placed large bets with information that the bookmakers had not known. It was perfectly innocent but had produced a sharp fall in the line.

However, that was simply an unexpected change in the gambling market. What are the genuine difficulties that the corruptors face in fixing the market? The first problem is that, in general, no long-term match corruptor, or a successful professional gambler, can place a sizable bet in their own name. Even honest professional gamblers, if they become consistently successful, will find it very difficult to place large bets. The American journalist Michael Konick wrote a book — *Smart Money*. It is a description of his working as a "mule" for a successful sports betting syndicate in Las Vegas. Konick claims that the casinos made it so difficult for anyone with a consistent winning record to place a sports bet that the successful syndicates resort to disguises or hiring outsiders, like him, to place their bets for them.

In general, two things happen to successful long-term gamblers at casinos and sports bookmakers: either they are prevented from gambling or they are allowed to place only small bets. You can do almost anything in most casinos, so long as you do not consistently win their money. In some casinos, failure to lose can result in a customer being escorted off the premises. In the second instance, successful gamblers sometimes are allowed to place small bets but those bets are then often copied by less scrupulous bookmakers for their own profit. Essentially, these bookies steal the research and calculations of the professional gamblers for their own personal benefit.

To get bets on the market both honest professional gamblers and dishonest match corruptors will use third parties to place their bets under disguised names. These third parties are known by various slang terms like "mules," or "runners". The most commonly-used expressions is "beard" after the alleged 19th-century practice of having these people wear fake beards to disguised themselves, when most betting was done in person. The strategies used by the "beards" to hide bets that could fill another book, but essentially they disguise the fact that they are placing the bets for other people (COR1, 3-5; B6-8, 20).

Figure 9.1 on the next page shows a simplified network that a gambling corruptor must put into place to successfully fix a football match. The top half of this chart we have seen in Chapter 7 when we looked at the need to establish decentralized networks among the players to actually fix the sporting event. However, the bottom of the chart shows that the gambling corruptors are effectively like spiders in the middle of a larger net. Their networks must also go into the gambling market and be disguised from the eventual victims, the bookmakers.

Figure 9.1, is a simplification of a sometimes very complicated fraud. There are a number of points that should be made. First, despite the popular press referring to corruptors as "bookies" or bookmakers, the bookmakers themselves are most often the financial victims of match-fixing. It is those companies that have to pay out for fraudulently rigged-sports events. The quote that began the chapter was about illegal bookies working in Britain in the nineteen-sixties taking fixed bets and then making a profit by passing them onto their competitors. Currently, there are also frequent anecdotal

Figure 9.1: A Simplified Fixing Network

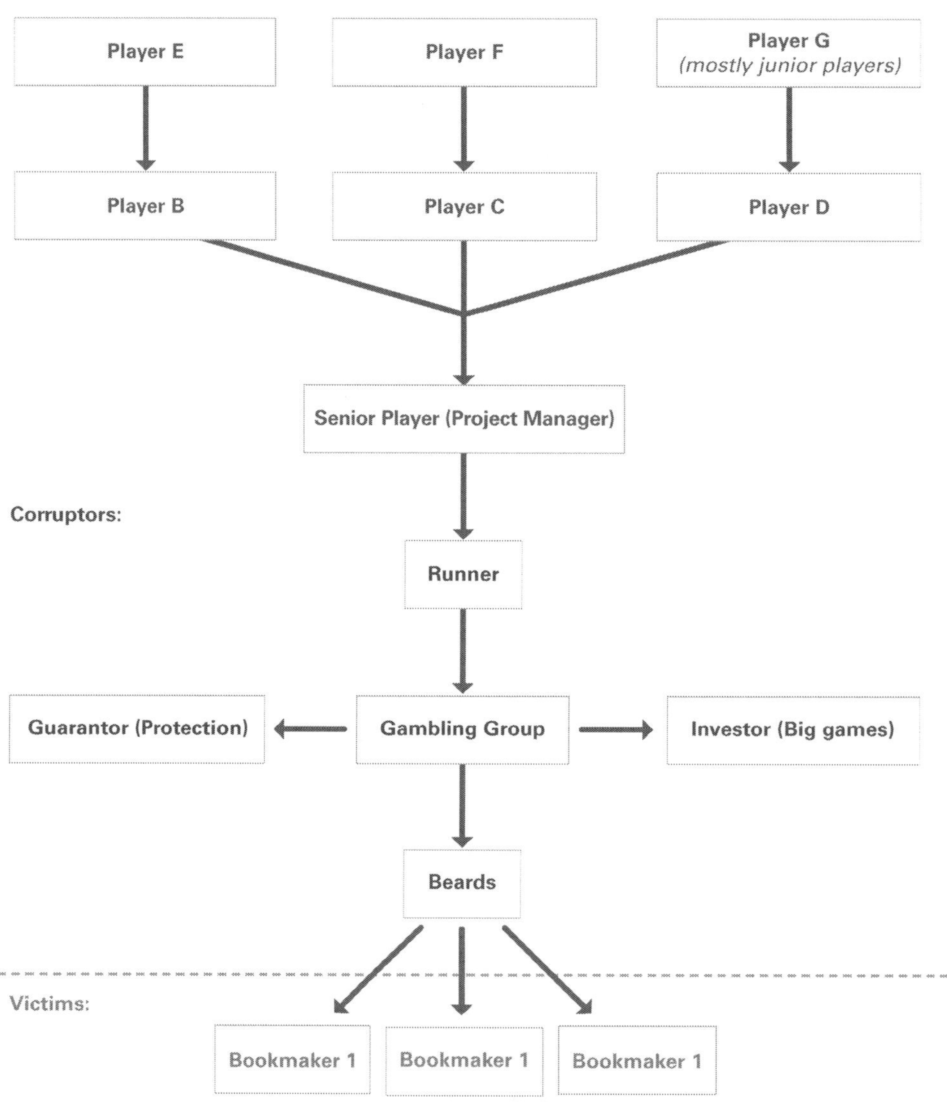

reports of current Asian bookmakers finding out about fixes and then "laying off" their bets onto other bookmakers so as to effectively pass off their losses to their competitors rather than lose money themselves. However, these are the exceptions. The whole point of a fix is to defraud bookmakers and make money for the corruptors, so even if every bookmaker were willing to defraud his competition, fixing would go on as corruptors sought to rig the market.

The corruptors' beards will themselves use different agents or other beards to hide what they are doing. For example, the London-based company SAMVO helps large punters and professional gamblers place their bets on the Asian gambling market in return for a percentage of their bets. In 2009, SAMVO's executives were questioned by both the British and German police because the company had placed a number of bets on the Asian market on fixed matches. However, the executives were able to convince the detectives that they had not known what was going on with these fixes because the beards had disguised the nature of the transactions so effectively.

Three, I include the units — protection and money — on each side of the gambling group. I do this to underline Gambetta's point about protection as a specific commodity in a corrupt deal. The corruptors have to make sure that no one betrays their deal. Many corruptors are quite capable of taking care of this side of the business by themselves. But some corruptors have to bring in "muscle" to ensure the deal goes through. This is not seen very often as the danger for the corruptor if this occurs is then the "muscle" can simply take over their entire fixing network.

The investors are brought in when the gambling group does not have enough money to pull off a fix themselves. This may occur in high-profile matches or with top-level, and more expensive, players. In 2006, I directly witnessed one group of corruptors needing to get additional funds because they were attempting to fix a sporting match that was so large (a World Cup tournament game) they simply did not have the cash available to pay for the fix. At this point, they became more like brokers establishing a deal for investors, rather than independent fixers. They attempted to arrange a match and then went to some rich investors who could bankroll the deal.

Given the general structure of Figure 9.1, what are the dishonest methods of fixing a gambling market? The first is to chose to fix a game where there is so much money (liquidity) in the market that no one studying the market can tell if there are significant swings in the odds one way or another. For example, the gambling market for one of the games in the World Cup Finals is measured in the hundreds of millions of pounds. It is almost impossible in most circumstances for anyone to detect unusual swings in such a large market. In other, lower-profile leagues, players and referees are cheaper to bribe, but the liquidity on the gambling market is so low that the profits are not particularly high. This does not mean it is easier to get the players to fix important matches; just that it is easier to fix the gambling market for these big matches. The reason why there has been an explosion in fixing of European football matches in recent years is that the liquidity on the matches has become so large with the globalisation of the world's sports gambling market.

A second method is for a corruptor to fix *with* the market in order to avoid detection. This method means lower short-term profit, but also less chance of detection. Academic game theorists describe this strategy as a "long-term" mode, as opposed to a "one-shot" game. For example, a weak team plays a strong team. The market expects the strong team to win. The corruptors fix the weak team to lose by a pre-set amount, pile on as much money as possible for the strong team, and few people will suspect a fix as the result occurs as the market predicted. It was seen in the fixing scandals in the British leagues of the 1960s, when one illegal bookmaker claimed to *The People* (the newspaper that broke the story), "In the eyes of the bookmaker, the perfect "fix' is the game which according to form should go one way... What the fixers do is make the natural and obvious result beyond any doubt but if they can get away with it." Another era — 2005; another country —

Finland; but the same strategy as this player testified to in a confidential interview with a popular newspaper:

> *I have taken money for a few games. This has been going on for years. The most recent case is from the last season. In this case it was just a normal league game.* ***We had gone to the game as the underdog and so the loss did not surprise anybody*** *[emphasis added]. (Staff writer, Ilta-Samsonet 2005)*

A match corruptor will also rig the market by using tactics similar to a fraudulent stock promoter "puffing up" a phoney company by placing false information in the market place. In this method, a corruptor will want the gambling market to lean heavily against the fix: so the team he controls is expected to win. To encourage bettors to bet *for* the fixing team he might spread a "credible rumour" that the other team has been weakened — an injury to a key player, dissension in the dressing room — or, ironically in leagues of high corruption, that he has fixed the *other* team!

Because much of sport B is either done during the game or in the two hours just before it begins, the later a corruptor can place his bet, the easier it is to place large money bets on the market and the more profit he can make (COR1). Say for example, a corruptor has established a link with players on Team A and he sees the betting market is betting heavily in favour of Team A winning the game. Ideally, the corruptor would want to bet heavily that Team A will lose, at attractive odds, (because if he comes in to the market too early, it can cause the odds to change) and then signal to his team to "open up the game" — lose — in the minute before the game is to begin. This would ensure the corruptor of the greatest profit.

However, in this scenario the corruptor faces a problem. How can he signal to his players without attracting any attention? How can they give him a signal that they have understood? All this happens in the final minutes before a big match. All the spectators, team-mates and officials are watching them. One solution to this problem was described by a corruptor who said:

> *What I do is have my runner stand beside the team box wearing a red singlet, if the team is to lose. When they come out onto the pitch, they stand at half-way line and salute the crowd. They see my runner wearing the red singlet and they know they must open up the game. If I wanted them to play hard, I would get my runner to wear a blue singlet. Now, when the players see the runner, they must put their hands on their hearts, as if they are saluting the crowd. This is their signal to let us know they have seen and understood the signal. They cannot pretend later not to have seen the signal. (COR1)*

The corruptor has now called the fix, ordered the players to rig the game in a certain way. Now it is only up to the players to deliver the right result.

## Performance

It is genuinely difficult for a player to fix a match. There are two principal constraints for corrupt players in ensuring a fix: how can they deliberately lose the match and how can they ensure that the audience — spectators, referee, team officials or fellow players — do not notice what they are doing? There is, after all, a certain limit to mistakes that a player can make. If they make too many they will be dropped from the team or make the fix too obvious; too few mistakes and the fix will not work. How the corrupt players and referees get around these constraints will be examined in detail in later chapters — suffice it to say there is a lot of acting that goes on! — but we will leave this stage for the moment.

## Payment

In the aftermath of the Lockheed scandal in the United States (where airplane manufacturers were found to be bribing foreign governments with American taxpayers' money) Neil H. Jacoby together with his colleagues Peter Nehemkis and Richard Eells, wrote, *Bribery and Extortion in World Business* (1977). In their work they included a comprehensive listing of the different forms of illegal payments and bribes practiced by U. S. companies. It ranged from the provision of prostitutes and scholarships to covert payments and kickbacks. However, the common denominator of these methods in bribing corrupt government officials is that payment is either hidden or "deniable".

The same challenges exist in paying corrupt players. The players are, for the most part, public figures. Their salaries are well known. Their lifestyles closely examined. Their honest team-mates work and play with them closely. How then can they enjoy the increased money without arousing suspicion? There are a number of strategies described in the databank. For example, *The Malay Mail* wrote that the corruptors often gave their players winning lottery tickets. The corruptors would buy the tickets from the winners, and then give the tickets to the players who had fixed the matches so that they could claim that the money had been won legitimately.

However, over 70% of the payments in Fixed Match Database to the corrupt players in gambling fixes were relatively unsophisticated cash payments (FMDB2). The discussion and strategies were much simpler than bribes to government officials, centring around where the payment would be made or if it would go through a runner or agent.

Generally, the gambling corruptors have two stages when making payment to the players. The first, as we have seen, is an advance or "coffee money" paid before the game. This payment is essentially symbolic. It settles the deal and shows that the player will take part in fixing the match. However, the main payment is reserved for after the game, when the player, has successfully performed the job. The place of payment is almost always a neutral location away from the football world — a disco, restaurant or airport.

There is another form of payment which successful, long-term corruptors ensure is paid to the player — the psychological one. This is similar to the pitches of the corruptors that as we saw are often couched in neutral languages. The corruptors try to ensure a long-term relationship with corrupt players. It may no longer be friendly, but it does need to be maintained in good account. Often players do not feel particularly good about underperforming in matches, so corruptors will provide them with "gifts" along with the payment. Frequently these gifts are women. Z1 took part in a number of fixed matches for the corruptor Chieu. One in particular match was against the Singapore team in Singapore in front of 50 thousand fans. Because of cultural rivalries it is very difficult for a Malaysian player to lose to Singapore, to lose in front of 50 thousand fans is even more difficult (the equivalent of Scotland losing to England). In Z1's confession he talks about the corruptor providing the corrupt players with women:

> *On the 28th of June in Singapore. We lost 5-0. I did not play all out. I went back to the hotel. The same night... Chieu had supplied four high-class prostitutes for four players...(Malaysian Police Confession, no. 2).*

In these last chapters, we have concentrated on how gambling corruptors fix matches. Initially, the challenges they face seem overwhelming. The games are often watched by tens of thousands of people. The team-mates of the fixing players, officials and spectators have an interest in seeing the games played honestly. However, we saw that a successfully fixed match is possible if a gambling corruptor first establishes an effective network by using a prominent player as his "project manager". This player should set up a corrupt network amongst his teammates. To establish this relationship the corruptor follows a pattern of five distinct stages of corruption: access, set up, calling the fix, performance, and payment. However, these stages of corrupting a fixed match need to be lubricated by two sociological mechanisms — coercion and trust — the next chapters show their importance.

## Chapter Review

- There is a significant relationship change between the gambling corruptors and the players/referees once they have accepted their bribes.
- This relationship change occurs because the gambling corruptor is now focusing on profit-maximisation.
- Gambling corruptors need to ensure that their fixes are not noticed by the gambling market.
- Their tactics include "puffing up" the game or suggesting they fixed the other team.

# THE PEOPLE OF THE GAME:
# PLAYERS AND REFEREES

# CHAPTER TEN
# PUSHED OR JUMPED?

*Because then you're fucking him around, and he won't like it, and he'll tell his Short Man... and then you get the chop and then you better watch it. You better get a bullet proof fucking vest, then... That's how fucking big it is... This is how fucking dangerous it is... When you're playing with fucking dangerous men, its fucking dangerous...*

*(Grobbelaar, cited in Thomas 2003, 185).*

The thesis of this book is that most sports corruption is driven by rational choice. In other words, corruption does not arise because of a specific nation or culture, but because it is largely in the self-interest of individuals to be corrupt.

However, what is self-interest? Are we speaking of "self-interest" from getting a lot of money? Or "self-interest" from not being killed? Mexican drug-dealers put it in a simple way. They ask "¿Plata o plomo?" — money or lead? — meaning that the potential collaborator has only two choices — accept a bribe or take a bullet to the head.

Diego Gambetta's book on adolescents deciding whether to stay in school came up with the framing question: "Were they *pushed* or did they *jump?*"

It is a good model to examine the popular myth that gambling corruptors frequently make players "offers they cannot refuse" so that they will take part in gambling match-fixing. It is believed that corruptors *push* players into fixing.

In the popular literature about match-fixing there is a theory that all corruption is generated by violence. There are lots of stories about tough, murderous gangsters. However, in this chapter, you will see that the evidence shows that although these situations may occasionally occur, far more often these stories are simply creations of the popular media, or an alibi created by the players to cover their willing involvement. This thesis is similar to the work done by Peter Reuter in *Disorganised Crime* in which he examined the illegal gambling industry in New York and found that many of the tales of coercion and violence were media creations.

There are three types of "coercion":

- *Violence* — an actual incident of physical force
- *Menace* — where players are threatened with force;
- *Intimidation* — where players indicate they are frightened or perceive a threat of some kind from the corruptors.

I add this last category to address the problem of analysing whether a business deal proposed by a professional criminal is always intimidating. In other words, if New York Mafia boss John Gotti had proposed a deal to someone, it did not matter how nice he was being. It was *always* intimidating.

## Coercion

At first glance, the data seems to support the hyperbole that gambling corruptors coerce players to fix matches. There are anecdotes about snakes being found in a player's car and of a goalkeeper dying in a "mysterious" car accident. Some of the confessions given by the Malaysian players to the police also seem to support the idea that violence was used as a recruitment tool:

> *September 1993 — it was during training time. Two Chinese men, maybe 5 feet 6 inches (167.6 centimetres), thirty years old came up to me and congratulated me. They said they knew Mike and Frankie [Two Singapore corruptors]. They were Frankie's men. They had just met some of the other players. They asked me to cooperate with a fix against Singapore. I refused. I left. The two Chinese [men] followed me and forced me to stop. One of them took out a Rambo-style knife and threatened to kill me and my wife, if I did not agree to help them.*
> *(Malaysian Police Confession, no. 5)*

This is described as a pattern by one coach in relating how gambling corruptors approach his players.

> *There is no nice chat, no long-term relationship stuff [i.e. no "counterfeit intimacy"]. They — the bookies — just ring up the players and say, "You do it or else." They will phone the players and say, "We want this game to be two-nil spread. You win. Or you lose." If the player tells them to fuck off — they say "we know where your sister goes to school" or "where your granny shops." (SO9)*

Stories of players being coerced by corruptors also exist among different sports in different eras. For example, during the President's Commission on Organised Crime that followed the U. S. college basketball fixing scandals of the 1970s, a player who helped fix games testified that one of the organised crime operatives connected to the corruptors had said, "You can't play basketball with a broken arm..." Another Malaysian player, Z1, claims a similar type of threat in this excerpt from his police confession, where in the midst of an apparently friendly business proposition with a corruptor, he was confronted with a threat of extreme violence directed at one of his colleagues:

> *May 6, 1995: XX [a corruptor] contacted me. He wanted me to sell the match. I was scared.... He then asked me to inform Z2 [a national team player also playing on Z1's team] that if he (Z2) does not cooperate XX will break his legs.*
> *(Malaysian Police Confession: no. 6)*

These excerpts seem to indicate that gambling corruptors frequently use coercion to persuade players to take part in gambling match-fixing. A more precise examination of the interviews, however, indicates that there is some suspicion that this is hyperbole. It is clear that none of the players who either fixed or played in fixed matches, regarded coercion as a motivation for themselves or their team-mates. This excerpt from an interview with one player is typical, when asked if players are threatened by corruptors he replied: "Oh no. It is like a business to them." *Question:* "So they don't threaten a player right away?" *Response:* "Oh no..." (P6)

The two other groups of interviewees who claimed that there was little coercion during recruitment were the law enforcement officers who investigated match-fixing cases and the corruptors themselves — the two groups who were closest to the corrupt deals. It could, of course, be argued that it would be in a corruptor's best interests to claim not to use violence as a recruitment tool. Or those corruptors who did use violence to recruit players were less likely to be caught. However, even in the covertly taped confessions, where the corruptor does not know they are being recorded, violence is not used as a recruitment tool.

A senior Singaporean policeman, who led many of the investigations into match-fixing cases, also claimed that for the most part the recruitment of players was done in a business-like manner:

> *I don't think many players were forced into the fixing. [In the] Initial stages anyone could have acted with impunity. After we started enforcement, then there was a lot more apprehension. And then they started to* ***enforce cooperation****, [emphasis added] but before we began operations there was no fear. It was only then that the players became fearful of the muscle behind the bookie (LE5).*

The groups of interview subjects who claimed that players had been forced into match-fixing were people all slightly removed from the actual corrupt deals themselves: journalists, commentators, or sports officials. Regarding the last group, it could be argued that it was far easier for players to pretend to league/association officials or their coach, that they were forced to take part in match-fixing, rather than admit they willingly accepted bribes. That type of lie may in fact be the reason for comments about violence like those of coach in the excerpt above.

But what about the confession databank: what does it say about coercion? First, the confessions that were quoted above should be analysed carefully. The police officers who interrogated the players wrote in their files that they felt the stories of violent coercion were often inaccurate and an attempt to excuse the players' actions. For example, Z1 — an excerpt of his confession is seen above — was, by the time of his arrest, the head of the corruption network for his team, so he needed a strong exculpatory reason to explain why he had become involved. According to the police, Z1's claim that he was the victim of violence was the player's attempt to excuse his involvement (Malaysian Police Confession: no. 6).

There are cases of coercion in the databank, and they are mentioned in interviews by all groups of interview subjects. However, a closer analysis of the American basketball case is typical of what we find in the databank, the gangster threatened the player *after* a "trial game" had not succeeded. In other words, it was coercion used to enforce the player's "continued involvement" rather than an initial recruitment ploy. So what happens if all the data is analysed using the following distinction: coercion used for recruitment vs. coercion used to enforce agreements?

Including the excerpts quoted above; there are thirty-nine different incidents of coercion mentioned in the gambling section of the confession databank. Only five of these examples report incidents of coercion being used as an initial recruitment tactic. However, of these five cases, three are the ones examined above, where the police felt they were dealing with a "cover" story. A fourth was explicitly denied by an organised crime confederate in an interview with the author (although, of course, this is what they would say). The fifth incident is a report of an anonymous player in the British leagues of the 1960s being forced to fix matches by a betting syndicate to pay for his extensive gambling debts.

The other thirty-four incidents of coercion follow the pattern where an arrangement did not work out and only then were the players threatened or felt that the possibility of extreme danger existed.

Table 10.1: Coercion for Recruitment vs. Coercion for Ongoing Agreement

**Source:** *Confession Databank*

But what about the players who said no to corrupt deals? Was coercion used against them? Were they threatened *after* their initial refusal?

Among the interview subjects and confession databank there are twenty-five cases of players who refused to fix matches when approached by gambling corruptors. Only one of them was exposed to coercive methods after he had turned down the first offer of fixing. Ironically, this came from his corrupt team-mates, rather than a gambling corruptor, who said in a 1915 fix between Manchester Unitd and Liverpool players, "If you score a goal you are — well, finished with Liverpool." The experience of Laurent Wuillot, a midfielder for the Belgian team Brussels FC, who was approached in 2005 by corruptors allegedly associated with organised crime is more typical:

> *Two days before the match, I received a telephone call from an old acquaintance. He asked me if I would accept to not play the game to my fullest... I refused immediately. I did not want to fall that low. But it was clear. The person and his commander respected my decision.* ***I had known them for a long time and I was never threatened, contrary to what people would have you believe*** *[emphasis added] ... (Delepierre 2006)*

There are two comments that should be made at this point. One, it is not that the data indicates that there is *never* any coercion between players and corruptors. There is data to indicate that internal corruptors *do* use coercion more frequently than gambling corruptors to *recruit* players to fix matches. Thus it is internal sports people who use coercion for recruitment far more often than outside criminals. This finding was substaniated by the 2012 FIFPro report on fixing in Eastern European football leagues. FIFPro is the international federation of professional players' unions. They conducted a survey of over 3 thousand of their current members on whether there was corruption in their leagues. To the authors' evident surprise, not only did more than 11% of the survey group reported being directly approached to fix matches, they also a reported a consistent pattern of harassment of the players by club owners. The authors stated,

> *Even the most battle hardened of us, who had worked in player unions for many years, were astonished at the scale of the problems the players face. Non payment of salaries, match fixing, violence, discrimination were all too common... Many players were too scared to respond and many of the players' unions face hostile reactions from the clubs who would not allow their players to participate. FIFPro would also like to comment the players who have agreed to be interviewed... many of these players have been threatened and bullied.... (FIFPro, January 2012, 4)*

Thus violence and intimidation is used by internal corruptors — team officials — more than external gambling corruptors. However, this does not mean that violence, or the threat of violence, is *never* used by criminals. In fact, the confessions and interviews do reveal that the players are often frightened of the corrupters and there were frequent incidents of coercion. However, most of this coercion was used to *enforce* corrupt agreements rather than for *recruitment.*

Why don't gambling corruptors — generally — recruit players with coercion? If we compare gambling match-fixing with other types of industrial racketeering, like the dry cleaning business in Al Capone's Chicago or corrupt U. S. Army procurement contracts in South Korea where violence was rife, the initial steps in gambling corruption are noticeably more peaceful. The difference in recruitment is partly due to the difference in the structure of the industry. Football is not dry cleaning. There is a high component of skill to it. In Capone's Chicago, one laundry operator could be replaced with another one relatively easily. But, because of their skill, football players are far more valuable to the corruptors than employees in a regular business. A better comparison is with artists rather than small businessmen. As Sepp Blatter, president of FIFA, declared, "You cannot consider a footballer like any normal worker... they are more artists than workers."

A second reason for a general lack of coercion in recruitment is a technical one. Frequently, organised criminals do not approach the players directly, preferring to use "runners" or former players who can set up a fix more easily. In previous chapters, we saw how gambling corruptors gain access to the players, and that in a large percentage of the cases in the databank, the corruptors used agents of some kind to approach the players. We can see this in the Belgian example quoted above, where the player speaks of his former associate and "his commander."

The third reason that corruptors tend to avoid coercion is that coercing a player into playing badly is a crime that carries a far higher risk of sanctions than simply bribing a player. Gambling corruptors are like predatory beasts, they may possess truly terrifying resources, but they pSee stalk their prey rather than seize them directly. In match-fixing, bribes work well and players seemed willing to take bribes often enough that there was little need to risk coercion.

In this chapter, we looked at the use of coercion and violence by gambling corruptors. The data, interviews and confessions, indicates that corruptors do *not* use violence or threats of violence to *recruit* players to fix matches. This finding seems completely contrary to the popular myths that surround match-fixing in football, where players are generally assumed to have been "made offers they cannot refuse." Rather, the evidence indicates that when coercion is used by the corruptors on the players, it is either by the club owners and managers or gambling corruptors use it to *enforce* already agreed upon corrupt transactions.

However, the essential sociological phenomenon that drives all successful corruption — be it match-fixing or bid rigging — is trust. In the next chapter, we will examine the concept of *trust* and analyse why the gambling networks have a high reputation of trust while fixing networks do not.

## Chapter Review

- Players are, generally, not coerced into fixing by gambling corruptors.
- Rather the violence occurs once they have agreed to fix a match and they attempt to renege on the deal.
- Internal corruptors (team officials) are more likely to engage in violence then gambling corruptors.

# CHAPTER ELEVEN
# TRUSTING ALL THE WRONG PEOPLE

*It was our coach and he said, "We have to be quiet, we don't have to say to anybody." So we didn't think it was something wrong because it was our coach who told us [to fix]. So we trusted him... And that's how it happened.*

*Player in the Belgian league, interview — August 2011.*

Trust drives societies. The more trust there is in a society, generally, the more successful it is. Trust propels a number of important concepts, from the postal system to invoicing for services to taxation systems. In his work on trust and corruption, Eric Uslaner claims that as general levels of societal trust go down, corruption goes up. However, there is one industry that actually shows the *opposite* effect — the illegal Asian gambling market. It is a multi-billion pound industry run, largely, by criminals who are flouting the law. Yet the reputation for quick-payment is exceptionally high even in countries whose general level of corruption is very high. An Asian athletics coach who said in an interview, "I have never heard of a bookie shitting on people," has a reasonably typical view of the Asian gambling markets. This chapter is an examination of this vast, illegal gambling market and, specifically, why it has a higher reputation for trust than its counterpart the fixing networks.

How, then, does the Asian sports gambling industry function? It is like the American porn industry: a vast, well-connected structure of indeterminate legal status that has connections with organised crime, as well as legitimate companies and generates enormous amounts of money. Some of the difficulty of estimating the size of the American porn industry is not only the connections to organised crime, but also the many very large corporations that make a lot of money out of the industry. Many of these companies do not want to admit that they do so. For example, some international hotel chains make a large proportion of their "in-room" profits on guests renting sex videos. There are similar issues with the Asian gambling industry, because it is often illegal, it is, like the porn industry, difficult to measure.

Here are a few rough estimates of its total size. A 2006 study in the American journal *Foreign Policy* valued the entire Asian gambling industry, both legal and illegal, at $450 billion U.S. a year. In comparison, the Asian pharmaceutical industry is worth roughly $106 billion U.S. a year. It is difficult to know how accurate the gambling figure is or how much of it is spent on sports gambling. For example, the Remote Gambling Association (RGA) (a trade group that represents many of the private bookmaking companies) in a complaint before the European Union in 2009, claimed that the total of all gambling and betting in the world is only $335 billion. However, the RGA added a statement saying:

> *Complete and accurate data on the gambling and betting sector, and in particular the remote gambling and betting segment, are not available. However, a number of sources offer sufficient information to provide an* ***approximate*** *[emphasis added] picture of the size and structure of the gambling and betting sector. (Remote Gambling Association, 2009, 16)*

The problem in getting accurate numbers on this industry is that much of it is run by illegal operators. The World Lottery Association (WLA), the umbrella-group of legal government-run gambling companies, claimed that the total amount of the illegal sports gambling world, with most of this market being in Asia, is approximately $90 billion dollars. Other estimates have gone even higher. Chris Eaton, the former head of integrity for FIFA claimed in 2011 on a television documentary that the Asian sports gambling market is roughly worth 500 million dollars. In the summer of 2012, Interpol — the international police organization — was even reported as claiming that the total world sports gambling market is worth $1 trillion dollars.

## A warning!

There may be some exaggeration in these last estimates. Part of the rise in the valuations of the market over the last six years could have occurred because of the rise in funds available to various organizations to "fight" illegal gambling. As in the "War on Drugs" which saw estimates of drug use and illegal importation shipping being, according to some commentators, vastly overstated so that various institutions could then claim more funding, so too it might be in the estimates of the illegal sports gambling world. Thus such figures should be taken with extreme caution.

However, putting aside any possible exaggeration, the market is still very large. Just as in the "War on Drugs" no one claims that drug importation was not taking place, so too the scale of the illegal sports gambling is vast. One example, in 2011 the gross turn-over of just one Asian bookmaking company was estimated to be four times higher than that of Adidas, the well-known sporting goods company.

Again, this is a comparison that should be viewed carefully, as the profit margins of Asian bookmakers are much smaller than traditional retailers like Adidas. But even so when the range of other countries that share gambling organizations — Indonesia, China, Vietnam, Thailand and Malaysia — are factored into the estimate, the size of the illegal Asian sports gambling industry can be safely estimated to be well into the tens of billions of dollars.

## The Structure of the Illegal Asian Sports Gambling Industry

The structure of the industry is there are about two-dozen bookies who are the heads of national gambling syndicates across Asia. Each of these syndicates controls one country or a substantial section of a country's business. One of their associates told me that they don't like the term *bookies*; they prefer *super-agents* and the people who work for them are *agents*. This is because bookmaking is still illegal in most Asian countries, so the term *bookie* attracts too much unwanted attention. But they really are bookies and they are based in Hanoi, Bangkok, Johor Bahru (a small city just across the Malay Peninsula from Singapore), Taiwan, Jakarta and, most frequently, Manila. The ownership, structure, and essential role of trust in this level of the illegal gambling networks is similar to the Asian heroin traffickers and relies on inter-ethnic Chinese community connections:

> *In the distribution of heroin throughout Southeast Asia, a very important role is played by the "mafia" of expatriate Chinese... They form networks of kinship and relationship extending across geographical frontiers into a dozen major Asian cities and a similar number in Europe... In this way, a clandestine financial network is set up, based on* **mutual trust** *(emphasis added) among the members of a single community — and on ruthless reprisal should that trust be broken (Lamour and Lamberti, in Arlacchi 1986, 198-199).*

In the gambling world, all of the *super-agents* of the national structures are also ethnically Chinese. They have very strong interconnections and they will balance their books by "laying-off" bets with one another.[12] Figure 11.1 shows an approximate structure of a national Asian gambling industry.

Gambetta wrote of established Sicilian mafias providing both political and financial protection to finance tobacco smuggling operations. A similar need for protection is seen at the higher levels of Asian gambling syndicates. The national-level bookies can potentially receive protection from two sources: a high-level politician or businessman who can provide them with political protection and the finances needed to cover an unexpected run of bad luck; and an organised criminal who provides the muscle to ensure that recalcitrant bettors pay up and that other crime groups do not prey on them. (According to the Asian crime experts Bertil Lintner and Gerald Posner, these two roles can often be played by the same person).

Below this level are regional bookies who aren't necessarily ethnically Chinese. They base their work in anonymous houses, or "counting centres, " distributed across the continent. I visited one in Klang, a costal port in Malaysia. It was housed above a car repair shop. There were no signs or advertising of any kind, but most people in the neighbourhood seemed to know of its location and existence. These counting centres are where the bets are tallied and the larger bets are passed up the chain of the syndicate. Underneath the regional bookies are a series of runners and the actual bettors who number in the tens of millions. The bettors can place money on a truly bewildering array of different bets, from football matches played in the Icelandic Second Division to local cock fights to Formula 1 car races.

---

*12 This term means when a bookie has taken too many bets on one result of an event, they (the bookie) will try to "lay off" the money with other bookies to balance his books. For example, Manchester United is to play Juventus, and the bettors in Vietnam, in general, bet heavily for United. The Vietnamese bookmakers will balance with their Thai counterparts who may have too many bets for Juventus.*

Figure 11.1: Structure of an Illegal Asian Betting Syndicate

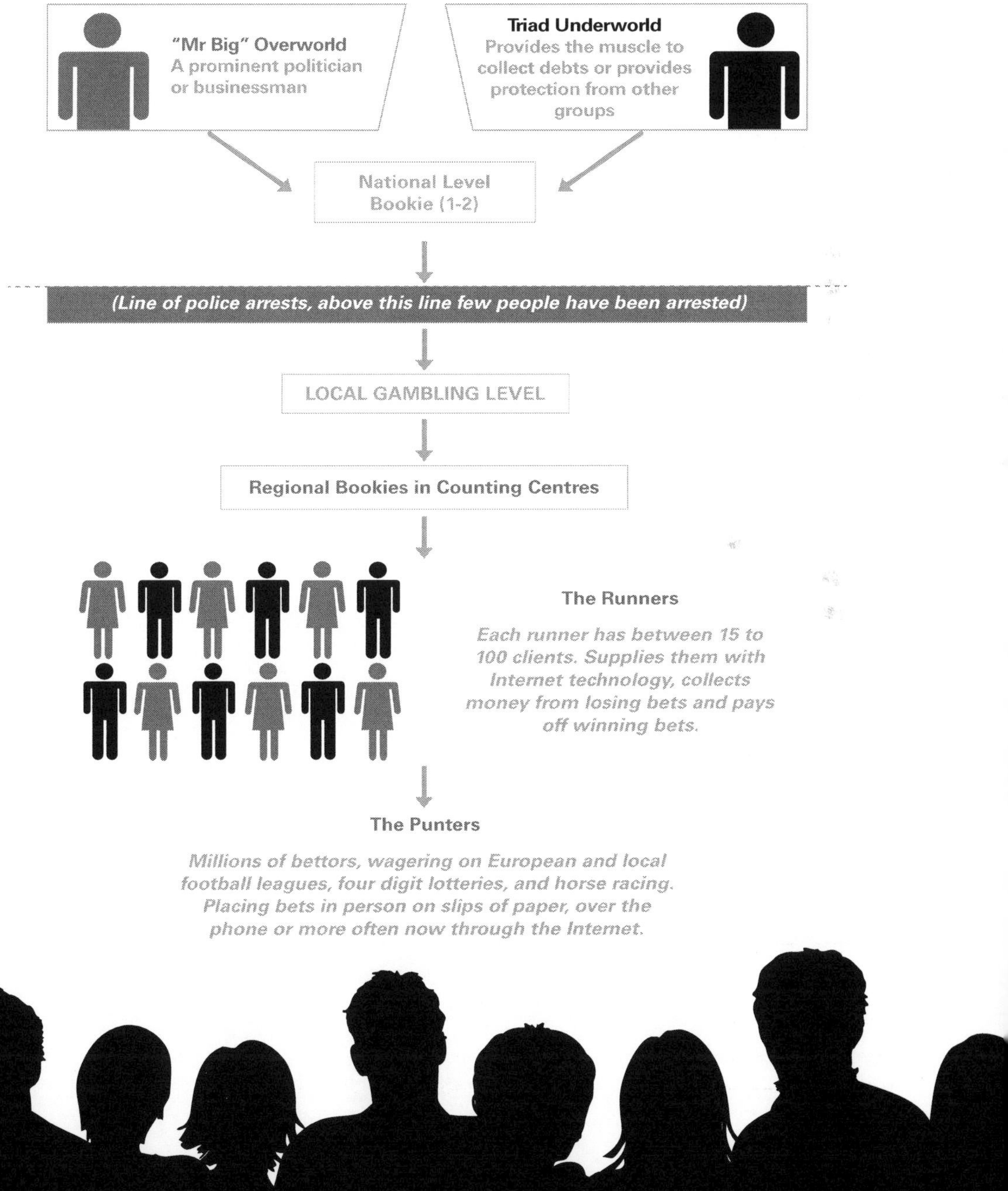

**"Mr Big" Overworld**
A prominent politician or businessman

**Triad Underworld**
Provides the muscle to collect debts or provides protection from other groups

National Level Bookie (1-2)

*(Line of police arrests, above this line few people have been arrested)*

LOCAL GAMBLING LEVEL

Regional Bookies in Counting Centres

**The Runners**

*Each runner has between 15 to 100 clients. Supplies them with Internet technology, collects money from losing bets and pays off winning bets.*

**The Punters**

*Millions of bettors, wagering on European and local football leagues, four digit lotteries, and horse racing. Placing bets in person on slips of paper, over the phone or more often now through the Internet.*

***Source:*** *Interviews with law enforcement and the informal gambling industry*

To add a further complication to Figure 11.1 is that a second wave of globalisation — conglomeration — has occurred in the Asian gambling world. In the early 2000s, a number of larger international corporations entered most of the betting markets in South East Asia. After a series of "table talk" negotiations with local bookmakers, these companies have introduced a new Internet-based technology that has added more concentration to the gambling market. Thus, while on a local level the structures of "agents" and "super-agents" are unchanged, there has been a remarkable degree of consolidation in the last few years at the head of the networks. At the time of writing, most of the local or national level agents pass their bets on to the larger offshore bookmakers, whose headquarters are often located in jurisdictions where sports gambling is legal, even though the bets of their sub-agents may be in jurisdictions where gambling is illegal.

Whatever the overall hierarchy, what is striking is that illegal Asian gambling operations, vast as they are, seem to operate under very strict principles of good faith and have a high reputation for honesty. SO2, one of the sports officials, spoke of this reputation.

> *They were — ironically — very honest. It is like where is the safest place in America to walk around with a big pile of cash? Las Vegas. The mafia would kill anyone who tried to steal or mug you in Las Vegas. They want to make sure that everyone feels safe and secure to gamble. It is the same with these guys here. They have to have a good reputation to pay out money. Otherwise word would go around and no one would bet with them (SO2).*

LE1 is a senior police officer who mounted a number of operations against the illegal gambling organizations. He claimed that trust is the "oil of their machine." He spoke of the lack of paperwork that engenders a functional need for this trust among the illegal gambling organizations:

> *Trust is key to the whole set up... With the punters and the bookies. I will show you some of the betting slips. There was nothing on them! Nothing! Just a blank piece of paper with just a few numbers written on it. Maybe four numbers. But that is all it took. With a regular bookie, my friends they just phone them up. Call them on the phone. That is all it takes (LE1).*

In fact, the reputation of prompt and ready payment by illegal Asian gambling networks is actually *higher* than their legal counterparts amoung professional gamblers. B7 is a professional gambler and his comments are typical:

> *The UK gambling market has no balls... I go to pick up my winnings and I am told, "Oh, our shop had an off-day. Sorry, but you'll have to come back tomorrow when we have had a chance to go to the bank." I can't place a big bet in my own name anywhere in London... but with the Asian syndicates, there is never any problem. In fact when XXXX [a British bookmaker] tried to set up in Asia during the World Cup, they were creamed by the competition. They were paying out bets six weeks late, which in the Asian market is unheard of (B7).*

This reputation of prompt and ready payment seems to be a universal feature of illegal gambling networks, even outside Asia. Joe Pistone was "Donnie Brasco," the police officer who worked undercover in two of the New York mafia families. As a mobster, he ran an illegal casino and bookmaking operation in Brooklyn for several years. In his interview, we spoke about the gambling operations. He said that this high emphasis on trust is based on good business sense:

> *[As a bookmaker] the odds of anybody beating me over the long run is very slim, very slim. And once the word gets out that you welched, no one's going to bet with you anymore, you know?...*

> *Somebody who has been in business for a while, is not going to do that because, like I say, over the long run the bettor's never gonna win. And, once you welch on one person, the word gets out and they're going to go to somebody else. (LE16)*

This is not to say that the reality of trust in Asian gambling organizations is universal for *all* bookmakers or that there is no violence associated with gambling organizations. Rather, interview subjects displayed what Dasgupta refers to as "a trust in the enforcement network." Meaning, they trusted that the gamblers would do something to them if they did not pay.

However, the opposite is reported about the reputation of the fixing networks: there distrust is common among corruptors and corruptees.

In the confession databank — the record of the corruptors talking about how they fix — the term "trust" or variations (trusted, trustworthy, trusts) occurs frequently. In fact, the words are mentioned more often (70) than such important football terms as "passing, passes, pass" (56) or tackling (11), dribbling (1) or even "teammate, teammates" (18). What is striking is that despite this emphasis on trust — or perhaps because of it — in the interviews and confessions of corruptors and players in the fixing networks, many of them are very suspicious of each other.

Chieu (name changed) was an immensely successful corruptor, however, in interviews he revealed himself to be highly suspicious of the runners who worked for him. He regarded them as capable of betrayal at any time. Nor was he the only corruptor who displayed this attitude. In the chapter "Calling the Fix", there was the example of an Indonesian corruptor who would signal to the players while they were on the field by having his runner wear a red or blue singlet to indicate whether or not a fix was to take place. In the interview, however, the corruptor went on to say that he frequently changed the meaning of the signals without telling his runner. The runner would think that red meant a fix was on, but the players would know that it meant that a fix was off. This way if the runner wanted to betray the corruptor and make a side bet, he would lose his money.

In an interview with a former Singaporean match-corruptor, COR2 also spoke about the distrust in the relationship between the corruptors and the runners:

> *A runner can also be a bookie. In North America, maybe you have a hierarchy in the mafia, but here money talks. They will do everything. Take money, gamble, fix games... see that their bookie is taking odds heavily one way, so go to the other side and take other odds that way or fix the game. There is no control over them (COR2)*

This sense of incipient betrayal and lack of trust is not confined to the corruptor and their runners. One player commented on the fact that there are times when relations with corruptors can become difficult, "These situations are where the bookies will get nasty (P8)." The "situations" the player was describing are those when players on a team would break their agreements and take on several corruptors at the same time.

> *Some teams have two bookies. That is why some people were threatening [sic] because they are saying, "you are doing other things for other people." So let's say, a team has two bookies and one bookie is trying to make a fix, make you lose. And the other bookie is trying to make you win. So the players they think, "Hey no problem! We lose, we get money: we win, we get money." (P8)*

This cheating on the part of the players, according to other interviews, was a relatively common occurrence. J6, an investigative journalist who helped "break" the story of Malaysian match-fixing claimed:

> *The players have no loyalty. They will work for different syndicates. In Selangor (a prominent Malaysian team) there was a fight in the dressing room when one group of players had sold the game to one syndicate, and another group of players had sold it to another syndicate. (J6)*

This seems to be the underlying attitude in fixing networks, betrayal is always an imminent threat and therefore coercion is used to enforce the already agreed upon arrangement. This is the explanation for the fear that players showed towards the corruptors that we saw in the last chapter: coercion is not used to *recruit* the players, rather to *enforce* corrupt agreements. For example, in an interview, a corruptor reported a situation between two of his teams (Rangers and Rovers). Initially, the Rovers were supposed to win but a few hours before the game the corruptor "switched" the game. Rovers were now to lose. One of the players on the Rovers — Z5 — refused to listen to the instructions:

> *I phoned the Rovers team and told them what to do [lose the game]. Z5 [the Rovers player] said he would not do it. I told him he would. He said, "No." I said, "You should." He refused. So I phoned the Rangers player. I told him, "You will win. But you must break Z5's leg. When he is on the ground you must kick his leg." He did and Z5 was out for six months. I told him, "This is what happens if you do not listen to me. (COR1)*

However, another corruptor claimed that he rarely had to use coercion to guarantee cooperation amongst the players. He preferred, what the American academic Susan Rose-Ackerman describes as, "reputational hostage taking." "I threaten them with a photo of the two of us together. And I say, 'Your name is all gone. Mine it doesn't matter, send me to prison, who cares? But you! Everything finished, your career, your football all gone!'" (COR2)

*Key Concept*

---

*Reputational Hostage-Taking: Susan Rose-Ackerman's term for blackmailing someone to do something or you reveal their secrets.*

---

Nor was betrayal of agreements only between corruptors and players. In the players' interviews and confessions there are frequent stories of junior players being significantly underpaid by the senior players. One example: in one of the confessions Z2 is the head of the corrupt network on his team. He pays off one of the junior players with a significantly lower sum than he was being paid: "When I passed the money to Z3... he was only getting 1,500RM. He was very unhappy. I told him, "If you are not happy. Go see the bookie yourself," (Malaysian Police Confession: no. 2).

So in the fixing networks there was little trust among the players, runners, and corruptors. The key question is *why* do gambling and fixing networks differ, so greatly in their reputation for trust? They are both illegal. They are both connected to organised crime. They are both profit-maximizing. The fixing networks were comparatively small, consisting of two or three clusters of individuals at most; the gambling organizations took in the hundreds of thousands of punters, runners and bookies in Singapore and Malaysia. Yet the gambling organizations have a reputation of being highly trustworthy and the fixing networks have exactly the opposite reputation, why?

## Profit-Maximisation

The solution to the question is that although both networks have the same goal — profit-maximisation — they differ in their methods of reaching maximisation of profit. In the gambling organization both the punters and the bookies want to establish what game theorists describe as "frequent playing mode," in other words they want to build long-term relationship. They both have to know that if they cheat, other people will discover it quickly and they will lose their customers or their ability to bet. Thus it does not do either side any good to cheat the other. If a bookie wants gamblers to place bets with their gambling structure week after week, they must honour any pay-out. If a punter in the gambling structure wants to place bets regularly, he must pay his debts promptly or he will find it difficult to place bets with any other gambling structure.

Even though the bookmakers and the punters are, in theory, in competition with each other, in practice there is so much information flowing through the network, that for the sake of reputation, each person must honour his commitments. In Singapore, a runner, B2, for a bookie was placed on trial for match-fixing. In part of the testimony B2's bookie testified as to why he had to support his runner financially:

> *B2 is closely associated with me. In bookie business, if his name goes down, my name would also go down... I have been in this bookie business also. I don't want my name to go down in the market. I have this reputation and since lots of people know that B2 was with me, I didn't want my reputation to go down and so I wanted to help him.*
>
> ***As what? A bookie?***
>
> *I am steady in my finance and money-wise, in betting, in the market, that I am a man of good reputation.*
>
> ***If B2 defaulted, [would people know about it?]***
>
> *If the debt is not honoured, it would be the normal practice to tell others.*
> *(Maran vs. Singapore PP, 1997)*

However, illegal fixing networks differ greatly from illegal gambling organizations. Illegal gambling organizations depend for profit on a high quantity of bets and imperfect information: the greater the number of punters and the less they know who will win the game, the greater the profit for the gambling syndicate. Fixing networks are the exact opposite as they rely on a small number of highly selective bets and perfect information. The smaller the number of people who know that there is a fix, the greater the gambling odds will be, the greater the profit. The more perfect the information — what the final result will be — the greater the profit.

Secondly, the fixing networks are attempting to commit a fraudulent activity within a fraudulent network. Their principal financial victims are not the spectators of the game — they are collateral damage — but the punters who have placed their bets opposite to the fixing network. A corruptor, if a player has betrayed them, cannot go to the market and complain about their reputation, as a bookie can do about a bankrupt punter.

Yet these differences do not explain why actors inside a fixing network should be more willing to betray the network than gambling syndicates. There are several reasons for this phenomenon. First, although there are a small number of players, there are even a smaller number of corrupt players who can affect a game, thus these players have more power than the average punter. They can sell their game to the highest bidder. They have no interest in necessarily maintaining a direct relationship with one particular corruptor; rather for profit-maximisation it is better to have several corruptors all competing for their interest. Thereby, the players ensure that corruptors pay them a greater return for their fixing work.

Figure 11.2 shows the trust relationship in the gambling structure is essentially a two-way dynamic, the punter and bookie can either pay each other or not (default). If they do not pay, they quickly lose their reputation and other people will not deal with them. However, the fixing relationship is characterized by a number of potential betrayals. A player can inform the owners (presuming they are not involved in the fix), make side bets with bookies, make deals with other corruptors or tell other players who are not involved who may sabotage the fix.

Figure 11.2: Potential Relationship Betrayals: gambling and fixing

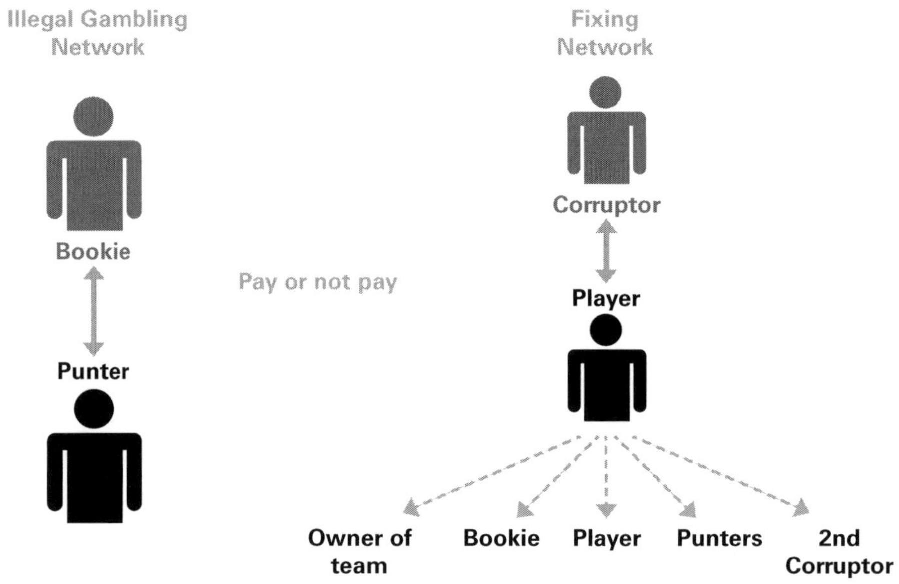

Illegal Gambling Network

Fixing Network

Corruptor

Bookie

Pay or not pay

Player

Punter

Owner of team

Bookie

Player

Punters

2nd Corruptor

Figure 11.2 shows that although fixing networks are small, the number of actors outside of the network who would wish to take advantage of a situation of perfect information is extremely high. Thus, a runner or any actor who has knowledge of a fix who wants to profit maximize has a built-in incentive to do so. Even a junior player, if informed early enough of the "direction" of the fix, can place a side bet through his regular bookie. That regular bookie would immediately change the structure of his odds if he were to see a player on one particular team betting in a certain direction. And once the odds lessened the fixing network would make less money. It is for these reasons that violence is often associated with fixing networks. It is very rarely used for recruitment purposes but it is used to ensure that the fixing networks continue to run smoothly.

In this chapter, we have examined the difference in reputation between illegal Asian gambling operations and fixing networks. In general, the gambling operations are massive operations that have millions of customers and are run, at the national level, by criminals. Despite these factors, the gambling operations have high reputations of trust. Fixing networks have extremely low reputations of trust. The reason for this difference is that fixing is a situation of perfect information that many actors would like to exploit. Gambling, on the other hand, is simply a corrupt transaction and one that depends for its profits on repeated exchanges. Because of these low levels of trust, once a corruptor has established a fixing network, he must use a mixture of coercion and reward to ensure that it stays "trustworthy".

In these last three chapters, we have examined match-fixing whether external corruptors use violence to force players and referees to be corrupt. The data indicates that, in general, this is not the case. However, the next chapter explores the issue -why - if they are not forced into corruption - do players and referees agree to participate in fixed matches?

## Chapter Review

- This chapter examined the difference in informal gambling markets (high levels of trust) and fixing networks (low levels of trust).
- Asian gambling industry is loosely comparable to the U.S. porn industry: enormous revenue often hidden by either hypocrisy or informal markets.
- Fixing networks are often held together by violence, even though the players/referees were recruited without coercion.

# CHAPTER TWELVE
# JUMPING INTO FIXING

*Since I first set my sights on soccer as a career I have met almost every known type of football fiddle. I have been involved in quite a few myself and I am not ashamed. I, like hundreds of others, have been driven to it by the miserly attitude of the authorities in their assessment of fair payment for services rendered... You can see why we look round for alternative sources of 'income'; why we are not above a little bribery and corruption so long as nobody gets hurt in the process.*

*Trevor Ford,* I Lead the Attack, *1957, 20.*

Why would a player participate in a gambling fix?

It is not an easy question if one uses theories from classic criminology. Criminologists are fascinated with the question of *why* criminals commit crime or as they call it "deviancy". For example, in the early part of the twentieth century, the Italian criminologist and physician Cesare Lombroso proposed that there was a genetic class of quasi-humans who were drawn naturally to crime. He came up with this theory partly by measuring the skulls of prison inmates and decided that most of their heads were of "unnatural shape".

Before you laugh too much, arguably the idea of a genetic make-up for a criminal class of people is underneath the currently popular "psychopath" school of thought, where prisoners and, ironically, upper management executives have been shown to have a high proportion of people lacking empathy, who commit criminal acts without being aware of the human cost.

In 1938 Robert Merton, one of the thinkers whose ideas have greatly shaped this book, proposed another idea for the motivation of criminals. He argued that criminal deviant acts are, largely, committed by working class males who lack status and respect in his society. The perpetrator has little or no legitimate means of acquiring that status and thus turns to a criminal pathway to gain the economic and social status that more privileged members of society can acquire. His article "Social Structure and Anomie" was immensely influential. At one point forty years after its publication, it was the single most frequently cited and reprinted paper in American sociology. The article and Merton's later modifications have produced its own school of though in criminology — "Strain Theory" and a host of modern-day disciples.

It seems that Merton and his disciples would say that professional athletes are exactly the last people to commit an act of corruption. After all professional sportsmen and women command an enormous amount of status in their societies. Many men, women and children idolise them. Their place of work is watched by tens of thousands of fans. They are, purportedly, well-rewarded by relatively large salaries. It is difficult to think of a professional that enjoys more status in society than an elite athlete. Yet across a range of different leagues, countries and cultures, athletes at the very height of their careers and prestige have taken the decision to commit a deviant act. We saw in the last chapter, that most of the time players are not coerced into corruption, so why would so many players decide to fix a match?

In this chapter, we will focus exclusively on players who are engaged in a particular type of match-fixing — gambling. The data from the FIFPro survey, among others, clearly shows that often players are coerced into corruption by their employers in an internal arrangement type of fixing. However, the data in this chapter shows that the best way to understand why some footballers agree to fix matches for gambling corruptors is to see them as economically-motivated criminals who choose to participate in fixing matches for a set of financial reasons. The best societal comparison of footballers is not disadvantaged working class males, but an eclectic mixture between high-level business executives and professional ballet dancers.

Let us begin with an incident that occurred during an interview with a player in Singapore.

## Financial Motivation

It was the day after a Champions League game. In Asia, most European games start at two or three o'clock in the morning. After the interview, we sat up to watch the game. P10 is an international player. At one time FIFA had ranked him as one of the most promising young players in the world. In the interview and conversation he seemed very honest. He spoke about his problems adapting to a lifestyle of easy fame and status. He had become a drug addict — mostly cocaine and amphetamines — had married and then divorced, after his wife had not been able to put up with his extra-marital affairs. P10 eventually dropped out of the game for some time, and with his parents help, had tried to turn his life around. He has now re-married, is a publicly professed Christian and has re-entered football.

He had taken part in fixed matches. Key matches where the manager or owner of his team had bribed players on the opposing team. But he claimed he had never taken a bribe or had anything to do with gambling match-fixing in his life.

The next day we met for coffee. He was leaving the city that evening. He had been playing for his club for five months and had received no salary. The owner of the team had signed a contract with him, promising to pay him a certain amount of money each month but the owner had refused to do so. P10 had played on and become the team's leading goal scorer. Still the owner had refused to pay him. Finally, the day before I met him, P10 had walked out of the club and, with his wife, was flying home.

As we drank our coffees and chatted about the game the night before, he leaned forward and said, "You know a lot of these fixers don't you?"

"Well. I have interviewed some of them, yes." I replied.

"Give me one of their phone numbers."

"What?"

"Give me one of their phone numbers." He repeated. "Look, I haven't been paid in four months. I have got a wife. I have got commitments. I could make a lot of money this way."

I include this anecdote not to shock the reader or moralise, but because it seems to sum up the state of many players who consider match-fixing. In general, they take part in corrupt deals not because they are coerced, but for financial gain.

This desire for money is showed throughout an analysis of the Fixing/Non-Fixing Player Database (the FPD database). The database has 117 players who responded either "yes" or "no" to a specific invitation to fix a football match: 25 who declined, and 92 who accepted. In the database there are 24 variables. One of these variables is "decision points" or a specific answer to a directly asked question, related to gambling-fixes — "why did you fix, or not fix, a match?" — for 76 of the players. These decision points come from varying sources in the database: some come from interviews; some are found in the equivalent of "life-histories"; in 23 of the cases, the players are answering this question in a court of law or a police confession.

The cases do show that the consistent, almost universal motivation, of match-fixing is money.

The precise motivation for acquiring that money varies in each case, from conditions of relative deprivation to simple greed. There are various reasons like private schools or clothes for children, investment in another business or inability to sell a house, given by the players to justify their decisions. The phrases that are repeated throughout the confession databank, in both leagues of high and low corruption, are variations of this theme:

> *You have to understand these types. They can make more money on one fixed game than an in an entire season, they are so badly paid at these clubs they are desperate to survive... (Delepierre 2006).*

> *It took a lot of heart-searching before I finally made up my mind to go through with the deal. I love football. It is my whole life. But I was in debt, and finding it difficult to manage. I thought of our money troubles... (Gabbert 1963, iii)*

> *I suppose I really decided to go "bent" because of the easy money there was to be made... (Gabbert 1964, viii).*

> *He had a fucking Rolex on his arm. I said, "Give it to me, I want to weigh it." It was the fucking business — three grand's worth of watch. He said, "This is yours, the next time you do the business [fix a match]." (Grobbelaar in Thomas 2003, 93).*

In the last chapter, we saw that few players are coerced into gambling match-fixing. However, this finding leads to two specific questions: if the players are bribed into match-fixing: *why* do the players accept bribes? And, *which* of the players will accept the bribes?

## Is it All Just Anomie?

One of the most trenchant criticisms of Robert Merton's thinking came over-twenty years after his original article when the criminologist Donald Cressey in his work *Epidemiology and Individual Conduct* (1960) asked a simple, but important question: "Why some and not others?"

In other words, it was all very well for Robert Merton and his followers to claim that deprivation was the source of a great deal of criminal deviancy, but many poor people, who have little access to status or high paying jobs, do not turn to crime. This particular question of who commits crimes and why was picked up by a host of other authors, and has become one of the dominant sociological puzzles of the field. So following Cressey's argument, if the main motivation for players to fix matches is financial, is it possible to come up with a set of common variables that delineate between corrupt players and non-corrupt players?

There are a range of theories that attempt to describe why some players chose to participate in gambling match-fixing. For example, the one most widely cited by Malaysian and Singaporean football officials is the "good-young-boys-entering-into-bad-circumstances."

They may not know it, but their idea is embedded in the French thinker Émile Durkheim's idea of anomie. For sociologists, Durkheim is one of the greats. You may disagree with him or worship his work, but his influence on the field is impossible to ignore. In 1897, he wrote a book examining why the rates of suicide were rising in France. His methods and techniques laid out many of the general working methods of sociologists for the next one-hundred-years. First, he looked at the statistics and found that — yes, the rates of suicide were rising in France, however, most of the rise was found in the industrial areas of the country where large numbers of people had moved to find work.

The rural areas of France, which were essentially unchanged for centuries, had no corresponding rise in suicide. Durkheim proposed the idea that the deaths in the new industrial areas were caused by "anomie" — or a state where both the individual and the larger community had few clear societal rules. The people living in these areas had no well-established routine, no clear safety network of family, friends and no known-community to support them.

### *Key Concept*

---

***Anomie:*** *a state of confusion or uncertainty that leads individuals to change their behaviour: examples would be religious conversions, having extra-marital affairs or committing suicide.*

---

Durkheim's original idea of anomie has been influential in a number of other academic fields. Robert Merton's famous breakthrough journal article takes much of its thinking from Durkheim's work. The two — Durkheim and Merton — have given rise to whole sub-fields in criminology called "Strain Theory" and "Anomie Theory" which still have many proponents today. In the specific case of athletes, it is that individuals from poor backgrounds do not have economic opportunities; they are suddenly given money, status and economic opportunity, the ensuing anomie causes them to commit acts of deviancy.

This argument is a version of the "sex, drugs and rock n' roll ruining the lives of young men" argument that has assumed various guises since the Biblical prophets mentioned it to the young Israelites. The idea goes as follows: the players are young men who suddenly receive attention and financial rewards beyond their wildest dreams. They hang out with bad company. They drive fast cars. They are tempted by faster women. It all goes to their heads. Suddenly, they are fixing football matches and ruining the integrity of the sport that has given them so much. SO1, a senior Malaysian football official, outlines the structure of this argument:

> *Most players are dropouts. Country boys. They would probably be working in the fields or rubber estates, if it were not for football. They are completely lost when they become big football players. They visit discos. It is all new surroundings. Lots of girls. There is a lot of naiveté. They are not hard criminals ... (SO1)*

This lack of economic opportunity certainly describes the background of many professional football players in Malaysia. They tend to be disproportionately from both poor backgrounds and socially marginalized groups like the Tamil community in Malaysia or the Malaysian community in Singapore. The argument of the sports officials is strengthened by the strong sense of hierarchy in professional football in Malaysia and Singapore.

The players, from their mostly disadvantaged backgrounds, are given little status within the football community. At times, they still have to kiss the hands, literarily, of some league officials. Club or league officials often do not hide their class-conscious contempt of the players. Another football official when interviewed said, "Most of the players are sharecroppers who without football would be cutting rubber trees in the jungle..."

To summarize this argument: a group of young, working class men, who normally would be unable to enjoy a middle-class lifestyle, are suddenly catapulted into a profession that gives them relatively large financial rewards, but uncertain status. The players have no set of firm rules or familiar norms that can guide them in this new situation. Their state of moral confusion is so overwhelming that they commit acts of deviancy and match-fixing.

If the theory of individual anomie leading to match-fixing were correct, match-fixing would be negatively correlated with age. Because players generally enter the league between the ages of 19 and 22, then the younger a player was, the more likely he would fix matches. Does the data support this hypothesis?

## Statistical Results

Percy Seneviratne's history of the Malaysian football league, (written and published with the financial backing of the Football Association of Malaysia) generally supports the idea of greedy young players losing their heads and fixing matches. However, as shown below in Figure 12.1, it also reveals that of the twenty-nine players suspended by the FAM in 1994, only five of them were twenty-four or under. The other twenty-four players were senior professionals with years of experience both as players and in enjoying "the high life".

Figure 12.1: Ages of Bribed Players in the Malysian League 1994

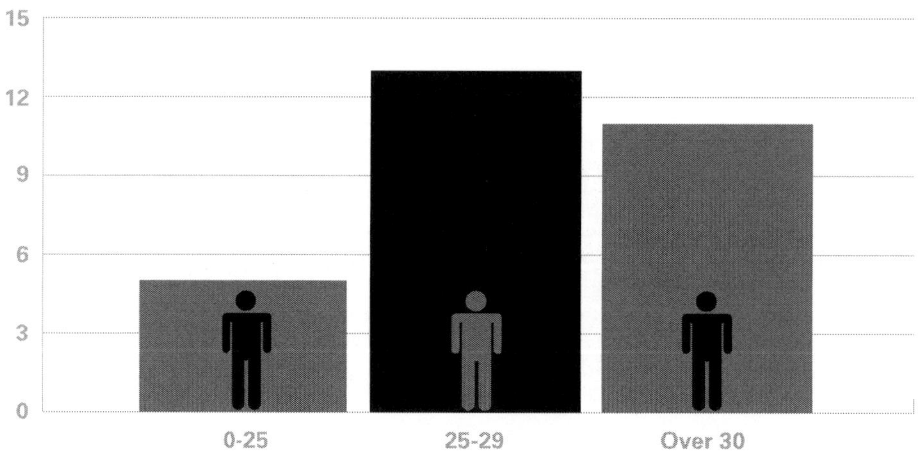


***Source:*** *Seneviratne, the History of Football in Malaysia, 1900-2000, page 115 (N=29)*

This finding is supported by the Fixing/Non-fixing Player Database for different leagues and playing eras. In the database there are 66 players who committed acts of gambling related match-fixing whose ages we know. When broken down, the figures of the Malaysian-Singaporean league are, roughly, replicated. They show that match-fixing is largely the purview of older players: of the players who fixed matches twelve (18.2%) were under the age of twenty-five; twenty-one (31.8%) were between twenty-five and twenty-eight; and a further thirty-three (50%) players were twenty-nine years old and over.

In Figure 12.2, these numbers are also contrasted with the age breakdown of players in a typical league of relatively high corruption — the Football League Fourth Division, operating in England & Wales in 1961 — as a control group. In that league 23.8% of the players were under twenty-four, 56.7% were between twenty-four and twenty-nine, and only 19.5% of players were thirty and over. Yet this last group — players thirty and over — accounts for almost forty-five per cent of the match-fixing players in the database. In other words, a player thirty and over is more than *twice as* likely to be engaged in match-fixing as a player under the age of twenty-five. These results are shown in Figure 12.2.

Figure 12.2: Ages of Bribed Players vs. Average Age of Players

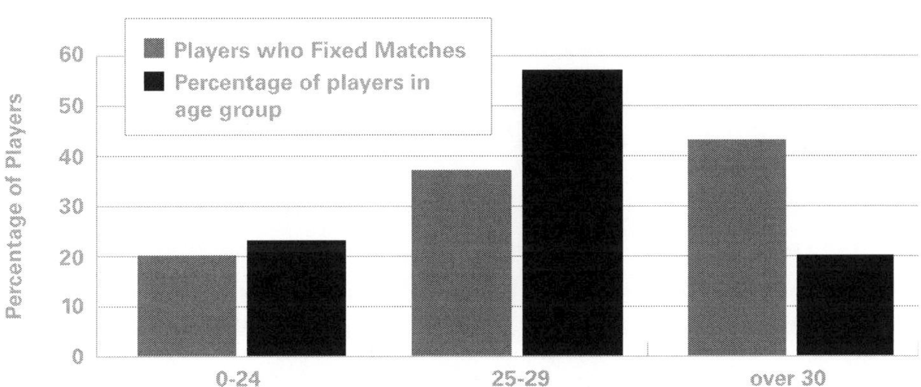


***Source:*** *Fixing/Non-fixing Players Database (N = 66)*

These findings do not, of course, mean that we can completely dismiss the theory of individual anomie. Figures 12.1 and 12.2 indicate only when the players were either caught or confessed to match-fixing, not when they *started* match-fixing. Players may have begun match-fixing at an earlier age because of individual anomie, but carried on fixing for other reasons. To further test the hypothesis that match-fixing is caused by youthful anomie, there was data for 41 of the players that give *both* their ages when they were *caught* match-fixing and when they *started* fixing. The results of this analysis are shown below in Table 12.1:

Table 12.1: Age Started Fixing and Years of a Career Before Fixing

| | Average age of player in League | Age when started fixing | Age when caught fixing | Years of fixing | Years Playing before fixing |
|---|---|---|---|---|---|
| Average age | 26.3 | 26.8 | 28.1 | 2.5 | 7.3 |

**Source:** *Fixing/Non-fixing Players Database (N = 41)*

Table 12.1 also does not support the hypothesis of individual anomie. The players who do match-fix had an average of 7.39 years playing professionally *before* they began fixing. The average age of the players when they started to match-fix was 26.8 years old; an age where youthful anomie caused by an introduction to a new career can be presumed to have passed. It is also striking to note that the average age when a player begins match-fixing is only a few months older than the average age of a player in the league. The figure seems to indicate that as a player moves into the back trajectory of their career, it is then that match-fixing begins.

We can see from the data that we must discount the hypothesis — that match-fixing is largely the purview of young players. Rather, match-fixing seems to be mostly done by players who are well-established in their careers.

This model makes sense. If a match is to be fixed, it is easier for a player with the most "playing capital" (the ability to most influence the game) to fix the match. It is the younger, less experienced players who, generally, lack playing capital, since their place in the team is uncertain, their talent is undeveloped, and their ability unknown.

The confessions and interview subjects also confirm that it was the senior players on the team who were generally the most prominent in fixing matches. These senior players were the players who had the longest amount of time to become used to the "high lifestyle."

## Sexual Anomie

There is one important qualification that needs to be made concerning the results above. The tables and statistics are accurate. However, they do have an underlying sample bias. The data is perforce, mostly from leagues of *high* corruption. The more corruption there is, the more players there will be who are fixing, the more fixing players there are from one league, the more the database will reflect situations of high corruption. However, there are four examples in the interviews and database of anomie leading to match-fixing. The examples are not related to age; rather they are linked to leagues or circumstances of *low* corruption. An example, from one of the corruptors who was, allegedly, able to corrupt matches at the Olympic Games:

> *There are some players who won't do it for money, but they will do it for women. I fixed the XXX team in 1996 against YYY at the Olympics in Atlanta. They wouldn't do it, when I offered lots of money. They said, "No, no, no... I am praying to God..." Finally, I got this beautiful Mexican girl. I paid her 50,000 dollars for the whole tournament. She would hang out in the lobby. She met him (the player from the XXXX team) and then went up to his room, did it [had sex] and then she proposed to him. Then I went*

> *in... "Will you do one game for me?" He said, "Yes." And they lose to YYYY. (COR1)*

The significance of this example is that sexual anomie was successfully created, not against a younger player in a league of high corruption, but against an older religious player in a competition where corruption was, and still is, relatively difficult. In other words, in leagues or competitions where corruption is widely practiced, the decision to fix games seems to come from the older players on the teams without recourse to anomie. However, in leagues or competitions with little corruption, on occasion anomie can be seen as a motivation to get players, again mostly older, to fix matches. In Chapter 8, we saw a similar trend in the data where gambling corruptors used a "fast bucks" approach in leagues of high corruption but, in leagues of low corruption, used 'counterfeit intimacy' as a way to approach players.

The general, correlated relation between age and match-fixing echoes other studies in the literature on economic crime and corruption ("white collar crime"). For example, in their study at Yale University, the sociologists David Weisburd and Elin Waring, examined the criminal conviction records of several hundred American executives. Weisburd and Waring looked at various variables such as house ownership, marital status and societal position — all of which produced no significant difference. However, the one variable that did show a positive correlation was age: the older a person was, the more likely they were to commit economic crimes. As Weisburd and Waring wrote:

> *... as offenders move into middle age they gain a growing awareness of time as a "diminishing, exhaustible resource" (Shover 1985, 211). Goals and aspirations change for these offenders as for other people as they get older. We suspect that such changes influence the willingness of offenders to be involved in criminality, irrespective of opportunity structures and other prerequisites for offending... (Weisburd and Waring 2001, 41)*

The British criminologist Dick Hobbs in his book *Bad Business: Professional Crime in Modern Britain* found a similar trend in criminals that he interviewed as this excerpt illustrates:

> *Whatever you got you want more — that's the way we all are. It's like anything else. You start off with something, and it seems like enough… But really it's family. When you got kids around you, you start worrying if they will be all right, and if the bills will get paid if you go away. The money don't go as far as it used to, and you start to feel like you should be stretching out for more… You want better things — motors and a proper home, if you got kids… the risk is there, but the money was more to the point. (Professional thief quoted in Hobbs 2003, 20-21)*

Advancing age is one of the things that make economic crime unique. It is in direct opposition to most "street" crimes — burglary, violent crimes, rape — where youth is directly related to the criminal's propensity to commit them. Unlike business executives whose prowess and propensity to commit crime is linked to their intellectual achievements and professional networks, a footballer's success is directly linked to their physical ability. (It should be noted that professional footballers effectively become "middle aged" in their sporting careers by their late twenties, and are often described as "elderly" if still playing in their late thirties.)

It is because of this *physical* factor that I write of the link between match-fixing footballers and professional dancers. For example, the British academics Steve Wainwright and Bryan Turner discovered in their study of professional ballet dancers, *Just Crumbling to Bits?*, that many dancers have an acute sense of "physical capital." In a typical excerpt a dancer says:

> *I retired at 38. I would say the last three years [I was] increasingly aware of aches that hadn't been there in the past, and also the fact*

> *that you take a little bit longer to get over from a particular exertion… as I got older my wife would always notice when I got out of bed and creaked! (Wainwright and Turner 2006, 244)*

Wainwright and Turner base their analysis of the interviews on the French thinker Pierre Bourdieu's ideas. However, I prefer a slightly different definition of physical capital, one more akin to the British sociologists Teela Sanders view of "sexual capital" in prostitutes in Britain, where a professional's ability to make money largely depends on their physicality ("the bigger your tits, the higher price the punter will pay").

Linked to this idea is the sense that physical ability is not only of relatively short duration, but also extraordinarily vulnerable. Harry Gregg, a successful goalkeeper of the era when match-fixing was relatively common in the British game (including on Gregg's own team), revealed in an interview, the attitude to injured players in the Manchester United squad: "…when you get injured nobody will talk to you…you shouldn't get injured. That was just the unspoken thing..."

Scottish international Ian St. John, another player of that time, echoed this when he wrote, "I wish I could write a book about all the great players of my era who were put on the rubbish heap when they were injured…"

It is this sense of the vulnerability and risk of imminent injury that is seen in the "fear of falling" that Stanton Wheeler writes of in his 1988 study of the motivation of economic criminals. Wheeler claims that it is not only money that motivates economic criminals but also a sense of imminent crisis or failure. A compounding factor for footballers is that, unlike other economic criminals, they are generally not particularly well-educated or have many opportunities outside their sport.

The FIFPro study, compiled by the players union, speaks of this sense of failing benefits and neglected education. Older footballers have a strong sense that their careers may be over in the next game or practice. They need to make as much money as possible *now*.

From this perspective, Robert Merton and his academic followers are correct in describing why a player might consider accepting a bribe. Their thinking is that footballers are under strain or anomie in their careers. The reality is that the players may not be considering their circumstances at the current moment. Nor are they thinking about trying to gain status or income, rather they are thinking about the near future, where they may be in a situation of anomie — no career, relatively uneducated and little opportunity to both the status and pay that they enjoyed as players. Given these circumstances, it then becomes a rational choice for the players to accept corrupt deals.

In the last few chapters, we have seen that, in general, players are not forced into gambling fixing. Rather the players that do decide to accept bribes make a rational choice they are coming to the ends of their careers to try and make as much money as possible, while they still can. However, it does not explain why *some* players decide to become corrupt while others do not. The next chapter explores more reasons as to why some players become corrupt.

## Chapter Review

- In general, players fix matches not because they are forced but because they want money.
- League officials often claim that the younger players are the most vulnerable, because they are suffering from anomie.
- The data indicates that it is actually older players who fix more frequently than younger players.
- The older players seem to be more willing to fix matches because they have a sense of a career that might end at any point and they need to make as much money as they can.

# CHAPTER THIRTEEN
# WHY SOME BUT NOT OTHERS?

*People I wouldn't want to be my company in life... there was millions of people who would pay millions of pounds to do what these guys were being paid to do... there were peoples with injuries, there were invalids, there were disabled people, people who would have given everything they had to go on a pitch and do everything these guys were doing and getting paid for it. ... To me, they were low-lives who were selling the club, the supporters and themselves for a shilling. I can't accept that.*

*Harry Gregg, former-goalkeeper of Manchester United and Northern Ireland on fellow players who fixed, interview August 2005.*

In 1939, a year after Robert Merton had published his ideas of deprivation and anomie creating deviancy, another American criminologist, Edwin Sutherland, gave a dramatic speech about the "white-collar" criminal. He took the opportunity of the American Criminology Society's annual conference, a few days after Christmas, to address his profession. Sutherland said that up to that point, most of their work had been both class-biased and wrong. He argued that crime or "deviancy" had been defined by academics as something poor people did. The rich and powerful were deliberately excluded from the academic analysis. He laid out the term "white-collar" criminal, but really he was speaking of thieves who were dressed better than street-level burglars or robbers.

In American academic terms, it does not get much more controversial than Sutherland's presentation and the ideas it produced. His later book, based on his speech, was censored by his university's corporate sponsors for over forty years and was only published in full after his death. The entire academic field of economic crime that Sutherland launched was heavily suppressed in United States during the McCarthy era of the 1950s.

The intellectual battle between two distinguished men in their field — Robert Merton and Edwin Sutherland — was one of the most important and enduring debates in criminology. As we saw in the last chapter, Merton, influenced by the French sociologist Émile Durkheim, thought that the fundamental motivation of deviant behaviour was anomie or lack of social opportunity, status or structure for potential criminals. In contrast, Edwin Sutherland (1947) and his disciples wrote of deviancy being a learned process of "cultural transmission". For example, the American criminologist Ronald Akers (1999) takes Sutherland's original idea of criminal "differential association" and writes that it leads to "social learning" of deviant activities.

### *Key Concept*

---

***Differential association:*** *is the idea that criminals gather together, separate from mainstream society to teach each other the techniques of gaining money illegally.*

---

In effect, Sutherland's school of thinkers is saying that crime is not the product of large society-wide conditions, but is specifically taught by established criminals to young people. This teaching is often done in small sub-groups isolated from the cultural mainstream. So a rich, but corrupt group of stockbrokers will teach — often unconsciously — others their methods and practices in the privacy of business association meetings or at an expensive golf club. Just as surely as a group of poor burglars will teach their apprentices how to crack safes.

In his original work, Sutherland wrote of "agents of cultural transmission" — or older criminals teaching younger criminals how to be more effective. In the Malaysian-Singaporean fixing, many of the players with the highest social standing in the teams — the senior, national team players — were Sutherland's agents of "cultural transmission." According to interviews the senior players passed on their methods and practices to the younger, less experienced players.

Many of the Malaysian interview subjects agreed with the idea of older players teaching younger players how to fix. They said that match-fixing was not only occurring in the domestic Malaysian Super League during that era, but also when the national team played in overseas tournaments.

LE2 was a senior police officer who investigated match-fixing in the league. He claims that during their investigations the police discovered that it was not a coincidence that many of the national team players were involved in the fixes. At the national team training camp many of the players were coming together ("differential association") to compare notes about money and methods of fixing:

> *It started with the international players. It snowballed from them... the international players would meet at the training for the national team, and then they would talk between themselves about how much money they could make [fixing games]. So that was a great way of networking for them (LE2).*

The key point is that the teaching of corruption by the players was not simply one of learning, it was also financial. In the confessions and interviews, the players are revealed to have established their own corrupt networks within their teams. On top of the structure was one of the senior players — or "project manager" as this role was described in Chapter 7 — with high ability to affect the outcome of the game. This player would recruit several other senior players, who in turn would get younger players to take part in the fix.

To return to a theme from Chapter 7, it is this network and influence that is part of the reason why younger players were drawn into match-fixing, rather than their "individual anomie" brought on by new conditions. So in a profession where the pay was uncertain and the risk of injury high, older players would school younger players who had the right attributes of corruptibility in an additional way of making money — fixing matches. However, what exactly were these attributes of corruptibility that made a younger player more likely to fix a match?

## Because they were asked

The factor of invitation has, of course, a self-contained irony. The Oxford professor Federico Varese wrote with the Israeli academic Meir Yaish the journal article *Importance of Being Asked*. It was an examination on what type of people helped Jews flee the Nazis during the Second World War. They found that one of the key explanatory variables to identifying who would help their persecuted neighbours was very simple — "were they asked to help?" It sounds rather simplistic, but again their data indicated that far more important than class, religion or age the key factor was being asked to help.

What is the significance for sports corruption? Well, the data indicates that in match-fixing there is actually a type of player who is more likely to be invited to participate in corrupting a game, and thus actually fix a match: those who can most affect the result of the game.

*Positions:* There are certain positions on a football field that affect the outcome more easily than others. If a goalkeeper makes a mistake it is more likely to lead to a goal than other positions, and goalkeepers are significantly over-represented in the fixing/non-fixing player database. Figure 13.1, seen below, illustrates this point. The three most common playing formations in contemporary football are: (counting from the back of the field to the most forward position) 1-4-3-3 (one goalkeeper, four defenders, three midfield players, three forwards); 1-4-4-2; and 1-5-3-2. In Figure 13.1, these ideal formations are compared with the actual proportions of players by field position, who were approached to fix matches as seen in the FMP database:

**Figure 13.1: Players Invited to Fix a Game by Position**

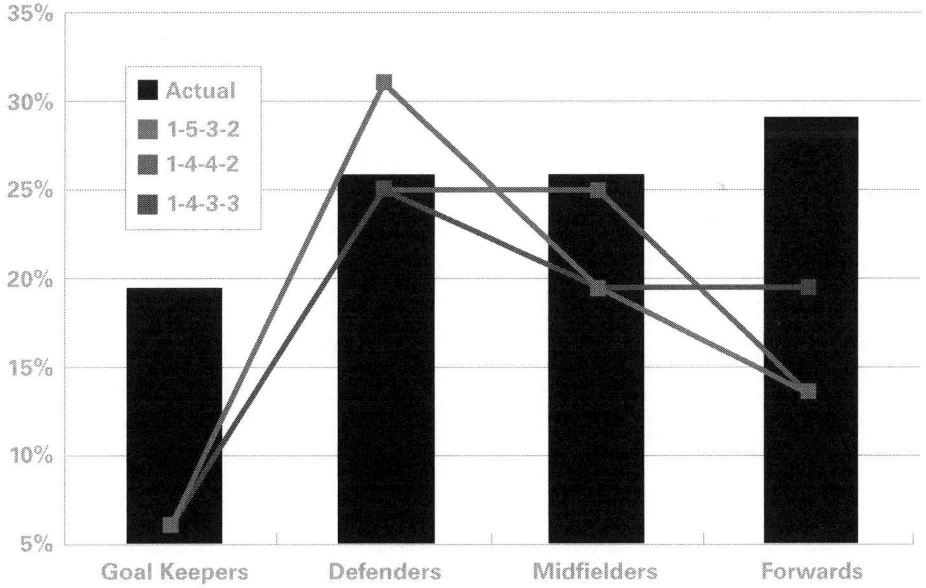

35%
30%
25%
20%
15%
10%
5%
Actual
1-5-3-2
1-4-4-2
1-4-3-3
Goal Keepers
Defenders
Midfielders
Forwards

***Source:*** *Fixing/Non-fixing Players Database (N = 98)*

In Figure 13.1, the solid blocks indicate the percentage of players who were invited to fix a match by position. The lines – red, purple and blue – are the number of players who *should* have been asked to fix a game based on the proportions of the most common formations of players. It can be seen that only goalkeepers and forwards are over-represented in the actual invitations to fix a game.

In fact, goalkeepers are almost three times as likely to be asked to participate in fixing a match as any of the formations indicate. The players frequently mention the importance of goalkeepers in the interviews and confession databank. Harry Gregg, the Manchester United goalkeeper, is typical when he wrote, "A goalkeeper is better placed than anyone to influence the result of a match and I suppose it was inevitable that the men involved in match-fixing at Old Trafford would approach me." In three of the cases where fixes did not work, it was because corrupt players felt they *had* to ask their goalkeepers to participate to guarantee the fix and the goalkeepers not only refused but went to the club management and exposed the fix.

*Star players:* The second group of players who are liable to be invited to take part in fixed matches are prominent players regardless of position. A Singaporean international player who took money from corruptors said in an interview for this book: "The goalie is the most important ...but really it is who is the *most influential* [emphasis added] player. The key players. When you going to be a good player, this will happen to you [being approached by corruptors]."

Rajendran Kurusamy, a Singaporean corruptor who fixed a wide number of matches in the Malaysian Super League, confirmed this idea in his court testimony. "In match-fixing, I won't be approaching people who are not regular players."

This is an important point: a player who could not guarantee his place on the pitch nor affect the outcome of the game, was much less likely to be invited to take part in the corrupt match.

This phenomenon of the best players being targeted by corruptors is also seen in the role of internationally-ranked players. One of the principal constraints to match-fixing mentioned in anecdotal discussions about match-fixing is the salaries and status of international players. It is supposed by some commentators, that these players would be very unwilling to participate in match-fixing and that match-fixing is the purview of the lower divisions and lesser leagues. The evidence from the database indicates that the exact opposite is true.

Of the average one hundred players in most national leagues, between one and 2% could be considered "international" players. In the Fixing/Non-fixing Database, over 53% of the players were international players; while of those that were not a further 20% were either the captain or lead goal scorer of their teams (Fixing/Non-fixing Player Database).

Table 13.1 represents the general characteristics of corrupt players. This is not, of course, to suggest that all players who have these factors are necessarily corrupt, simply that the finding indicate them *more likely* to fix than others.

**Table 13.1: General Characteristics of Corrupt and Non-Corrupt Players**

| *Non-corrupt* | *Corrupt* |
|---|---|
| Below 25 years old | Above 29 years old |
| Bad players | Star players |
| Midfielders | Goalkeepers, Forwards |

## Public Expression of Morality or Religion

There is a final question: are players who publicly express religious or moral views more or less likely to fix a game?

The popular myth that surrounds match-fixing is that players who take part must be, in Harry Gregg's words, "lowlifes"; while those who decline to take part have a far better moral code. I do not want to argue questions of specific morality here, as the Norwegian academic Jon Elster observes morality is very difficult to measure accurately. It is, for example, quite possible for people to be guided by two or more moral codes simultaneously. However, what is clear in the specific case of match-fixing is that *publicly* professed personal morality is not a primary indicator on whether a player would fix a match; in fact the exact opposite may be true.

As with coercion, morality does at first seem to play a part in the decision to fix a match. In the database there are twenty-five instances where a player chose not to fix a match. In all of them some form of publicly professed morality is mentioned as a reason for turning down the fix. A few examples:

> *Money would have been given to me if I had been willing to secure the loss of my team. The negotiations ended quickly. "I answered right away — no thank you. I can't hear you."* ***This kind of idea is so strongly against my morals that it wasn't a temptation*** *[emphasis added]." (Staff writer, Ilta-Sansomet 2005)*

> *In the dressing room before the start of the game, he [the goalkeeper] was cornered, told what was about to happen and asked quite bluntly. "Do you want in?" Hastie Weir [the goalkeeper] went berserk [saying no]...* ***Weir was raging and ranting like some fire-and-brimstone preacher*** *[emphasis added]. (St. John and Lawton 2006, 64).*

> *Two days before the match, I received a telephone call from an old acquaintance. He asked me if I would accept to not play the game to my fullest… I refused immediately.* ***I did not want to fall that low*** *[emphasis added]. (Delepierre 2006).*

However, a closer examination of this evidence suggests that morality is not the only factor that prevents these players from corrupting matches. In all of these examples, as in most of the cases in the database, the "confessor" goes on to describe that in their own case they had enough money not to be tempted. The first example is a Finnish goalkeeper who reveals later in his confession that he had just signed a contract for several years with a professional team. In the second example, the financial position of Hastie Weir, the goalkeeper who turned down the fix, like "some fire and brimstone preacher" was compared to the other, poorer, fixing players:

> *He [Hastie] had a good job as a works manager and when he joined us from the amateur club Queen's Park, he reputedly signed for £10,000, which was rather more generous than the bonus received by the rest of the dressing room… The pros [who were organizing the fix] joined for a mere £20. (St. John and Lawton 2006, 63).*

The Belgian player, whose confession was the final one listed, said, "Me, I had a chance. I made a career that took me to foreign places [i.e. he was well-paid]. It made it easy for me to refuse." A good summation of this mixture of morality and finance was given by Maurice Cook, a player for the English team Fulham, who was approached by representatives of Everton to fix a match in 1961. Cook claimed in his affidavit that, "Because of the smallness of the sum and my reputation for being a completely 'straight' player I could hardly believe that [the offer] was serious". In other words, it was both the lack of money *and* Cook's own internal morals that did not allow him to take the corrupt offer seriously.

This is not to say that all morality has a price, or that any player who refuses to take part in fixed matches is practicing a morality that is only achieved with financial security. But it is to say that the data from the confession databank is inconsistent on whether it is only morality or a combination of other intertwined factors that make players refuse to fix matches.

As we saw in the anecdote from Chapter 12, the player — P10 — is a publicly-professed born-again Christian, yet he wanted me to help him contact corruptors to fix matches. Another sport, a similar example, Hansie Cronje was the bible-quoting, star captain of the South African national cricket team who was revered for his clean-living lifestyle, until the New Delhi police revealed that he had been corrupting international matches for Indian bookmakers. In Malaysia, there were several players, who at least when caught, quoted Biblical or Islamic scripture.

In contrast to these examples, interview subject P6 was a self-described, hard-drinking, womanizing player who according to his own description "loved a bet". Yet P6 risked physical injury from his corrupt — and publicly religious — teammates when he threatened to beat any of them up if he thought they were match-fixing. In later chapters, we shall see how many of the match-fixing players use "deceptive mimicry" to disguise their corrupt activities. It may be that in assuming a public stance of religious morality a corrupt player is able to hide his activities.

There is a similar comparison in the wider literature on corruption where Johann Lambsdorff, the German academic expert on corruption, points out that "corrupt people tend to be involved in a variety of charitable institutions". Thus the situation may occur where publicly professed morality can actually be an indicator of corruption, however, the specific data on match-fixing, at this moment, is simply not clear enough on whether this is accurate or not.

In these last chapters, we have examined why some professional footballers would agree to participate in gambling match-fixes. The data indicates that, generally, players are not coerced or forced into this type of fixing. In corrupt deals of this type, the players combine both the betrayal of trust that corrupt business executives or government officials display in committing acts of economic criminality and the powerful sense of vulnerable physical capital that characterizes many professional dancers.

In Chapter 10, we saw that the data indicates that if corruptors use violence, it is to enforce agreements or cooperation, not to recruit participants. In the last chapter, it seems that the solution to the question, "Why do players participate in gambling match fixes?" is almost always money. In nearly all the interviews and confessions analysed, the principal motive for the players' participation was financial.

The analytical problem was to determine *which* type of players would be more likely to be bribed than other types of players. For example, in Chapter 12, we saw the idea that fixing is practised mostly by young, inexperienced players who are caught up in a maelstrom of personal anomie is generally not true. In fact in many cases the older players worked as Sutherland's agents of transmission in teaching and training the younger players on how to fix a game.

We then examined the players most likely to be asked to fix a match and showed that goalkeepers are *three* times more likely to be invited to participate in a match than their position would indicate. International players comprised over 50% of the fixing/non-fixing database while their actual numbers should be less then 2%. These findings indicate that corruptors seek out players who can most effect a game and tend to ignore lesser players. Finally, the data for expressions of personal morality and corruption are inconclusive. We cannot conclude that publicly practicing religious or moral players are more or less likely to fix a match than non-publicly religious or moral people. These last few chapters have been an examination of *why* players may agree to participate in match-fixing, in the next chapter, let us turn to the question of *how* players, and referees, actually perform a fixed match.

## Chapter Review

- This chapter examined the question "who would fix a game?"
- The debate between the criminologists Robert Merton (deviancy comes from lack of opportunity) versus Edwin Sutherland (deviancy is taught) was examined.
- The factor of being asked was found to be extremely important. Goalkeepers and star players were most at risk.
- Public morality is not a protection against corruption.

# CHAPTER FOURTEEN
# SINS OF OMISSION

*That is the whole problem of trying to prove match-fixing from the playing point of view. The point is footballers are human beings and they make mistakes. So it is virtually impossible. You might think there is something going on, but the player will say, "Hey, I just misjudged the ball." You know. There is no way of proving it, unless you have a player on tape talking to a bookmaker and arranging to play for a certain amount of money.*

*Player from the Malaysian Singaporean League, interview December 2005.*

It is genuinely difficult for outsiders to know by simply observing a match being played whether players or referees are fixing. Imagine you are one of the judges in a jurisdiction like Singapore, the Czech Republic or the British House of Lords and you have spent considerable time examining different experts claiming that the players were trying to fix or not. There have been scores of legal pages written on this very problem. Instances of players or referees actually confessing to fixing games are rare. There are no statistical studies that have been done that can be used to determine how a fix takes place, while expert testimony is frequently unreliable, and any witnesses are usually deeply subjective. Yet fixed football matches do frequently take place and, in some leagues, they occur on a very wide-scale.

It is also genuinely difficult for players and referees to actually fix matches. They face two principal challenges in ensuring the fixes: they have to either deliberately lose the match or help one team lose and they have to do it in a way that the audience — spectators, team officials or fellow players — do not notice. After all, there is a limit to the number of mistakes that they can make. If a player makes too many mistakes he will be dropped from the starting squad or make the fix too obvious and with too few mistakes the fix will not work.

So how then do the players and referees perform the fixes?

This is the question that we will examine for the next two chapters.

There are ways of doing it badly. Almost all of the Genoa and Venice teams, in the Italian leagues, arranged a match between them in the spring of 2005. The arrangement was that Genoa would win the game, which meant that they would get promoted to the top division — Serie A — and that Venice would get a lot of money. But in the second half, the Venice manager got a call on his mobile phone from the Genoa coach,

"What the fuck is going on? Your player just scored a goal!?" he screamed.

"I know, I know," replied the Venetian manager, "The players are crazy! They scored by mistake!"

To the Genoa's great relief, Venice managed to let them score another goal and the game ended as arranged. So Genoa was promoted to Serie A. Or rather they would have been, if the entire arrangement had not been caught on tape by Italian investigating magistrates.

Different era, same league, same problem. In his autobiography, *In the Mud with the Soccer God*, 1970s Italian forward Carlo Petrini described the problem he and his Bologna teammates had when they arranged a fix against Juventus in a Serie A match. The plan was that the teams would draw the match 0-0 and bet on that particular result — a draw — on the illegal Italian sport lottery. All was going well until the fifty-seventh minute, when a Juventus player took a shot at the Bologna goal. It had been snowing, so the Bologna goalkeeper could not hold the ball. It slipped past him into the net. One-nil to Juventus. The Bologna team was furious. There was, according to Petrini, almost a fight in the middle of the pitch between the two teams. However, a Juventus midfielder calmed them when he called out, "Don't worry lads, we'll score an equaliser for you." Ten minutes later there was a corner against Juventus. One of their team rose magnificently in the air to head it into his own net. The game ended in a one-all draw. Everyone went away happy, except the fans who were so enraged with the game that they pelted the players with snowballs.

At the international level there were the same problems in delivering a fixed match in Singapore in 1986. The Merlion Cup was a tournament featuring the national teams of Indonesia, North Korea Singapore, and Canada. An outsider may have thought of all those teams, the one least likely to accept a bribe would be the relatively rich Canadians. However, within the Canadian team a forward had arranged with a group of his fellow players to lose the semi-final to North Korea. He was furious when Paul James, a player he thought was in on the fix, played honestly. *"What the hell are you doing?"* He screamed at James for passing so well that the Canadians almost scored a goal. However, all went well in the end for the fixing Canadians and the Koreans were allowed to win 2-0.

## Two Types of Corruption Performance

In their monograph *An Empirical Typology of Police Corruption*, Thomas Barker and Julian Roebuck, one a sociologist, the other a former police officer, laid out eight specific types of corruption that police officers can commit. However, upon closer examination all the corrupt acts they list — planting evidence, soliciting bribes, deliberately ruining cases — can be divided into two general types: active and passive. The active corrupt acts are extortionate: for example, a police officer can say to a suspect, "Pay me something or I will *find* evidence near you." Passive police corruption is when an officer does not do something he should have done: for example saying to a motorist, "Pay me something and I will *not* give you a traffic ticket".

The exploration of football corruption in this chapter mirrors this essential division between active and passive corruption. For the terminology of the chapter, let us borrow from the concept in Catholic theology expressed in the Prima Secundae Partis of Thomas Aquinas' *Summa Theologica*. Aquinas writes of two types of "sins": omission and commission. Sins of omission are passive misdemeanours that come from *not* doing something that one should do: "my neighbour's house is on fire and I do *not* phone the fire brigade." Sins of commission are misdemeanours that come from actually *doing* something: "my neighbour's house is on fire because I set it alight".

This chapter is entitled "Sins of Omission," because this is what the players and referees are often doing when they are fixing.

## Deceptive Mimicry

In the work *Perspective on Imitation*, Gambetta describes the pattern of "deceptive mimicry" that some criminals engage in. It is the same for match-fixing players, the under-performing players not only have to play badly, they also have to *pretend* to be playing to the best of their ability.

Jackie "Mr. TV" Pallo was a popular British professional wrestler for three decades. He was famous as a "baddy" who delighted in tormenting the "blue eyes" (wrestlers who played heroic roles) and the audience. However, at the height of his career Pallo was excluded from a lucrative television contract. Accordingly, he wrote a tell-all autobiography entitled *You Grunt, I'll Groan* where he claimed the entire sport was a fraudulent theatrical exercise. He described in detail many of the fixes in wrestling and how they are performed (My personal favourite is the chapter entitled "Six Commandments of Wrestling"). He claimed that he had participated in a large number of fixed wrestling bouts and the most important part was the need "to sell" a fix. After each wrestling move the fighters will try to convince the spectators that it is a genuine with screams of either anguish or triumph.

There is a similar theatrical aspect to fixing in football. A former Serie A player, when interviewed for this book, said "I hate fixing games. You know why? Because I am a player, not an actor." He was expressing his dissatisfaction with the way players must act, on and off the field, as if the idea of fixing is the last thing in their minds. P6 was a player in the Malaysian Super League who did not take part in fixes. However, he played in a team where it was discovered that at least six of his fellow teammates were involved in fixing games. He reports, and this is echoed by other players, that even though he knew something corrupt was going on, he could not be sure of which players were taking part.

> *It is all the verbal bullshit before a game; they shout lots of stuff, "Come on, come on," then during the game it is just little tiny things like just mistiming a sliding tackle or letting a guy go through. These guys became experts in making it look like they were out there giving blood to their team. Coming in after the games and throwing themselves on the floor and screaming (P6)*

Few people — even trained coaches — can actually tell if players are really fixing the game. This human fallibility became a problem for the Singaporean police when they were trying to investigate the issue, as this officer commented in his interview:

> *Another difficulty is that football is very subjective. So people can have a bad game, but not because they are playing badly. Even if they are bribed to under-perform. Who can tell? The assessment is often so speculative that it is difficult to figure out (LE7).*

Even fellow players who are playing with them find it difficult to tell what, if anything, is going on. P7 knew there was some fixing going on in his team. He spoke confidentially to a team-mate about his fears. Later it turned out that the very player in whom he confided was actually one of the corrupt ones. P6 played with the match-fixing team for an entire season and could never figure out who was in on the fix or what was going on:

> *That is the whole problem of trying to prove match-fixing from the playing point of view. The point is footballers are human beings and they make mistakes. So it is virtually impossible. You might think there is something going on, but the player will say, "Hey, I just misjudged the ball." You know.* ***There is no way of proving it*** *[emphasis added] (P6).*

A similar problem exists in trying to assess referee's performances. R3 is the head of the referee's program for a section of FIFA. He is an international referee with years of experience and training. He watches all of the games played under his jurisdiction, either in person or on tape. He watches the games specifically to judge the referee's performance. Yet even he cannot tell if a referee made a mistake by design or by accident. In an interview - and this is substantiated by other refereeing officials - he explained that much of the problem of assessment is that no one expects referees to be universally perfect. "We say that if a referee can get 85% of the decisions right, he is having a good game." (R3)

Edílson Pereira de Carvalho was a corrupt referee in Brazil's elite league who used this subjective uncertainty to his advantage. He clearly used deceptive mimicry before matches to disguise his dishonest activities. As de Carvalho was an evangelical Christian, he would pray — very publicly on the field — creating an identity of extreme honesty and piety, before attempting to fix games (however, as we do not know *what* de Carvalho was praying *for*, it might be assumed that he was asking for divine intervention in helping him fix the game!) Whatever he was publicly praying for, it was the same type of mimicry that Hansie Cronje, the match-fixing South Africa national cricket captain, purportedly indulged in, when he was accused of "theological ventriloquism".

## Strategies — "Sins of Omission"

However, if the dishonest players and referees spend a lot of time acting to ensure that no one discovers that they are fixing, what can they do as individual actors to actually help the fix? The key concept of this section is that of *underperformance*. Whatever the players do on the pitch, they must not do it to the best of their abilities.

The principal data source for this examination comes from a previously unexamined police confession. Z1 was a prominent player in the Malaysian Super League. He was involved in match-fixing and was arrested by the police in the summer of 1995. His interrogating officer was also interested in the question of how individual players underperform. During his interrogation Z1 and the officer went through a list of all the things that players in various positions could do to ensure the fix. I put his words in italics at the beginning of each section about individual positions, below.

However, there are a number of similar sources in the confession databank that outline match-fixing techniques. For example, there is a similar confession by an anonymous British player from the 1960s and Jean-Jacques Eydelie, the player who helped arrange fixes for Bernard Tapie at Olympique de Marseille, wrote of fixing methods in his book *I Do Not*

*Play Anymore: A Footballer Breaks the Omerta.* A number of interview subjects and confessions also discuss match-fixing tactics. I amalgamate the information to show the performance strategies of match-fixing players according to these sources.

Overall, Z1 claims that the fixing player's principle strategy is simple inept play (Eydelie describes it as "lifting your foot from the pedal a little..."). Here players have a choice, they can make themselves look bad or they can sabotage a fellow team-mate. For preference, many players choose the latter. Z1 explains, "You can do a perfectly good pass to a team-mate, right position, everything, but if you spin the ball, it is difficult to control." The anonymous British player of 1960 described a more brutal tactic, the "hospital pass": "It's a short ball to one of your team placed in such a position that he has to go for it and face collision with a defender who can reach it at the same time... This is the dirtiest pass in football. It not only risks the future of your colleague, it usually starts off a blood-match..." If the player decides to underperform on his own he can either give a gift to the other team or control the game in such a way that his team cannot play well. Here are the strategies of each position, starting with Z1's comments.

## Goalkeepers

This is the most important position in terms of delivering a fixed match. As we saw in Chapter 13, goalkeepers are three times more likely than other positions to be involved in fixes.

> *On a breakaway the goalie will deliberately leave the goal and play so far up that the goal is clear. (Z1)*

A Finnish player who fixed games in his country's Veikkausliiga Premier League in 2004, described a similar method in which a corrupt goalkeeper roams out of his penalty area: "...goalie screws up again. He comes outside the penalty area to collect a pass but he comes up against a forward. The forward now has an easy job to put the ball in the goal."

*Goalkeeper puts himself in the wrong position…(Z1)*

A good fixing goalkeeper doesn't have to act like an idiot; they don't have to wander around on the other side of the goal simply standing 1 metre further away from where they should be is enough. As the forward shoots, being slightly out of position allows the keeper to throw themselves bravely, but vainly, as the ball whistles just past their outstretched hands.

*Goalkeeper drops the ball, he could catch it, but he just pats it away… (Z1)*

The third strategy is the most obvious and it is, of course, the exact opposite of what every childhood coach tells their young student: "catch, smother the ball with your body." By pushing the ball out into the area or dropping it, the fixing goalie can cause all kinds of problems for his team-mates. P6 remembers one incident very clearly:

*There was one game. The other team had a corner. I was on the goalpost. I was defending. And the corner came in. And it was floating. It wasn't played with any pace. I was standing right beside the goalkeeper. And it was like something in slow motion. The goalie went up, caught the ball, and then dropped it right at the feet of their player who scored. And I was so frustrated that I went up and pushed him. I was boiling and I actually physically pushed him. And I shouted "You cunt! I know what you were doing! And he said, "Oh come on…" And you know* ***they act all innocent*** *[emphasis added]. But I was convinced I knew what was going on. (P6)*

## Defenders

Defenders are another position that can greatly help in creating a successful fix. One corrupt goalkeeper in the English League in the 1960s, failed to deliver a fix because the honest defenders on his team simply did not give him a chance to allow a goal. Along with giving away penalties there are lots of strategies that a corrupt defender can use. In their 1960 exposé the *Daily Mail* revealed one nasty tactic — the "suicide pass."

> *The ball is placed by a defender too far away for the goalkeeper to clear it or gather it, but near enough to the opposing forward for him to nip in and score a "gift" goal… Every Soccer fan has seen this happen, but sometimes it is not an accident…(Borissow et al., 1960, ii)*

The strategies described by Z1 are less violent. These tactics are, like the goalkeeper dropping the ball or patting it loose in a crowded penalty area, the exact opposite of what every football coach has taught young players not to do since the ball was first invented.

> *Left back and right back will not assist the sweeper when he is being attacked. The sweeper will not assist the left or right back when they are being attacked. The defence will not play all out and will purposely allow the attackers to get by us (Z1)*

## Forwards

This position is also important for fixers. As the great British manager Brian Clough said in his playing days when confronted with fixing players on his team. It is no use letting goals in, or earnestly making mistakes if some keen and honest forward is scoring lots of goals. Therefore forwards are also called upon to employ a number of tactics in order to deliver a fix.

> *Keep the ball for a long time, and then allow the opponents to take away the ball. Dribble the ball straight at the opponent, allowing them to take away the ball. Missing goal opportunities by either kicking directly at the keeper or missing the goal all together. (Z1)*

Fred Pagnam was a young Liverpool forward in 1915. He was one of the few players on his squad that decided not to throw a game against Manchester United. The game was at the end of the season, Liverpool had nothing to play for while Manchester United was struggling against relegation. The First World War was on and in a few months, most of the players would be in the Army. Many of them decided to rig the match to give United the points and themselves a little more cash. Fred Pagnam was told on the way to the match by his corrupt team-mates to follow similar instructions to Z1: at all times lose the ball and if he was in front of the goal — miss.

## Midfielders

So far, we have not examined the corrupt strategies of midfield players. This is not because midfielders never fix matches. It is because their principal job in fixing matches is not inept play (although they can do that), but a much more important job — controlling the fix. To lose a game against a strong team that really wants to win is not particularly hard, but for a strong team to lose, credibly, against a weak team is actually very difficult. Give the ball to an incompetent, but honest, team and there is no telling what they will do. They can even make such stupid mistakes that the fixing team will have to score.

So controlling the game is as important for fixers as simple ineptitude and breaking the rules. It is also a much more complicated and important task. One corruptor described having to coach his teams to lose by holding on to the ball for a few seconds, then passing backwards, each corrupt player doing the same thing. Nothing is obviously amiss, but in the corruptor's words, the corrupt players "buy time..." (COR3).

Z1 described a similar series of movements for corrupt midfield players:

> *The midfield will keep the ball for a long time and then allow the other team to take it away.*
>
> *The midfield will interrupt the system of playing by passing the ball back to the defence.*
>
> *The midfield will make a pass that is 50-50, so that the opponents will get the ball.*
>
> *The midfield keeps the ball in his own area, will not allow the ball to get open.*

SO15, the coach of a Singapore team who fixed a number of games in the early 1990s, described the most blatant method of controlling that he saw by one of his corrupt players in a game against a much weaker team:

> *The betting was that we would win by more than three [goals]... but we were missing goals from 2 yards out. In fact there is one incident that I clearly remember when one of our players was in with their goalie at his mercy when X [a corrupt team-mate] ran across him, took the ball off him and passed it off to the right wing! (SO15)*

What SO15 describes in this interview excerpt is an important factor for gambling corruptors. They ask their players not just to lose a game, but to also change their game depending on the time of the match. The reason is that the really skilful gambling corruptor wants to make the maximum amount of money. They can do this by winning bets that have far higher odds than just predicting a win or loss: things like predicting the number of goals scored in the match or the time in the match when those goals are scored.

Throughout this chapter, we have seen the actual words of the players as they spoke about fixing. In general, they present a picture of *not* doing something to ensure a fix, however, is that true? In the next chapter, we shall test this idea using statistics to see if there are underlying patterns of sports corruption.

## Chapter Review

- It is extremely difficult for outsiders to recognize if a fix is occurring.
- There are two types of corrupt performance: passive and active.
- A key part to passive fixing is "selling" the fix by acting that one is trying hard.
- The strategies of successful underperformance vary position by position.

# CHAPTER FIFTEEN
# SINS OF COMMISSION

*This happened to a friend of mine. He was an Aussie lad. Good guy. Never get into this stuff [fixing]. But he was a forward playing in the league. And the centre back on the other team comes to him and says, "Get in the penalty area." He thinks, "What?" But the centre back says again, "Get in the box." Sure enough he runs into the penalty box and the centre back just chops him down, the ball wasn't anywhere near him. Bang! Referee gives a penalty. My friend says, "Crikey! This is fucking magic!*

*(SO9)*

In the last chapter we saw how corrupt players claim that underperformance is essential to a successful fix. In this chapter, we will test this idea using statistics.

Some of the inspiration for this work comes from two great American economists, Charles C. Moul and, Stephen Levitt — the latter of whom became famous for his work in *Freakonomics.* These men, independently of each other studied, the statistical patterns produced by collusion in the Soviet Chess system (Moul) and Japanese Sumo wrestling (Levitt, with his colleague Mark Duggan). Their work was very good; however, neither of their studies specified *which* particular matches or sumo bouts were fixed. They only examined the sports — chess and Sumo wrestling tournaments — and described the statistical patterns that made them think that there were dishonest practices going on.

In this study, I have tried to go further. I have collected a sample of football matches that were fixed and I compared them to honestly played matches. I wanted to see if there are key patterns or features in fixed games that can be used in the future to help recognize or predict them.

It is impossible to measure "sins of omission" that we examined in the last chapter. Lots of people may think that a player should have done better in making a tackle or passing a ball, but their opinions are completely subjective. However, when something is actually *done* — "sins of commission" — events that occurred in games that can be measured in an objective manner. In football matches, three primary events that can be easily seen, suggested themselves. Penalties, own goals, and sendings off known popularly as "red cards".

## Penalties

A reasonable expectation is that there would be more penalties in a fixed game than in an honestly played match. If the players were corrupt, they would attempt to foul the opposition (an example begins this chapter). The *Daily Mail* reported that fixing players told them that "give-away" penalties were common in fixing matches:

> *The give-away penalty is almost as simple, providing the player concerned is prepared to risk the wrath of the home crowd. There are numerous variations to this cooked theme — a push in the back, a trip, handling the ball — all's fair in the penalty box for the man with his bet on the other side.*
> *(Borissow, et al. 1960, ii)*

A similar situation is reported by a number of referees in interviews.

This excerpt from an interview with a former international referee is typical:

> *It was in 19-- in -----. The match was between XXX and YYY (two national teams), but if YYY lost the third team would go through. So fifteen minutes before the match "a big man" connected to the third team came into the dressing room. He was very blunt. There was no beating around the bush. He just said:*
>
> *"So what do you want cash or cheque?"*
>
> *I said, "What?"*
>
> *"Cash or cheque?"*
>
> *"I don't understand."*
>
> *"I can have the money delivered to your hotel…" then he said to me, "10 thousand dollars."*
>
> *I said, "No, I want to do [sic] good match."*
>
> *"I want you to do good match too. I just want one penalty. One penalty for XXX. That's all. 10 thousand dollars cash."*
>
> *I said, "No" and I left the dressing room. I was very upset. (R4)*

In the interview excerpt, we see that the would-be corruptor, "the big man," considers a penalty as the essential tool for a referee to effect a game. He is explicit in his offer to the referee. The referee can, in his words, "do a good match": correctly give offsides, fouls, and other small decisions. But the "big man" wants one penalty in the match, which will favour his team.

There are similar stories around other examples, for example, the British journalist Brian Glanville reported that a similar offer was made by a corruptor from the Italian team Inter Milan before the 1966 European Champion Clubs' Cup Semi-Final match against Real Madrid.

However, football commentator and journalist Simon Kuper in his book *Football Against the Enemy* writes of a Russian "insider" who claims that a "good" corrupt referee is far more subtle than the awarding of penalties: "Bad referees give penalty kicks or offsides, but good referees know how to stop an attack while it is still in midfield." In effect, the referee can underperform throughout the match to achieve the fixed match, rather than give away a large decision like a penalty.

Which strategy most accurately reflects reality? Do well-trained, corrupt referees eschew a small number of big decisions like penalties or red cards — which bring unwanted controversy and scrutiny to their corrupted matches — in favour of a strategy of a large number of small decisions favourable to one team. If this second strategy is the general modus operandi of corrupt referees, there would be no statistical difference in the rate of penalties between fixed matches and honestly played games.

At first, the data shows very little difference in the rate of penalties. In honest games, slightly more that 24% of them feature penalties. In fixed games the rate rises to 32%. The difference is not statistically significant. But when the data is analysed with reference to *corruptees*, there is a significantly positive result. Figure 15.1 shows the result. In Control Group One, there were ninety-five honestly played matches where we have information on whether a penalty was given. In these matches, twenty-one featured a penalty kick — a rate of 24%. In fixed matches, where the principal corruptees were players, we have information for fifty-eight matches: in these matches, ten featured a penalty — a rate of 19%, which is not statistically different from either control group.

Figure 15.1: Penalties: honest vs. fixed matches (corruptees)

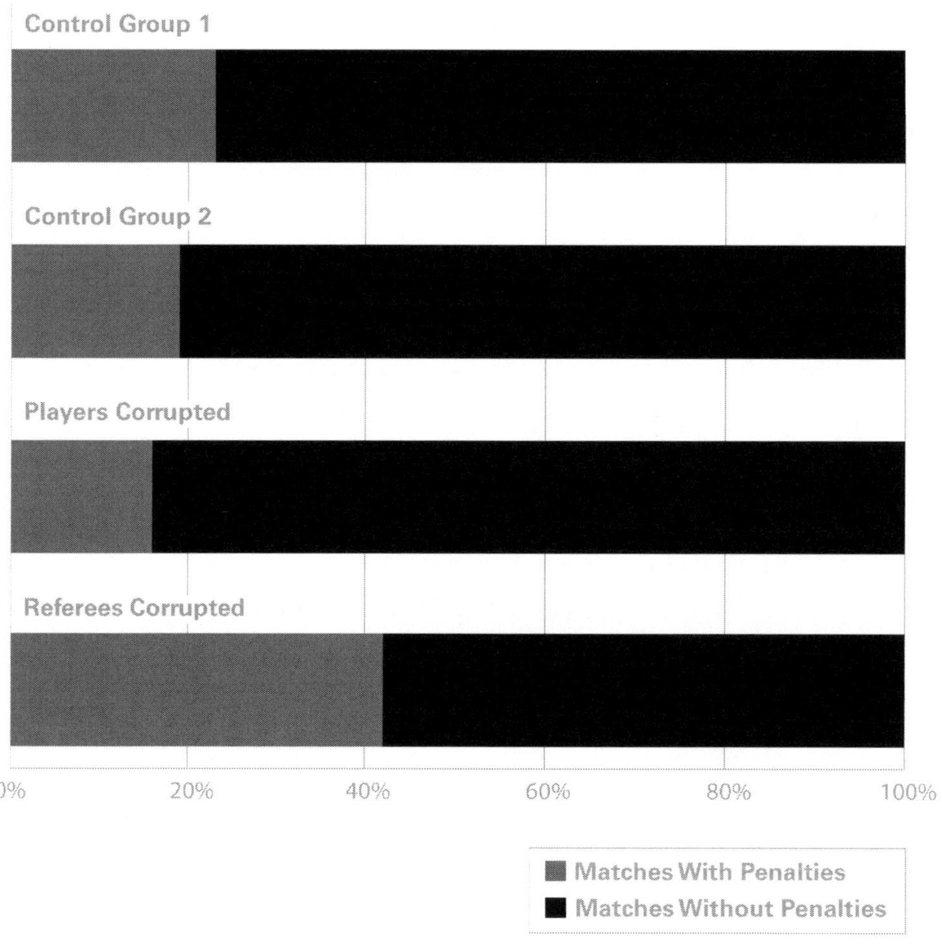


**Source:** *Fixed-Match Database 2 (N = 209)*

However, in the fifty-six games we have information of where the referee is the corruptee; twenty-four matches featured a penalty — a rate of 42%. The p value is .00016 — or less than one chance in a thousand that the difference is due to chance. And there is a 60% greater chance that there will be a penalty awarded in a game with a corrupt referee.

These results seem to indicate that when players are fixing matches they prefer a more passive approach to fixing. So a defender, rather than deliberately fouling an opposing player in his penalty box, will simply allow the opposition to slip by for a shot on goal. Presumably, this is because to give away a penalty draws undue attention to the fixing player. The unavailing slip, the attempt to get the ball, the mistimed tackle — all accompanied with what the wrestler Jackie Pallo would have described as "selling of the fix" grunts and groans — are as effective in accomplishing the fix and less conspicuous.

Referees, however, seem to use penalties as a tool to deliver fixed matches. This does not mean that Kuper's informant is not correct. There may be crooked referees that use a series of smaller decisions to affect a game. But the analysis indicates that, in general, referees often use penalties to corrupt matches.

A further note may be of interest. In the composition of the test, there is a second control group made up of the average rate of penalties, red cards and own goals from six major European football leagues for the 2005-2006 season: England/Wales, France, Germany, Scotland, The Netherlands and Italy. In five of these leagues the rate of penalties is between .19 to .24 (or roughly a penalty in every four to five games). However, after the 2005-06 season, an Italian Football Federation Commission of Inquiry found that in their league there had been a large number of fixed matches featuring bribed referees. This corruption seems to be confirmed in the data as Italy had a significantly higher rate of penalties than the other leagues at .32, far closer to the rate of penalties in games with a corrupted referee of .42.

## Own Goals

There is one obvious phenomenon that the Malaysian player, Z1, does not mention anywhere in his confession about fixing matches: own goals. One might think that would be the most common way for a player to fix a match: knock a goal into his own net, hang his head in public shame ("deceptive mimicry") and then go pick up the payment the next day. After all, are not all dishonest goals scored in fixed matches, in their own particular way, own goals? Popular mythology certainly speaks of the own goal and fixed matches. The British players who contributed, anonymously, to the *Daily Mail's* 1960 report, allegedly also mentioned "the crafty own goal."

However, the Asian corruptors who have fixed a wide range of games in different leagues, claimed in an interview that he hated when his corrupted teams scored own goals. One of them declaimed against a Vietnamese gambling ring who had fixed their national team to lose in the South East Asian (SEA) games in December of 2005: "They don't know what they are doing… but they were stupid. Scored an own goal almost, very stupid [sic]. Too obvious." (COR3)

There was one problem that made testing this theory more difficult. Own goals are, even in honestly played matches, commonly under-reported. In part, the reason for under-reporting has to do with the high feeling of shame attached to own goals that results in statisticians not ascribing them. However, another reason is the assumption among many football statisticians that in an honest game there are few *real* own goals. A player may accidentally score in his own net, but only because of pressure by an opposition player, who is, accordingly, credited with the goal.

The problem of under-reporting also exists for fixed matches. For example, the confession databank contains the unpublished, police confession of a captain of a Belgian League team that was fixing matches. In his confession, the captain claims that he headed up a fixing ring on the team for an Asian gambling corruptor. In one of the fixed matches that the team lost, the opposition scored a goal. The official match report claims it as a goal from a direct shot. However, in a journalistic description of the game it is reported that the shot took a "strange deflection" off a defender. How strange was the deflection? Was it a deliberate attempt to fix the game or mere chance? In compiling the database, there was no attempt to enter into this debate only the officially marked own goals for both honest and fixed matches are presented, even if this had a risk of under-reporting.

In the first stage of analysis, there is little difference in the number of own goals scored in honest matches and fixed games. There is accurate information for eighty-eight honestly played games, ten of which featured an own goal — a rate of just over 11% (There is no information for own goals in the second control group of European leagues). For fixed matches in general, there is accurate information for ninety-six games, fourteen of which featured an own goal. There is then no significant difference in the rate of own goals — about 14.5% in fixed matches — between honestly played and fixed matches.

However, as shown in Figure 15.2, there is a significant difference when the fixed matches are analysed by type of corruptee. If referees are fixing the game, there continues to be no difference in the rate of own goals per fixed match versus honestly played matches. But if the players are fixing the game, the number doubles to almost 20% of the games. There is a key point that must be stressed. Even though there is an increase in the total numbers of own goals, the p value does not go below .05, rather the p value is .068. What this means in everyday language — is that the results do not reach the threshold of 95% possibility that the rise is not due to chance — the generally accepted social science norm.

Figure 15.2: Own goals: honest vs. fixed matches (corruptees)

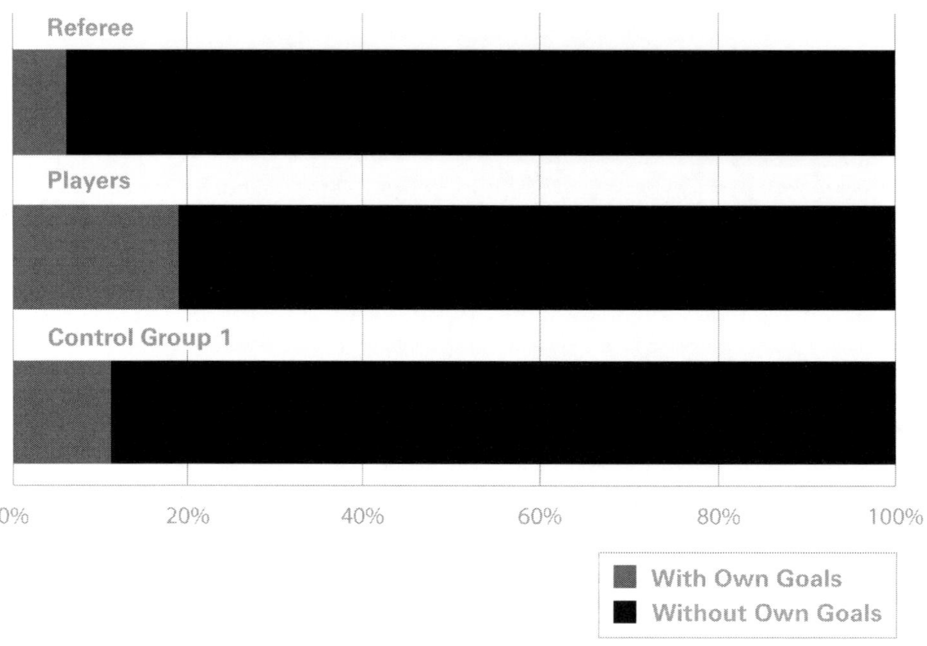


**Source:** *Fixed-Match Database 2 (N = 184)*

This figure suggests that while certain players score own goals to help the fix — a factor that we know from the anecdotal evidence — causing a rise in total numbers; overall, own goals are not a *consistent* tool used to corrupt matches; unlike penalties use by referees. The principal feature is *not* that 20% of the games featured own goals; rather it is that 80% of the matches did not.

## Red Cards

A "red card" is the football expression for when a player is sent off the field by the referee for a serious misdemeanour. The player is not allowed to be replaced and thus places their own team at a disadvantage compared to the opposition. It would seem to be a perfect way for a dishonest player to help

Figure 15.3: Red cards: honest vs. fixed matches (corruptees)

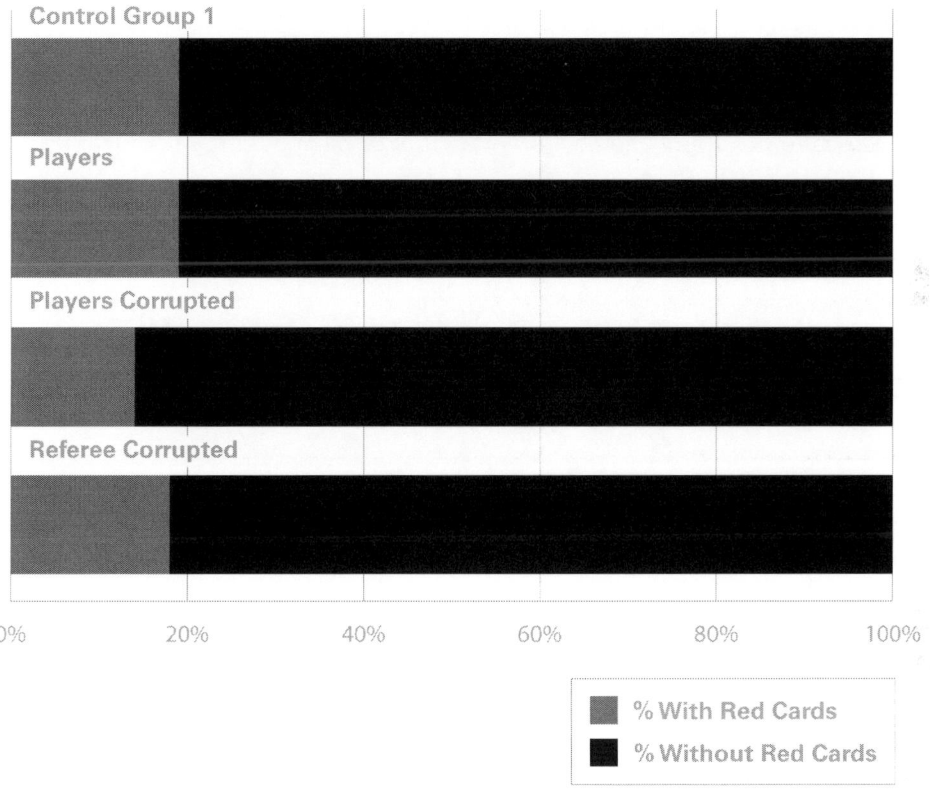


**Source:** *Fixed-Match Database 2 (N = 170)*

corrupt a match: shout abuse at the referee or get sent off the field and the other team wins with a one-player advantage.

It also seems a perfect tool for a dishonest referee. Removing the star player from the team that they are trying to make lose would surely aid the fix. Robert Hoyzer, the corrupt German referee certainly did it when he successfully fixed a game.

Again, in conducting the research there was a problem of under-reporting. Match reports that featured the disciplinary records (red cards and yellow cards) were difficult to find, particularly from older games. If no yellow cards or red cards were mentioned the cases were excluded. This exclusion means that red cards may end up being over-represented. However, the results show that red cards are *not* a tool used by either corrupt or dishonest referees in fixing matches in a statistically significant way. The rate shows no significant increase whatsoever in either corruptee. Dishonest referees who fix matches have a rate of approximately 19% of their matches featuring a red card, while honest matches have almost exactly the same rate.

Figure 15.3: Red cards: honest vs. fixed matches (corruptees)

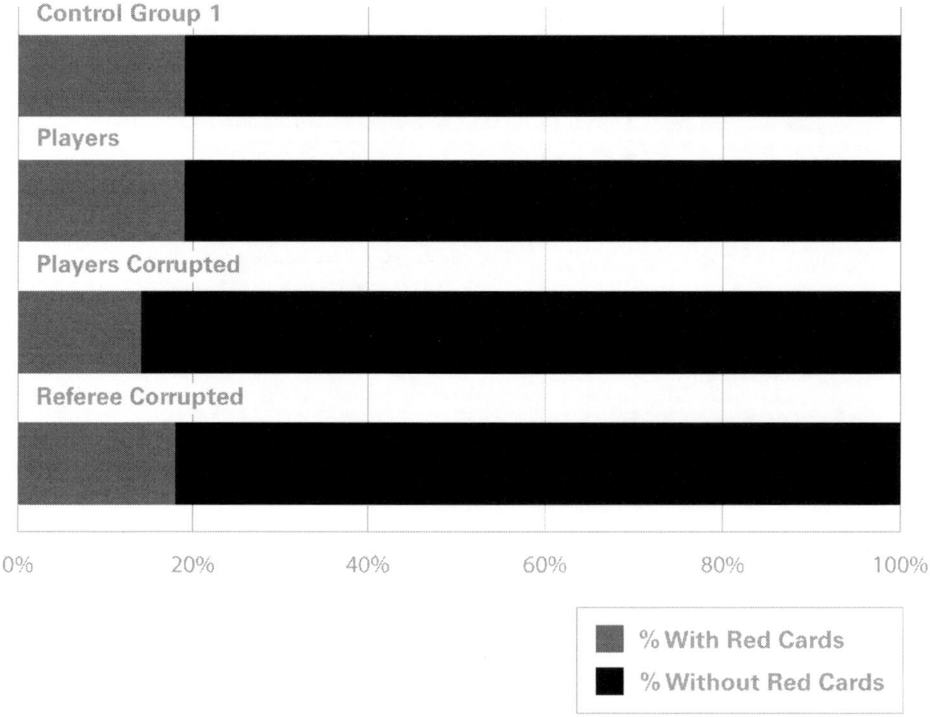

Control Group 1
Players
Players Corrupted
Referee Corrupted
0% 20% 40% 60% 80% 100%
% With Red Cards
% Without Red Cards

***Source:*** *Fixed-Match Database 2 (N = 170)*

What is interesting is that dishonest players seem to have *less* red cards in fixed matches than players do in honestly played matches. What this trend seems to indicate is that dishonest players are either not trying hard enough to warrant a red card (frequently, red cards come about from over-enthusiasm while trying to win a match), or they are deliberately trying *not* to get sent off the field. Presumably, being on the field is better than being off the pitch if one aims to fix a match.

## Timing of Goals

Is there another way of recognizing a fixed match? Are there definite patterns that distinguish a dishonestly played match from a regular match? We have already seen that there is a statistically significant difference between total goals scored in fixed matches and honestly played matches (matches that are fixed by gambling corruptors have, on average, 20% more goals scored than honest matches). The key to recognizing potential dishonest patterns might be to examine *when* the goals are scored in the matches.

One of the many myths that surround match-fixing is that of the "last minute goal". Popular literature is strewn with references to "last minute penalties" and "late goals." The inference being that the referee or corrupt players wait until the last few minutes of the game and then score or award a penalty late in the game to achieve the desired result.

One coach spoke about his players fixing a game in this way:

> *We were playing an away match and we were two-one down with five minutes to go. I thought frankly the way we were playing it was a decent result. The other team was much better than we were. But suddenly we lost a corner, the ball came over and my goalie flicked the ball into the net. Two minutes later — and it was close to the end of the match there was a shot from 35 yards out.*

> *The goalie let it go through his legs…* ***The goalie was swearing and acting like it was a terrible thing*** *[emphasis added]. But I talked to one of my players later and I found out they had a bet on the spread. They had bet 15-1 that there would be a three-goal difference in the game. So that means with five minutes to go they realized they would never score three goals themselves to win the bet, they deliberately let in two goals and won the bet (SO9).*

An interesting story, but is it true on a more general level? Joe McGinniss in his brilliant description of the Italian Serie B team Castel di Sangro fixing their game against Bari, claims that the corrupt players discussed the timing of the goals in the following way:

> *Then a player said, "'The first [goal] must come immediately. Even be-fore the people take their seats. That way it is not noticed so much. And then two more, as they develop, but all in the first half.'"*
>
> *"And in the second?"*
>
> *A player laughed. "In the second we all lie down and take a nap."*
>
> *"But this will not look bad?" a younger player asked, sounding worried.*
>
> *Another laughed. "Look bad to whom? ... Do not worry. No one pays attention at these times. Everyone looks the other way. Only be careful never to shoot at the Bari goal tomorrow. That would be a mistake."*
> *McGinniss 1999, 391 — 392.*

The complete transcript of the players discussing *how* to fix the match makes for interesting reading. It is a good example of Edwin Sutherland's transmission theory, in that the older players coach and teach the younger players how to play in a convincing fixed match.

There is another theory — that a match-fixing performance is also, at least partly, opportunity based. In other words, finely laid plans are all very well in theory, but in the reality of a game, players simply have to take the opportunity to fix when they come. The Castel di Sangro players hint at this when they describe the second and third goals coming "as they develop..."

Is it possible then to test the structure of a successfully fixed match? Do corrupt players depend on opportunities, or are there specific patterns to the timing of the goals? Did they come later, earlier or at approximately the same time as goals scored in non-fixed matches? To test this idea, the games were divided — both fixed and control group — into 10-minute segments (there were nine variables for each match indicating whether goals had been scored in minutes one to nine, ten to eighteen, etc., and how many goals). Figure 15.4 (overleaf) is a frequency chart that shows the results of this analysis.

The *Y-axis* is the percentage of goals scored in fixed or honest matches. The *X-axis* the time, in ten-minute sections, of the game. The *blue line* represents when goals are scored in a corrupted game that is an arrangement fix — when team officials are likely to be the corruptors. The *red line* represents when goals are scored in a corrupted game that is a gambling fix. The *green line* represents when goals are scored in the control group of honestly played matches. From the tenth minute of the game to the eighty-first minute, there is no significant difference between the types of games.

There are a number of significant points in Figure 15.4. The first point is in the initial ten minutes of the game. Here, in arranged fixes — like the Castel di Sangro vs. Bari game — goals are scored at a far higher rate than in either gambling fixes or honestly played matches. There is a possible reason that may explain this propensity for early goals in arranged fixes.

Figure 15.4: Timing of Goals in Fixed vs. Non-fixed Matches

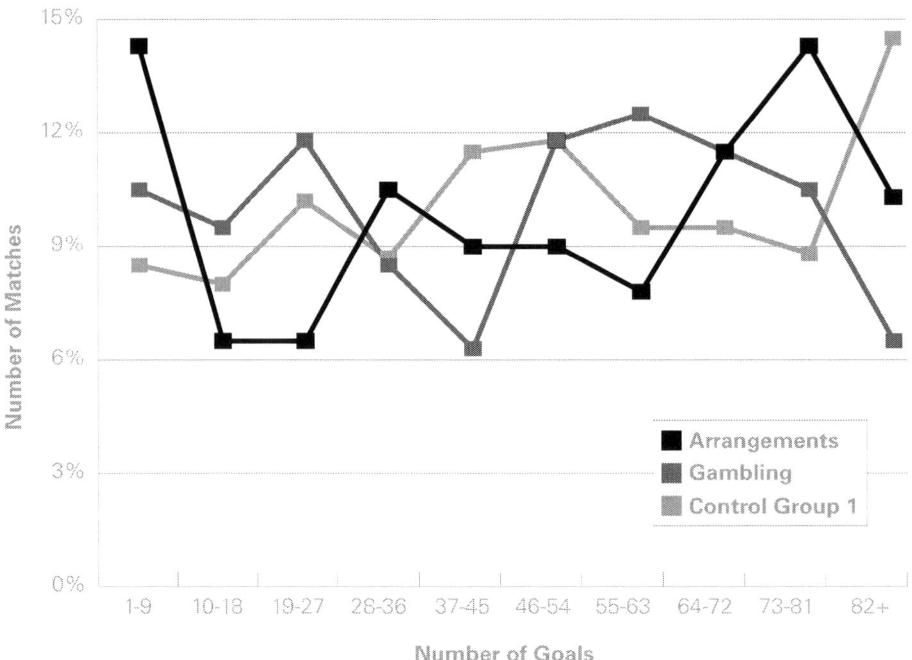


**Source:** *Fixed-Match Database 2 (N = 237)*

The assumption is that goals that come during the course of play may seem more *natural* than other goals. So goals that are scored early would be more likely to be criticized by spectators. However, frequently (80% of the cases), in arranged fixes, the team administration is also helping to organize the fix.

In other words, the players do not have the constraint of hiding the fix from their coaches or managers so they can either score or allow a dishonest goal earlier during a game without risk of it being discovered. In gambling fixes the corruptor is frequently either a player or an external agent (85%), but the team administration is not aiding the fix. So the dishonest players may have to delay their goals in order to hide them from their managers or coaches.

The second point is that for the majority of the match (tenth to the eighty-first10-81st minute), the rate of goals for all types of matches — gambling fixes, arrangements and honestly played matches — is all roughly within the same confidence level. This means that there is virtually no statistical difference between the goal rates in these types of matches. Clearly if there are dishonest goals being scored during this time they are following an *opportunity based* strategy of dishonest play.

The final point is that honestly played matches actually feature a rising rate of goals as the game nears its end — fixed matches are the exact opposite. In a fixed match, the number of goals scored actually *declines* in the last ten minutes. Presumably, this occurs because the dishonest players or referee finds it easier to arrange dishonest goals before the end of the match, avoiding a frantic search for a goal in the last few minutes. This finding overturns the cliché of a fixed match that they feature "last minute" goals or penalties. This is not to say that they do not occur, it simply means that they mostly occur in desperate situations where the equilibrium point — the fix — has not been reached by the fixing players.

---

In the last two chapters, we have examined a question that has perplexed judicial and sporting experts: how to determine if a football match has been fixed? In the first chapter, we saw from interviews and "confessions" that dishonest referees and players used a variety of methods. All of them are based on the principle of passive corruption or *underperformance* — or not doing what they could do to the best of their abilities — to deliver the fix. This underperformance was disguised by a deliberate and conscious pattern of "deceptive mimicry" on the part of the dishonest actors.

In the second chapter we saw the results of a number of quantitative tests. The tests were based on analysis of a fixed match database: 137 fixed matches were compared with 120 matches that were presumed to have been played honestly, to see if there are any differences in the number of penalties, own goals, or red cards. In these three tests, we saw that although there was a statistically positive result for the number of penalties awarded by dishonest referees there was no significant result for dishonest players in these three categories. However, the rate of own goals scored in games featuring corrupted players does have a large numerical rise, but not one that is above the rate of statistically probability used in the social sciences.

In other words, dishonest players are dealing with the constraint in fixing a match: they must lose the match, but they must not be seen to be trying to lose the match. So players respond to this challenge by choosing a strategy of many small mistakes rather than risking large controversial decisions, like giving away a penalty or scoring an own goal. They accompany this with the appearance of extreme honesty — cheering on their team-mates, nodding fervently at their coaches' instructions or throwing themselves on the floor in frustration after a loss. Presumably, it is this combination of small mistakes and "deceptive mimicry" that make it very difficult for outsiders to judge if a game is fixed or not.

However, there was one significant difference in the pattern of fixed matches: timing of goals: fixed matches have a higher rate of goals scored at the beginning of the game than honestly played matches. The rate of goals then declines in the final ten minutes, while in honestly played matches it increases. This is the first discovery of its type in the study of the mechanics of football match-fixing. In the final chapter of the book, I lay out a series of measures that could prevent most match corruption, so that eventually every match could be checked to identify similar "red flags" of corruption. However, in the next section of the book, we will turn to the question of why some football leagues collapse due to high-levels of match-fixing, while others do not.

## Chapter Review

- In this chapter, there were a series of tests to see the difference in fixed matches from a control group of presumed honest matches.
- Penalties: there was no statistical difference when players were corrupted; however, there was a significant rise when referees were corrupted.
- Own cards: although there was a slight increase when players were corrupted, it was not statistically significant.
- Red cards: there was no difference when either players or referees were corrupted.
- Timing of goals: the scoring of goals actually declined in the final ten minutes in matches that had been fixed.

# PART THREE
# THE SYSTEMS OF CORRUPTION

# CHAPTER SIXTEEN
# A CRITICALLY CORRUPT LEAGUE

| | |
|---|---|
| *Policeman:* | *I do remember that one of the police officers: one of the lead guys in the [Malaysian match-fixing] investigation. We caught him meeting with one of the bookies that we were trying to investigate. We put a tail on him and we got a phone call from the people who were tailing him. He was meeting with the Chinese bookie.* |
| *Hill:* | *Do you arrest him?* |
| *Policeman:* | *No, it would have been too embarrassing* |

*Malaysian police officer, interview, November 2005.*

On October the 2nd, 2004, Yang Zuwu the manager of the Chinese team Beijing Hyundai did something odd. In the 85th minute of the game with the provincial team Shenyang Jinde, he ordered his team to walk off the pitch. He then stood outside the dressing room door and announced that his team was not only refusing to take part in the rest of the match, but also refusing to take part in any more matches in the Chinese Super League (CSL). Beijing Hyundai was sponsored by the Korean car company and was one of the richest teams in the league. Yang Zuwu and the protestors were infuriated because in less than five months, a league with capitalization of hundreds of millions of dollars (U.S.) had proven to be rife with corruption and match-fixing. The bribing of referees, players and teams had, they claimed, become so widespread and so blatant, that it was impossible to play honestly in the league. Five years later, the Chinese government finally agreed with Mr. Zuwu and began an investigation that eventually saw over 180 people, including the president of the league, jailed.

The collapse of the CSL follows a trend across south east Asia. In the last fifteen years, along with the example of Singapore, Malaysia that we saw in the previous chapters, the football leagues of South Korea, Vietnam, Thailand and Indonesia have all suffered similar embarrassing scandals.

This third section of the book focuses on the overall conditions inside these leagues and analyses the following questions:

- What are some of the conditions inside a league where corruption has become normal?
- What are the social mechanisms that lead to high corruption inside some leagues but not in others?
- What does "collapse" mean and what factors lead to a sports league collapsing?

The data shows that widespread match corruption is not a cultural phenomenon: Malaysians, Singaporeans or Asians in general, are no more willing to take bribes because of ethnic or cultural reasons than any other group.

The data indicates that when similar conditions exist in a football league in a different country with a different cultural background — England in the 1950s — those players also engaged in match-fixing.

This is good news. It means an honest sports officials who wants to ensure clean sport, does not have to go about changing general expectations of corruption in their society, but simply has to ensure that within their specific league the key conditions which lead to large-scale corruption do not exist.

Before we go any further, two definitions are needed: first, leagues that are "highly corrupt" have the following characteristics:

- divisional championship and relegation competitions that were influenced by bribery.
- regular illegal gambling match-fixing that occurred throughout the season.
- a nexus between gambling corruptors and internal corruptors that led to an institutional paralysis.

Second, a "collapsed" league is:

- a league where there is a widespread public perception that the sport is not a competition, but effectively a theatrical exercise.
- This public perception is marked by a significant (over 40%) decline in attendance, an equally large loss in private sponsorship money and a reordering of the administration of the league.

Given these two definitions, what does a league with a high level of corruption look like? What does it feel like to live or work within one? This chapter begins with a description of an incident that occurred when interviewing a senior Asian sports official.

We were talking about the anti-corruption efforts needed to clean up the game. It was at the most prestigious sports club in the city. As the interview went on, we sat on the balcony watching a game of cricket. The interview was with one of Asia's top sports officials. He drank Scotch and water. I drank a pot of tea. I was talking about a football match that I had seen the night before on television.

"The game was great. 4-2. One team scored all its goals in the second half. It was a fantastic effort! A never-say-die attitude from the players that I loved watching!"

He looked at me incredulously.

"You want to see more matches like that?" he asked. "You should stay around! You think that game was played honestly? One team scored all their goals in the second half! Ha Ha! If you like games like that, this is the place for you. Never-say-die attitude! Oh dear..."

He laughed uproariously into his drink at my naivety. A businessman came up to him.

"Hey, Chin [name changed], meet this fellow. He thinks that football players here are very honest. He thinks they never give up!"

The businessman began to laugh too. He nodded at me politely though, and then handed the sports official a brown envelope. The official opened it, took out the bank notes that were inside, checked them, and then said,

"Thanks, come and join us for a drink."

"No, I can't. I have some more meetings like this one."

They both laughed. Then the businessman left and the sports official continued to tell me about the anti-corruption measures the leagues were enacting.

In earlier chapters, we examined the American criminologist Edwin Sutherland's work and particularly his idea of sub-cultures influencing individuals to criminal acts. In other words, not the culture of a country, but the culture of a specific industry motivating people to be criminals or corrupt.

To repeat these are not general Malaysian-Singaporean cultural norms, but the norms that existed in their joint football league. So the key question for this final examination of Malaysian-Singaporean match-fixing in the context of Sutherland's ideas is: was match-fixing tolerated and accepted by many of the people inside the sub-culture of football?

To be blunt, the answer to the question is — yes. Match-fixing did not arise suddenly with the advent of professional football in the late nineteen eighties, it had long been a part of the established culture in Malaysian football. In interviews, football officials and others were very clear that match-fixing had a long history in Malaysian football, dating back at least to the nineteen sixties. In fact, several of the senior officials in charge of running the league and ensuring that it was free of bribery, admitted to having played in fixed matches themselves. SO3 was both a player for his club and national side during the nineteen sixties, he spoke openly about the prevalence of match-fixing:

> ***Was there match-fixing in the Malaysian League when you played?***
>
> *Oh yes. But it was different... there was nothing obvious. Some of the senior players would tell us the difference should be in the goal difference. In other words, don't win by three goals just win by a few goals less. (SO3)*

According to the interview subjects the number of players who were actually caught and punished in the 1990s, large though it was, is felt, to be an under-representation of the real number of match-fixing players. All the interview subjects in the Malaysia-Singapore cohort, from the senior football officials to the players, claimed that many players had escaped arrest because of the sheer size of the investigation. Even the league officials who publicly led the investigation claimed:

> *We lost nearly an entire generation of players, but if you are going to tell that there is no corruption now I wouldn't believe you.... We had circumstances where the entire team, including substitutes, were in on the fix. (SO1)*

A player who had been in the dressing room with many of the match-fixing players said:

> *They arrested a lot of the players. But they definitely missed a lot of the big boys. A lot of the big boys. And there was no doubt those guys were involved in fixing. And those guys are still involved in football in some capacity in coaching or whatever. But they definitely missed some of the big boys. I would say that what has been involved is just the icing on the cake as far as the players who were involved were concerned... (P6)*

The British academic Matthew Bond writes of the "inner circle" of interconnected elites who fund political parties in Britain. There was also a widespread belief by both spectators and players in Malaysia that a similar type of "inner circle" of socially and politically connected elite football and political officials were involved in both gambling and fixing. For example, one Malaysian sports official is a prominent gambler, well known for his trips to the casinos of London and Las Vegas. Every interview subject, with the exception of then-current officials of the Football Association, described him in negative terms as being involved in gambling (though not in fixing). However, many of the players go much further and describe the possibility of corrupt sports officials or politicians being in someway involved in match-fixing. One example of this belief is expressed by a former player:

> *Our team was run by a group of top politicians and I am not saying they were fixing, but I am saying that there were very strong rumours and suspicions around them for several years. I can't accuse him. You have to get proof. These guys are untouchable. You are talking about corruption at the highest level of society. If there is corruption going on at the level that there is no hope, the game has absolutely no hope. (P6)*

The Malay Mail whose initial articles "broke" the story of widespread match-fixing also alleged that members of the Royal Families of a Malay State had been questioned by anti-corruption police in regards to match-fixing. The players' confessions also show that a number of players were told by the corruptors that state or high-level football officials were on the take. In Z1's confession the gambling corruptor tells his team-mates when approaching them the first time to fix a game:

> *Okay easy to talk. But I control your coach. I brought in your two foreigners. I paid the transfer fees for them, not the state FA. (Malaysian Police Confession: no. 1.)*

Another player who fixed matches was explicit about team officials — like the coaches or managers — ordering him to under-perform in certain matches:

> *Hill: Was the [team] management ever involved in the fixing?*
>
> *Player: Yes, sometimes the management gets involved. They start to get involved in fixing. You think 40K in 90 minutes, is not tempting? Sometime the owners will tell me, 'Look I bet 40K on 8 ball...' You ask the other players they will tell you this. (P9)*

The *Malay Mail* also wrote of the involvement of team officials in the rigging of matches:

> *It has been learnt now that players aren't the only ones fixing matches. Officials have got into the act, too. Some of them unscrupulous, some of them going for wins and throwing matches that aren't detrimental to their team's chances of a title or a place in the Malaysia Cup.*
> *(Malay Mail, July 29, 1993, 17-18)*

One of the league's prominent football officials, a man with direct connections to dozens of the players, claims that this type of linkage between corruptors and sports officials continues to the present time. Even one of the gambling corruptors, when interviewed in 2005, claimed that he had worked with at least three different sets of political leaders and football officials to help them fix matches in a way favourable to their team.

Nor is the Malaysian-Singaporean league alone in this problem, the Chinese example which began this chapter, has had a number of investigations and high-profile "confessions" linking senior football officials with corruption and match-fixing. And Peter Velappan — the former General Secretary of the Asian Football Confederation (AFC) — is quoted by the The Malay Mail as saying that the FA officials were directly linked to the bookies, "they are sweeping it under the carpet. I have not come across any FA in this region who have faced the problem squarely". Following on this theme, in the winter of 2012, FIFA announced that their former head of integrity had also received similar information, as this statement to the media shows:

> *We can confirm that Chris Eaton, as our Head of Security, has led and managed a global investigation of allegations of match fixing which has included Malaysia. As FIFA take every allegation seriously, we also confirm that FIFA have inconclusive investi-*

*gative information suggesting the involvement of some football administrators. We are looking forward to cooperating with FAM [Football Association of Malaysia] and the Malaysian authorities in order to share this information with them and then to proceed with our global investigations. (FIFA, official media statement, February, 2012)*

This is not to state that every football official, or even the majority, could be corrupt. Allegations of high-level corruption are, at this point, difficult to prove, but at the very least, it may be a question of perception influencing reality. For a player who was considering match-fixing, the widely-held perception that corrupt politicians and sports officials were benefiting from match-fixing, must have, in some way, effected their decisions to take part in the corrupt activities.

In Noel Coward's words, if "everybody's doing it…" the players would be more inclined to join in or feel like they might miss out on a profit-making venture; particularly, if the player was surrounded by senior colleagues who were making large amounts of money from fixing and these players were willing to teach and involve him in the fixes.

The players and football officials were not the only people involved in corrupt activities. The interview excerpt that started this chapter shows that even the police investigations into match-fixing were hampered by senior police officers, allegedly, passing information to gambling corruptors. Some of these same gambling corruptors also employed journalists to work for them, using them to pass information to players. This allegation was repeated frequently by journalists and a number admitted this practice to me in interviews. This excerpt is typical:

*I worked a couple of times for the bookies. They asked me to go and speak to some player. During the practice. I just went and said, 'Mohammed [name changed] asks OK?' 'And the player replied,*

> *OK.' That was it. No more. They had their agreement. They were just confirming it (J8)."*

At this point, another incident from another interview with a high-level, Asian sporting official may be appropriate. He was seemingly honest and deeply committed to helping clean up corruption in sport. We had a long, insightful interview. At the end of the interview, I asked,

"How much does it cost to fix a football game?"

He replied, "I really don't know. But hold on a moment, I have a friend who does this kind of thing all the time. Let me phone him and ask him."

He punched in his speed dial. His friend answered.

"Hello? Yes, I am here with a fellow from Oxford. How much does it cost to fix a football match now days? No, no. It is all off the record. No problem. What's that? About 10,000 Malaysian ringgit? Right. No, no. See you next week. Thanks."

He put the phone down and turned to me.

"My friend tells me that when he and his bookie friends fix a game here, it costs about 10,000 Malaysian ringgit ($2,500 U.S.)"

---

Jens Andvig writes of "Grand corruption," or a stage of corruption "when the overall apparatus of the administration is corrupt" and every institution and everyone seems to have been corrupted. I prefer the term "critical mass of corruption" to describe this situation. At this stage of corruption, where everyone is thought to be doing it; a curious phenomenon is observed in some of the interview subjects. It seems to be genuinely difficult for even relatively honest people to psychologically appreciate what is corrupt. Corruption has become a norm.

To repeat, not everyone is corrupt; but there is a widespread behaviour of what Leon Festinger (1962) coined as "cognitive dissonance": or the ability for a person to have one belief — "I am a non-corrupt person" — while acting in a manner that contradicts their own belief.[13]

Both the journalists who carried messages for the gambling corruptors, and the high-placed sporting officials that I wrote about in the behavioural observation sections of this chapter, claimed to be highly moral, honest people. That one would have accepted a pile of cash in a brown envelope or another would have on his speed dial, the number of a person who could fix football matches, seemingly, did not strike either as unusual.

But many people seemed, as Festinger would have predicted, to be changing their own beliefs to fit their own personal facts (or vice versa). For example, in a number of interviews people who received money from corruptors said that the corruptors were the people that made the league competitive and that they were good for the development of the sport. It is the same phenomenon that the British academics and journalists John Sugden and Alan Tomlinson reported in their interview with one of the organizers of the UEFA Championship League who claimed that some football associations were "so corrupt they do not know they are being corrupt".

This is the situation that is the best way of describing sport in Malaysia in the 1990s. In examining the context of the Malaysian-Singapore league and we

---

[13] *Festinger's original example was the person who smoked knowing that millions of people die from cancer, but persuading themselves that they would not die from smoking.*

see that not only were the players corrupt, but also a whole range of other people, from top sports officials to journalists to individual police officers were suspected of corruption. It is this norm, where every institution seems to have corrupt elements that is a critical mass of corruption. If this chapter shows some of the conditions that exist when a league reaches this "critical mass of corruption", then the key question for the next chapter is why do some leagues get to this stage of corruption.

## Chapter Review

- This chapter examined the features of leagues of high corruption.
- It found that in leagues of high corruption the officials were generally assumed to be corrupt. Whether they were or not, this expectation of corruption became a motivating factor for more corruption.
- There was a cognitive dissonance displayed by some of these officials, so that while they may be doing corrupt actions, they do not perceive themselves to be corrupt.

# CHAPTER SEVENTEEN
# WHY SOME LEAGUES BUT NOT OTHERS?

*Sometimes you would have three or four different bookies [corruptors] working on the same team. One senior player would have a relationship with one bookie. Another senior player would have a relationship with another one. Maybe even a third player would work with another one. They would have two or three players working with them. And if the bookies all wanted the game done in a certain way — no problem. But sometimes there would be fights inside the dressing room. If the bookies wanted different results. Even on the pitch, the goalie would scream at the defenders who were trying to do different fixes.*

*Malaysian coach, interview, May 2005.*

Donald Cressey's query — "Why some and not others?" — still hangs over the fields of criminology and corruption studies. After all, if sports corruption were linked to general societal corruption, trying to figure out which football leagues would be more corrupt would only be a question of looking at their countries' ranking in the Corruption Perceptions Index (CPI). As countries declined in their levels of perceived honesty and transparency, so their football leagues would become more corrupt. In this way, we could predict that Singapore, which has a higher ranking in general societal honesty than Canada, would have a more honest football league than Canada or any other country below it on the CPI.

However, the case study of Singapore and Malaysia shows a more detailed analysis is needed. The two countries are geographically contiguous, however, their cultures are vastly different. Malaysia is an Islamic democracy; Singapore an almost aggressively agnostic state. The per capita Gross Domestic Product of Singapore is approximately three times higher than its neighbour. Malaysia has a series of royal families and a crowned monarchy. Singapore has no titled aristocracy and its head of state is a President.

More pertinently, in the 2012 CPI ranking, Singapore's position was fifth; only New Zealand and three other countries have a higher ranking for honesty in the world. Malaysia, on the hand, is ranked fifty-fourth , roughly equivalent to Turkey and below Botswana or Cape Verde, in the anti-corruption league. However, they do share a similarity, their shared football league collapsed due to match-fixing and both leagues are still generally assumed to be full of match-fixing. What then are the common features of the leagues that allow corruption to flourish?

For a precise response to this question, an examination of another football league is useful. Its leagues used to have high levels of fixed matches, but now there are comparatively few. The country also has a relatively high standing in perceived honesty — Britain.

In the popular literature, there are few books on British football that mention match-fixing. In general, the game is portrayed as a noble pastime, free from the pettiness and spite of everyday life. This idealization is particularly true of books on British football in the 1940s and 50s. For example, James Bartholomew, in his book on the general decline of British society, wrote a chapter lionizing this purported golden era, From *Stanley Matthews* to *Vinnie Jones*[14]. Bartholomew writes that football of that time was a halcyon sport played by gentlemen like Stanley Matthews, who enjoyed a tough, clean game: but now the game is played by teams of cheating thugs.

The primary sources indicate that this view, at least of the British game in the 1950s, is simply a myth. Harry Gregg, one of the interview subjects who played for Manchester United of that era, replied when asked of Bartholomew's views: "I don't know what sport he is talking about, but it certainly wasn't the one that I played."

Ken Chisholm, Trevor Ford, Brian Clough and Harry Gregg were all relatively prominent internationals of that era who each represented the national teams one of the "Home Countries": Scotland, Wales, England and Northern Ireland. Each of them played in the First and Second Divisions of the Football League; and each would write of the match-fixing that occurred in that era. All of them would claim that match-fixing was relatively common. Here is an excerpt from the writings of Ken Chisholm describing a fixed match he participated in between Leicester City and Cardiff City in 1953:

> *Before people get hot under the collar this kind of 'arrangement' was commonplace [emphasis added] towards the end of every season in those days, and I know of many similar cases where points were given away to save clubs who commanded good support from being relegated, and also to get promotion...(Quoted in Inglis 1985, 149)*

*14 Stanley Matthews was considered the greatest English player of this generation. His name was also a by-word for gentlemanly conduct. Vinnie Jones was the player mentioned in Chapter 3, whose photo grabbing the testicles of another player was so widely popular in the UK.*

Clough and Gregg also wrote of the gambling match-fixing that was going on in their own teams. Gregg's case is possibly the more interesting because he played for Manchester United who were, and are, the most popular club in England. Their testimonies are not exceptions. For example, Ian St. John, a Scottish international player, wrote of his own match-fixing in the Scottish League. P3, an interview subject, who also played in England in the 1950s said:

> *I played in the UK for XXX and YYY. In those days match-fixing was very obvious. It was easy to call a manager to arrange a match. In those days it was very obvious. (P3)*

In the interviews and confession databank, there are another 26 players' confessions from that era discussing either why they fixed matches or how they were approached to do so. But perhaps the most convincing of the primary sources is one of the highest league officials of the time, the Secretary of the Football League, Alan Hardaker, who wrote:

> *There are many men in football today among them respected and celebrated managers, who have good reason to remember the great bribery scandals of the early 1960s. They were deeply involved in the mess but escaped because the Law and the League could not get the evidence to nail them. Corruption was rife in the League [emphasis added]. I received calls from directors, managers, players, bookmakers and the pools. The trouble, moreover, did not stop at coupon swindles [gambling fixes]. There were club-to-club payments being made to swing matches affecting promotion and relegation. I did not believe all I heard. Much of it I guessed to be rumour or hearsay, but even if only a portion of the information fed to me were true, it still meant that there was a significant problem. (Hardaker 1977, 99)*

It is difficult to quantify with any precision how many games were fixed in the British leagues of the 1960s and whether they were greater or lesser in number than present-day Asian leagues. However, the general trends were roughly comparable to some of the contemporary Asian leagues: there were gambling networks fixing matches throughout the season; at the end of the season, many of the divisional championship and relegation competitions were affected by match-fixing; and the corruptors, both gambling and team officials, were forming links between themselves to profit-maximise. Currently, British football is assumed to have far less match-fixing — what has changed since that era?

Illegal Gambling: The first condition that leads to widespread match-corruption is the presence of illegal gambling networks. SO11, an interview subject, grew up in 1950s England:

> *I remember in England in the 1950s there were illegal bookies on every street. The only way you could make a bet legally, if you lived in Birmingham, was to go to the Doncaster Races. So, every street had their own gambling ring. (SO11)*

Wray Vamplew and Simon Inglis in their excellent examinations of corruption in English Football in the earlier parts of the last century, show that even the Pools companies (who organised a form of sports gambling regarded as relatively benign in contemporary times) in the period between 1930s and 1960s had to print their coupons in The Netherlands or Belgium to get around British laws. Betting in person in a shop, which is now a societal norm in Britain, was completely outlawed until 1961.

The academics Ian Preston and Stefan Szymanski, in their model of match-fixing in cricket, show that the presence of illegal gambling networks is a strong contributory factor to gambling match-fixing. Their theory is that if gambling is illegal, than the people who run it will be criminals.

Professional criminals will be more likely to turn to match-fixing than established legitimate companies. This is also the view of the Football Association of Singapore who, after the collapse of their football league, campaigned for the establishment of a government run sports gambling industry. According to a number of interview subjects, the fact that match-fixing continues in the Singaporean football leagues is an indication that the government run company has been unable to compete successfully with the illegal gambling industry.[15]

In the other Asian countries where their football leagues collapsed — China, Malaysia, Vietnam, etc — sports gambling is vastly popular, but for the most part, officially illegal. It is this dynamic which gives both organised crime and match-fixing much of its impetus. This is similar to the situation in the prohibition era United States when alcohol consumption — a vastly popular pastime — was declared illegal, which the American academic Peter Lupsha and others claim fuelled a massive rise in American organised crime.

*Relative Deprivation:* If 1961 signalled the beginning of widespread, publicly available, legal gambling in Britain, it was also the year of a significant controversy in professional English football whose *latent function* was to reduce the prevalence of match-fixing.

*15 The illegal gambling industry has a number of competitive advantages over government established betting companies. Generally, the pay-outs are quicker and higher in the illegal market. There is also the important element of credit betting; which means that a bettor can simply phone his bookie and place a bet on the phone, whereas the bettor with a government established company has to physically go to the betting shop (B1-2, 8 - 12).*

*Key Concept*

---

***Latent Function:*** *is the idea that often phenomena in societies have hidden benefits that few people will discuss. The most controversial and often given example is that the publicly available prostitutes help reduce the risk of rape and incest.*

---

George Eastham, a forward playing for Newcastle United, wanted to play for the London-based team Arsenal. His club, as was the industry norm, refused to allow him to transfer. He took them to court and won. This legal decision was the beginning of the end of a system that has been called "legal slavery" by some commentators. I do not want to over-simplify a long and complex socio-economic battle that lasted from the Eastham Decision, through a threatened large-scale labour action by the players, right up to the Bosman case in Belgium in the 1990s.

Essentially, however, before 1961 professional footballers in Britain had very few employment rights: the clubs controlled if they played or not; how the players dressed; if the players were injured the clubs frequently paid them no compensation or benefits. Even when their contracts ended players were prevented from signing for another club unless they had permission of their first club. All players — regardless of experience or playing ability — had a maximum wage salary cap that determined how much they were paid.[16]

Some of the players responded to these conditions by fixing matches. Ian St. John, a footballer in the 1960s Scottish First Division (whose conditions were

---

[16] *This is a simplification of a complex debate, because frequently the clubs would pay over the maximum wage to their best players. However, they would do so by fraudulent means, which further increased the "corruption" of the league (Ford 3-7, 1956 and Hardaker 101-102, 1977, have a discussion of some of the common types of corrupt practices used).*

roughly equivalent to the Football League in England and Wales of the time), sums up these motivations in his description of his team arranging a fixed game with corruptors from a "razor gang" in Glasgow:

> *The temptation for lads gleaning such meagre rewards, who despite drawing huge crowds had no security, no chance of buying a house, was maybe stronger than it should have been... (but) did one match matter against the chance of having a little money in the bank, the possibility of putting something down on a small car or taking a holiday in the sun, something beyond any of our dreams as we were growing up? All we had to do was throw a game... (St. John and Lawton 2006, 62)*

Are players who fix matches simply being greedy or do they genuinely need the money? This is an examination of general themes, rather than individual motivations, but some people would argue that when players fix matches, no matter what their conditions, they are simply being greedy. To return to the Malaysian-Singaporean case, Patrick Ang was a club official in Singapore in the early 2000s who expressed a relatively common view of football players from the owner's perspective:

> *Where on earth can you get 5,000 Singapore dollars (around US$3,900) a month without a good education? If not for the S-League industry (the Singaporean soccer league), I believe that when I call 62-35-35-35 (the phone number of a well-known pizza delivery company in Singapore), some of these players will be the riders delivering the pizza to me. They are earning good money in a time of recession. They must do their part of the bargain and behave like good, honest professionals. (Meng, 2003)*

Ang's views may have been partly due to frustration. In the months preceding the interview, the players on Ang's team had taken part in a novel form of labour protest. They had won the Singaporean League Championship but Ang and the other owners had *not* paid the players their promised bonuses for doing so. In the Cup Final the following week, the team "lost" the game 8-0.[17] There was widespread suspicion that the game had been thrown in protest for the unpaid bonuses. However, Ang is not alone in his views of players as uneducated, working class upstarts who have won the lottery of life. We have already seen the common attitude of many Malaysian sports officials that "Most players are dropouts. Country boys. They would probably be working in the fields or rubber estates, if it were not for football (SO1)."

Along with this class contempt, there is also the issue of non-payment of wages, a common occurrence in both contemporary Asian and British leagues of the 1950s. P6 played with corrupt teammates, but as a foreigner he received a regular salary, many of his team-mates did not:

> *One thing I should add is that back in those days some of those guys didn't get paid for three months. It was fundamentally the excuse they gave, "Look we have to pay rent or mortgages. We have to pay for our cars. We have to put food on the table for our families. We haven't been paid for three months. And someone comes up to us and offers us ten thousand Malaysian ringgit (around $3,000 U.S.) for one game. We have no choice. We have to take the money. (P6)*

Even one of the senior policemen — LE4 — who helped lead the investigation into match-fixing was sympathetic to the players that he caught fixing games:

---

[17] *This was not the only possible fixed game that arose from labour protest, Tengku Abdullah ibni Sultan Ahmad Shah, Deputy President of the Football Association of Malaysia suggested a similar tactic when the Malaysian team lost 6-0 to Indonesia at the 1999 SEA games (Straits Times, November 1999).*

"I don't blame the players. There were two systems — foreigners were very well paid. Domestic players were not particularly well paid" (LE4).

There were similar conditions in the four divisions of the Football League in England & Wales in the 1950s. Harry Gregg, in his interview, described a discussion on the idea of labour specialization and skill that occurred at a 1961 meeting among the Football League's players, held to decide whether the players would launch a strike. The meeting was in an auditorium at the White City, in west London. On the stage was a table with the organizing committee. In front of them was a room crammed with many of the league's players, from the famous Stanley Matthews to the journeymen players of the lower divisions. At the beginning of the meeting there was a general discussion about the merits of industrial action, with the leaders on stage urging for a strike. Harry Gregg remembered what happened:

> *One young man stood up and said, "I do not agree with you. My father works down the pit and he only gets 8 or 10 pounds a week and I think that my father does a better job and we should be happy with what we get." The young fella killed the room completely. It went dead. Tommy Banks, the Bolton [Wanderers] left back, a really broad Lancashire man, said, "Mr. Chairman, can I answer that man? Lad, tell thy dad that I'll do his fucking shift down the pit between three o clock and twenty to five on a Saturday afternoon, if he can mark Brother Matthews here…" (Gregg interview, 2005).*

According to Gregg and others (P32), most of the players in the room laughed in agreement with Banks and soon afterwards agreed to take a strike vote.

However, the underlying point about this story is that the players were trying to determine what Walter Runciman and other commentators call their "professional reference group." In the discussion about whether they should go on strike, the young man thinks their reference group should be coal miners. It is the older player —Tommy Banks — who points out that the players have professional skills and talents that the ordinary person does not have, and should be rewarded appropriately.

Incidentally, in an interview with Tommy Banks he confirmed this specific incident and made three points: one, Banks supported the claims of Gregg, St. John, Ford and others of widespread exploitation of the players of that era and that match-fixing was prevalent: two, he had worked as a coal miner and so could have done the father's job; and three, when news of his speech and its impact on the other players was printed in the newspapers, he was fired from his team and never played professional football again.

### *Key Concept*

***Professional reference group:*** *If keeping up with the Jones is what a person wants to do. Then the question is "who are the Jones?" Most people do not compare themselves to the Queen of England. But who is the person or group of people that you compare your professional salary, employment conditions to — this is your professional reference group.*

The relative exploitation of the workers in football is the second phenomenon that drives widespread match-fixing. In earlier chapters, we saw how, despite the popular myth, very few football players are coerced into gambling fixing. Rather, their motivation for fixing is principally to gain money. There are two key points that must be reiterated. This is not to say that paying players more money means that there will not be some players who will continue to accept bribes to underperform. There are always people who are motivated by greed; it is just that by raising wages one can reasonably expect to reduce their number, so that widescale fixing is more constrained.

This is the concept of the relative exploitation of workers. This is the labour situation that many contemporary Asian players contend with: it is not that they are paid particularly badly; it is that they are paid badly compared to the total money generated by the sport.

Given those caveats, there is a key factor that drives widespread match-fixing in a league. The two conditions — relative deprivation of the players and referees combined with the existence of an illegal gambling market make much of the large-scale fixing possible.

### Key Concept

---

*The main dynamic that drives fixing is the **interaction** of the two markets. The first is the legal sports market, which pays its actors poorly for doing their jobs well. The second is the illegal gambling market, which is willing to pay those same actors very well, for doing their jobs poorly.*

---

*Expectation of Corruption:* If people expect corruption, they often get corruption. This is the closest that rational choice analyst comes to using culture as a motivation for corruption. So in the story about the senior sporting official from the last chapter, perhaps the most significant point is not that the top sports official was accepting a cash payment in a brown envelope, rather, it is that he expected any unusual play in a match to be the result of corruption. I, as a newcomer, *expected* the game to be played honestly. If, in general, people expect there to be corruption, there will be corruption. It is similar to the point that Pino Arlacchi makes in his exploration of the continuing power of the Sicilian mafia:

> *Once they exceed a certain level... mafia murders begin to develop a powerful multiplier effect, which has devastating consequences for the structure of society. The mechanism by which mafia*

> *murder sparks off other murders... is not based on any superficial imitation; it derives from a range of socio-psychological tendencies deeply rooted in collective and individual life. (Arlacchi 1986, 158)*

This is not to contrast the moral severity of murder with match-fixing. Rather, it is to show that there are similar societal mechanisms at play in these cases. In his essay on "the self-fulfilling nature" of corruption, Diego Gambetta makes an important point: beliefs fuel corruption. So when individuals in certain societies, be they inhabitants of Sicilian villages or football players in a particular league, feel that deviant acts are actually the norm, they may feel that they have to join in.[18]

There is, however, an important distinction in the particular case of match-fixing. In both 1950s Britain and current-day Singapore, there is a widespread belief that societal corruption is low. However, there was, and is, chronic match-fixing in both football leagues. So the expectation of corruption in this case is *not* societal, rather it is the *specific* beliefs within an industry that drive corruption. The specific belief that drives widespread corruption in football leagues is that there is *official* complicity.

In other words, it is not enough that players and referees believe that other players and referees are corrupt; it is that they believe some officials who run the sport are also corrupt. We already saw in the last chapter that almost all interview subjects — including players, referees and sports officials — believed that club officials were sometimes involved in gambling and fixing in Malaysia and Singapore. So the situation is that the players and referees are relatively badly-paid, they perceive that their bosses are involved in corrupt activities and there is an alternate market — illegal gambling — that is willing to reward them.

---

[18] *Gambetta makes a second important point when he states measuring those particular beliefs is very difficult.*

Later in the book, we will see how honest sports officials can rectify this situation and stop most match-fixing from occurring, but for now, Table 17.1 lists the factors that lead to wide-scale match corruption:

Table 17.1: Factors Leading to Wide-scale Match-Corruption

| *League* | *Relative exploitation of players* | *Expectation of Corruption* | *Large illegal gambling networks* | *CPI ranking* | *High levels of Match-fixing* |
|---|---|---|---|---|---|
| Singapore | Yes | Yes | Yes | 5 | Yes |
| Malaysia | Yes | Yes | Yes | 47 | Yes |
| China | Yes | Yes | Yes | 70 | Yes |
| Vietnam | Yes | Yes | Yes | 111 | Yes |
| England (1960) | Yes | Yes | Yes | n/a | Yes |
| England (2013) | No | No | No* | 15 | No* |

One comment about Table 17.1, is that with the rapid globalisation of internet gambling, some of it run by Asian organised criminals, illegal gambling networks are beginning to be seen in a number of leagues. There are anecdotal reports on the gambling market of corruption in the contemporary British leagues. However, whether this will necessarily bring about a situation equivalent to the Asian leagues is unclear at this moment.

Overall, the data in this chapter indicates that there are three essential reasons that lead to high corruption in football leagues: a wide network of illegal gambling, a high degree of relative exploitation of the players and "an expectation" of official complicity with the corruption. These factors feed into each other. If the players were simply badly paid, there may be some match-fixing, but not a great deal. If there were an illegal gambling market and the players were well-paid, again there may be some match-fixing but not a great deal.

What really creates wide-scale corruption is that while the players are badly paid, another market — the illegal gambling market — is willing to reward those same players. At the same time many of those players perceive the officials as being involved in corrupt activities. It is this expectation that some of the officials are either complicit or corrupt themselves that helps drive the final stage of corruption. In the next chapter, we shall see what happens when corruption reaches this point and sports "collapse".

## Chapter Review

- Corruption in sport is not culturally dependent. The case of Singapore shows that a society can generally have low levels of corruption, yet a sport can high levels of corruption.
- The features which drive industry specific corruption are: the exploitation of workers: high levels of informal gambling networks and a competing market that will reward the workers for performing their job badly.

# CHAPTER EIGHTEEN
# DEATH OF A LEAGUE

*No one [in the sports world] wants to know about this case. Everyone wants to believe in a clean game. So the Football Association does not want to talk about this case.*

*(Prosecutor involved in a match-fixing case, interview, 2007)*

Throughout this book I have written about the "collapse" or "complete disasters" of football leagues in Malaysia-Singapore and across Asia. Those are sensational words; however, football leagues did *not* collapse only because of high corruption. As we saw earlier in the chapter, the Malaysian-Singaporean league had a culture of match corruption, both gambling and arrangements, dating back at least thirty years before its demise. In the Chinese case, several years before Beijing Hyundai's dramatic walk off the pitch, both a team owner and a referee had announced that there were high levels of corruption in the league.

The owner, a provincial real estate magnate announced publicly that he was retiring from football and going back to the more honest world of the construction industry. He made the choice, he claimed, because football was too corrupt. This chapter focuses then on the specific question of what factors causes leagues to collapse.

Here is the important point of this section. An equilibrium level of corruption

— where corruption is the norm, rather than a deviant act — did not cause the failure of these leagues. Rather what caused their "collapse" was the wider public's *awareness* of corruption.

If we return to Diego Gambetta's model of corrupt actors that we used to analyse corrupt deals in the first part of the book, there are three types: --

- corruptors who offer the bribe;
- corruptees, who are the fiduciary agents who accept the bribe to underperform their professional duties;
- a truster, who has placed their trust in the fiduciary agent to carry out their responsibilities honestly. The public, in the case of match-fixing, is the truster. They put trust in the league to deliver an honest product. Once they have lost trust in the sport they withdraw their support and thus the league collapses.

However, the key point is that the public has to *know* the extent of the corruption before they will begin to switch their interest away from the sport.

The author Simon Inglis argues along similar lines when he writes of the "institutional public trust dilemma" which faces many leagues: if they investigate match-fixing in football they erode public trust in their "product," if they do nothing they run the risk of allowing the value of game to erode Stefan Szymanski and Tim Kuypers write that the game is a "product" — the players "workers," the spectators "consumers." Under this analysis then, match-fixing is the equivalent of selling a "tainted" product to an unsuspecting consumer. But, like the owner of a meat factory who discovers the workers have produced unsafe meat, there is a strong incentive for sports administrators not to publicize the deed outside of an inner circle. Who, after all, wants to eat unsafe food?

Given this negative outcome, how are the people who inform the public of corruption treated by football associations?

## Whistleblowers

There are lots of cases to suggest that generally, whistleblowers are not well received. After all, if corruption is the norm, outspoken honesty becomes a deviant act. William Whyte was an American sociologist who lived for three-years in an Italian working-class neighbourhood dominated by the U.S. Mafia in the 1930s. From this deep "behavioural observation" study, he wrote the classic book — *Street Corner Society* — about the community and how it functioned. One of Whyte's observations was of the loneliness of the one honest policeman in the corrupt precinct. The officer was ostracized and isolated not only by the community, but also by his colleagues.

Many whistleblowers in the football world know exactly how that policeman must have felt. For example, when the tabloid newspaper *The People* exposed the widespread match corruption of the British leagues in the 1950s and early 1960s. The Football Association acted not by helping the newspaper but by banning their journalists from any football ground in the country for the following two seasons.

Another example, from another league: after the construction magnate announced that he was leaving the sport Chinese football officials claimed they were going to clean up the game. They announced a general amnesty for any corruptee who would admit to match-fixing. Gong Jianping, a FIFA ranked international referee, promptly took them up on their offer. The Chinese officials just as promptly broke their word and had him arrested. His subsequent trial featured accounts of sex bribes for referees and poker games with high-ranking Chinese Football Association officials. Jianping claimed that there were corrupt norms *inside* the Football Association that led to match corruption.

For example, he testified that an ambitious referee was supposed to play cards for high stakes with the officials, and then deliberately lose the game so the officials would receive his money. The referee would then receive the best international games to referee. The only way the average referee could afford to play in these card games was to accept bribes. For his apparent honesty Gong Jianping received a "lenient sentence" of ten years in a prison labour camp. He died a few months after entering prison. Since then no other referees have taken up the Chinese Football Association's offer of amnesty for exposing potential match corruption.

However, a police investigation — personally ordered by the Chinese head of state — later confirmed much of Gong Jianping's statements and led to the arrest of six Chinese football executives and almost two-hundred players, coaches and club owners.

However, the above examples are anecdotes. What do statistics tell us about the response of football officials to the public's perception of corruption?

Figure 18.1 (opposite)— shows the role of "detector," or the individual who first reveals on match-fixing in football leagues.

The sample section was from the Fixed-Match Database-2 (FMDB-2), or the 137 matches that we know were fixed with a high degree of certainty. There were seven categories of "detectors": police investigation, media investigation, football administrators, spectators at a game, confession of a participant, confession of an outsider and betting patterns.

There is, of course, a selection bias in the results, since the FMDB-2 consists only of games that are certain to have been either fixed or been attempted to fix. Most of that certainty comes from a legal decision and, obviously, cases that were investigated by the police are more likely to have come to court. Therefore, to reduce that bias by as much as possible, each case was examined to see *how* they began.

Figure 18.1: Who Detects Match Corruption?

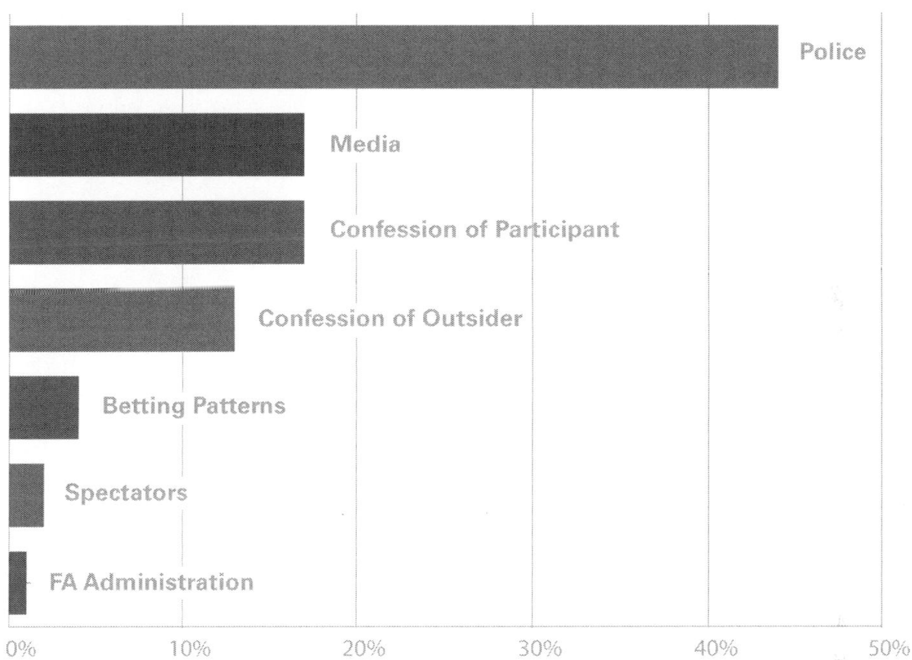


***Source:*** *Fixed Match Database 2 (N = 137)*

For example, in the Moggi case — or games in Italy that were arranged by the internal corruptor Luciano Moggi — began when police were investigating a seemingly unrelated Camorra gangster who was arranging matches with various players. The police eventually took their findings to the Italian Football Federation (FIGC). The football officials did nothing for several months, until the police leaked the transcripts to journalists. After a number of high-profile stories the Federation began a series of hearings that found Moggi guilty of match corruption. However, in the MFDB-2, the detector is listed as a police investigation, because it was their work that *initiated* the inquiry.

There may also be a selection bias in MFDB-2 towards the media. If a participant wants to garner maximum publicity to expose match corruption they may choose to go to the media. For this reason, I have included three categories: "media investigation," where journalists actively investigate match-fixing; and "confession of a participant" and "confession of outsider," where corruptees or observers go themselves to the media to announce match corruption.

Figure 18.1, shows that the largest number of fixed matches — 42% — was revealed by police investigations. The next rankings are shared equally between the confession of a participant in the media or independent media investigations — approximately 18%.

The detector who is the very least likely to reveal match-fixing, with only one case in the entire database, were the national football associations.

This data reflects the situation up to September 2008. Since that date, a number of things have changed. The publication of *The Fix* helped to catalyse the establishment of an integrity office within UEFA. In general, there has been an added emphasis on developing effective connections between sporting associations and the gambling industry to determine if there were unusual betting patterns on specific events. There are now two main companies — *Early Warning System* (EWS) and *SportRadar* — that have contracts with sporting associations to reveal any possible gambling fixes. Finally, a number of European-wide police investigations have revealed the extent of the network of fixers and Asian match-brokers working across the continent.

However, despite these excellent initiatives, there has been no overall change in the fundamental numbers of who reports corruption. The national football associations are still far behind the police agencies in revealing potential fixing and UEFA, despite its excellent start, is now on its third Chief Integrity Officer in four years.

There are some legitimate constraints on football associations that keep them from revealing to the public, corruption in their leagues, and may partly explain this low rate of initiating public investigations. A European football official stated that part of the reason for the low rate was legal:

> *I must repeat there is a big difference between knowing something and doing something... Knowing and saying are two different things. There are many things I'd like to say, but I can't. Otherwise the lawyers would kill me! (SO28)*

This is not an idle threat, Peter Limacher is a Swiss lawyer who was the founding head of UEFA's integrity office. A year-and-a-half after Limacher started the anti-corruption initiative, he was injudicious in trusting a journalist in what he thought was an off-the-record briefing about an unfinished investigation. The journalist published a story on Limacher's statements and he was both fired and sued by the club he had been investigating.

However, some leagues seem to go further than merely being bound for legal reasons not to mention match-fixing. They aggressively defend their product by actively sanctioning players or coaches who suggest that any match corruption may be going on. An example of this form of sanctioning occurred in 2012, when a Serbian player Dragiša Pejović, publicly announced along with FIFPro the existence of what he described as widespread fixing in the Serbian league. The Serbian authorities, like the Chinese reaction to Gong Jianping, promptly started a criminal investigation against Pejović and threatened to ban him for life.

A state prosecutor, who tried to convict players for match-fixing had a similar experience with a national football association in Europe:

> *We [the law enforcement agencies] received no help from the football association. In fact quite the opposite, they closed ranks. They do not want to admit publicly that it [match-fixing] goes on. (LE9)*

Another reason for lack of public discussion of match-fixing is that some football associations themselves may be corrupt organizations. This is not to suggest that *all* league officials of every league organization are corrupt. But we have already seen the alleged links between officials and gambling corruptors in some of the Asian cases. And the same European official suggested that similar situations existed in other European countries:

***Hill:*** *How much trust do you have in the national federations?*

***Officials:*** *(laughter) We will be honest — sometimes they are the problem! In some cases the leagues run the federations — and the leagues are run by the clubs. So there is a conflict of interest right there. And we know that in some of the places there are irregularities in the leagues…In fact, unless you want to get killed — I would avoid Romania, Ukraine and Turkey. Very dangerous places the mafia runs the place. (SO29)*

This last allusion to organised crime involvement in football associations is not new. There are many cases of a football association's involvement in criminal corruption: Juan-José Bellini, the former president of the Colombian Football Federation (FCF), was prosecuted by the US Drug Enforcement Agency and jailed for sex years for "illegal enrichment" and money laundering for the drug trafficking group, the Cali Cartel. The former president of FIFA João Havelange and his son-in-law Ricardo Teixeira, the former president of the Brazilian Football Confederation, have been linked to illegal gambling gang leaders. Several of the highest officials in FIFA have been convicted in a Swiss court of accepting multi-million dollar bribes for the international television rights of the World Cup tournament.

This is not to say, that all football associations are always engaged in corruption. But it is important for the reader to realize that the governing institutions of football can be corrupted and this corruption will lead, inevitably, to a critical mass of corruption.

However, the suppression of information about match-fixing even by dishonest football associations may have an important hidden benefit. If the associations publicized the existence of match-fixing it may lead to more match-fixing as the expected rate of corruption goes up. Suppression of information may make it both unexpected and more difficult to reach corruptors.

To counteract this suppression of information, for a football league to collapse, its society must have a reasonably free media, so that the public can become aware of the corruption in sport. Presumably, there are many countries where corruption in sports is widespread, but the press is unable to report this fact. However, football in Asia provides an interesting industry-specific exception to general societal conditions. The human rights organization Freedom House ranks countries around the world from "free" to the bluntly "not free" in terms of press freedom. Both China and Vietnam rank very low on their scale.

However, in articles about corruption in match-fixing in south-east Asia, many writers made a point of drawing a distinction between the reporting on general societal corruption and corruption in football. This excerpt about Chinese football, from the *Guardian* is typical:

> *Its governing body, the CFA [Chinese Football Association], is accused of complicity in match-fixing, bribe-taking and gambling. These claims have been widely investigated because the media are given* ***more freedom*** *to cover football — the country's most popular spectator sport —* ***than almost any other subject*** *[emphasis added]. (Watts, 2004)*

The final factor, which leads to the collapse of football leagues, is one of an alternative market. It is not just that the public becomes aware of high-levels of corruption; it is that there is also a viable alternative market that is presented to the public at approximately the same time. Soon after the public exposure of high-levels of corruption in Asian football leagues, various new television stations began broadcasting European football matches from the Premier League (EPL) and the UEFA Champions League.

There is a wide gap in quality level between football in Asia and Europe but if the local leagues had not been deeply compromised by corruption, the new football programming probably would not have had much effect. There were a number of logistical and cultural challenges that European football faced in Asia. For example, most European games, if they are broadcast live, come on in Asia in the middle of the night. There are few Asian players playing for European teams to give fans local heroes to cheer on. European football also misses the local sectarian rivalries which give football much of its piquancy there are no Singapore vs. Malaysia or Shenyang (Manchuria) vs. Beijing (Mandarin) games to draw people in. However, because the reputation of the local leagues had become so tarnished, the Premier League became widely popular at the same time as the attendances for local matches declined so dramatically.

---

Wilson Li is typical of a large number of ordinary Asian fans. He has a tattoo of the English football club Liverpool over his heart. It was pretty clear, because at the time of meeting him, he was bare-chested, waving a Liverpool flag and singing loudly in an empty Singaporean car-park (Liverpool had just won a major championship) with eighty of his fellow fans. However, when asked Li if he and his friends supported their local Singapore team, he replied:

> *We used to. Maybe ten years ago, we used to drive up to Kuala Lumpur when Singapore played. It was great; there would be 60,000 people in the stadium. But, now? There is too much bribery. The fans, they pay good money for the game, suddenly their team loses 2-0, 3-0 for nothing. Waste of money!*

---

Li is not alone in either his enthusiasm for European football or his dismay for the local leagues. A November 2007 Arsenal vs. Manchester United match attracted over 100 million viewers in Asia. In comparison, in much of the Malaysian Super League matches in the 2005 season there were generally fewer than 3 thousand spectators in the stadium. Figure 18.2 shows that this is a universal trend.

Figure 18.2: Total Attendance in the Malaysian Football League 1989 - 2005

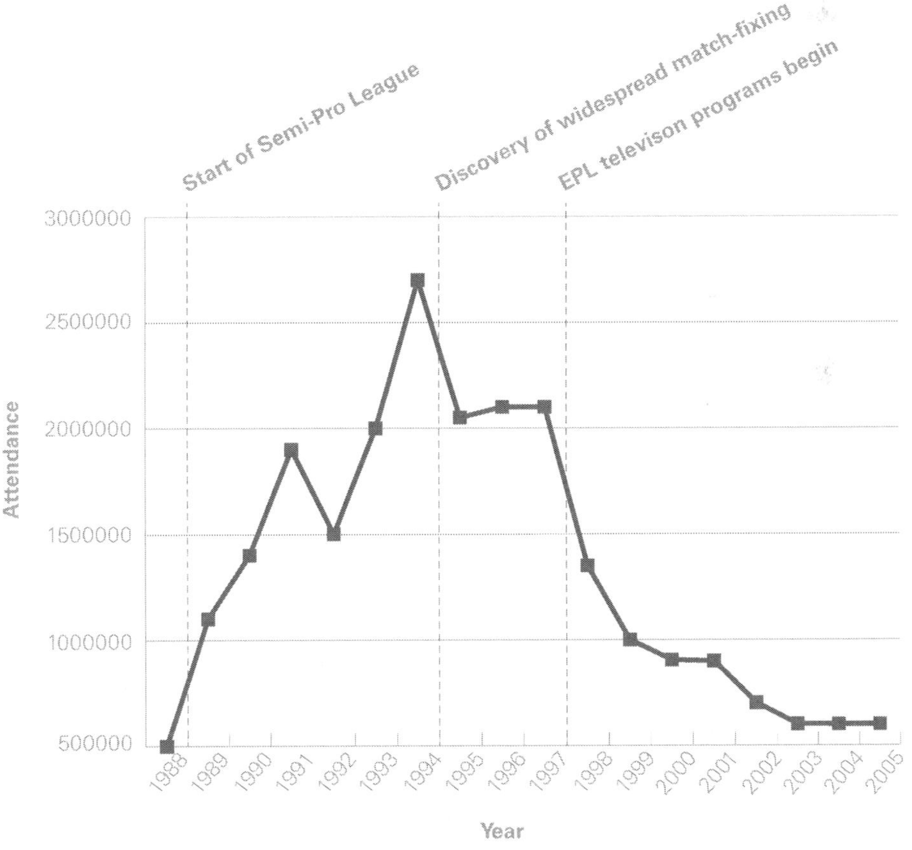


**Source:** *Football Association of Malaysia*

Before 1989, Malaysian football was largely an amateur game played only between the country's constituent states. In 1989, attendance at games began to rise as the new professional league, featuring teams from across Malaysia and Singapore, was founded. 1994, was the peak for this league, however, at the end of this season the police discovered widespread match-fixing and attendance began to decline. The absolute decline was acerbated in 1997, when new satellite television stations began to show live Premier League matches. It is this introduction of new competition which did *not* happen in England in the 1960s that ensured that the league in that country did not collapse.

Table 18.1 summarizes the factors that we have seen in this chapter that lead to a "collapsed" league:

Table 18.1: Factors Leading to the "Collapse" of Football Leagues

| League | High Levels Match Fixing | Public Awareness of the Fixing | New Alternate Market | Collapse of league |
|---|---|---|---|---|
| Singapore | Yes | Yes | Yes | Yes |
| Malaysia | Yes | Yes | Yes | Yes |
| China | Yes | Yes | Yes | Yes |
| Vietnam | Yes | Yes | Yes | Yes |
| England (1960) | Yes | Yes | No | No |
| England (2012) | No | No | No | No |

In this chapter, we see how situations of high corruption where corruption is the norm, do *not* lead to the collapse of football leagues. Rather, it is the public exposure of these situations that lead to their demise. It is because of the importance of public perception; many football officials deliberately suppress reports of match corruption. They do so either by failing to report it, or actively sanctioning any actor, internal or external, who raises the possibility of match corruption. However, wide public awareness is not enough to cause the demise of leagues; it is a competitive relationship with another market that causes the demise.

Just as we saw in earlier chapters that low payment for the players and referees was not enough by itself to cause corruption; what was needed to cause widespread corruption was another competitive market — the illegal gambling one. In this case, just as the public was becoming more aware of corruption in the local leagues television stations began broadcasting a new product — European football matches. These two factors led the attendance and sponsorships in the league to fall by more than 50% In the next chapter, we will examine how the disease of failing sports leagues due to corruption is becoming a global phenomenon and how it has led to a number of murders, suicides and suspicious deaths.

## Chapter Review

- High corruption levels do not lead to the collapse of leagues. Rather it is the widespread knowledge of the corruption combined with a market alternative that causes the collapse.
- Possibly for this reason, the sports world tends to treat its whistleblowers badly. Many sports officials do not want to discuss corruption and have the lowest level of reporting corruption of all the institutions examined.

# CHAPTER NINETEEN
# THE DEATH OF A SPORT

*For their part, Dan Tan and his group constitute a criminal network that is both dangerous and quick to violence in case of anyone who breaks their rules. This is stated in the testimony of one of the members who said it takes very little in the case of treason by one of the group to risk their murder.*

*Judge Guido Salvini, Cremona State Prosecutor, December 2011*

His body was found at the foot of his apartment building. He was one of the casualties in the widespread sports corruption that has been featured in this book. A few years ago, Lee Kyung-Hwan had it all. He was a good-looking, young soccer player with a professional contract for a team in Seoul, South Korea. Lee was even being considered for a spot on his national team. However, like thousands of athletes around the world, he made a mistake.

Dissatisfied with low pay, Lee and some of his team-mates decided to take part in fixing matches with a gang of criminals who were linked to international match-corruptors. They were discovered. Lee was convicted and then banned from the sport he loved. A few weeks later, it is presumed that the shame became too much, and he jumped off the balcony of his fourteenth floor apartment in Seoul. Lee leaves a widowed mother.

Lee Kyung-Hwan was the forth South Korean sports person to commit suicide over the issue of fixing. In the last three years, there have been other deaths — either murders or suicides — linked to sports corruption in half-a-dozen countries. There are now over thirty national police or judicial investigations around the world into the problem from the National College Athletic Association (NCAA) of the United States college system to football games in the UEFA Champions League to pre-World Cup matches in South Africa.

This is the phenomenon that we have seen throughout the book. The first part of the book laid out basic definitions and ideas. The two key concepts are: first, the "underperformance" of fixing is a universal deviancy that is fundamentally different from cheating: and second, that there are arrangements and gambling fixes.

The next section of the book was about the individuals conducting the corrupt deals. First, was an exploration of the role of corruptors from inside the sport and then as external criminals entering the sport. Then there was an examination of the motivations of players and referees, particularly why they would agree to participate in such fraudulent actions.

The third section of the book is about systems of corruption — or leagues and industries where corruption was so prevalent it has become the norm. However, throughout all three sections of the book, the data shows that for the most part corruption is driven by a set of industry specific conditions, not a set of cultural or national mores.

This chapter outlines the final piece of evidence that demonstrates that sports corruption is not specifically cultural or ethnically based. It is that this new wave of globalised corruption has shown that athletes and sports officials in a range of different countries when faced with the same circumstances have chosen to fix.

The source materials for this chapter are mostly qualitative, interviews that have been supplemented by a series of police and judicial investigation reports from jurisdictions as wide apart as Zimbabwe, Finland, Germany and the Greek Anti-Corruption Bureau. However, below is an outline of the universal factors that drives this phenomenon of international corruption.

## Collapse of the Asian Sports Leagues

*"The Chinese soccer league is a national disgrace."*

These are not words blaring from tabloid newspaper headline, nor are they words of Zuwu Yang, the outspoken Chinese coach leading his team off the field in protest against corruption. They are the words of the former Chinese President Hu Jintao, who declared in the fall of 2009, that there was so much match-fixing and corruption in their football league that it was an embarrassment to China

We see similar circumstances in the soccer leagues across Asia: Vietnam, Hong Kong, Indonesia, Laos and Thailand, have all faced similar scandals in their own leagues. In Malaysia and Singapore, the specific leagues that have provided much of the material in the book, the corruption was so bad that in the 1990s a cabinet minister there estimated that 70% of the matches in their leagues were corrupted: meaning it was more usual for spectators to watch a corrupted match than a regularly played game.

There are many other stories of corruption in other Asian sports. Possibly the best example of the current level of corruption is the case of the South-East Asian Games of 2005. The South-East Asian Games are a kind of mini-Olympics of the region. In November 2005, a few days before the tournament began the Vietnamese sports executive in charge of the team held a press conference.

At the conference, the Vietnamese journalists expressed concern that their team was not particularly strong and would not win a lot of medals. "Don't worry," said the sports executive, "It is all fixed." He then explained how many medals each national team would get and for which sports. Most of the Vietnamese press corps showed that independence of spirit that makes Communist regimes such bastions of freethinking and democracy and did not report the story.

However, one Agence France Presse (AFP) reporter at the press conference did write an article. It went out over the international wires where the Filipino journalists, who as a whole suffer from many problems but timidity is not one of them, splashed it all over their front pages. The Thai Prime Minister of the time, Thaksin Shinawatra wearily responded when asked about these events at a press conference, that everyone knew that the SEA games were corrupt and they should think about abolishing the games. The Vietnamese government faced with a barrage of public embarrassment carefully reviewed the situation and realized what the problem was — the AFP reporter. So they pressured her to rescind her article. She apologized for "causing national embarrassment" but did not withdraw the substance of her story.

At the end of the SEA Games in December 2005, two things happened. One, many Filipino journalists took great delight in pointing out that the medal tally of the games correlated exactly with the predictions of the Vietnamese sports executive. And two, eight Vietnamese footballers were arrested for fixing matches with an international gambling ring.

There are a few uncorrupted sports in Asia, but they are often the honourable exception: from Taiwanese baseball to Japanese Sumo wrestling to Pakistani cricket; sports officials and corruptors linked to the illegal bookmakers have fixed leagues on that continent to an extraordinary degree. Asian sports fans are not stupid. They know what is going on. They are not happy about all the corruption in their sports, in fact they are very angry. So what are they doing?

In the last ten years, for the first time in their societies' history they have had a competitive alternative. As we saw in Chapter 18, international television broadcasts are now bringing sports from around the world to Asia. The games are, generally, of higher quality and enjoy a widespread perception that they are not corrupt. Thus Asian sports fans are turning their allegiances to teams in these other leagues where they think the contests are not corrupt. This is part of the reason why you cannot walk down a street in China and not see many people wearing Houston Rockets or Manchester United shirts.

## The Globalisation of the Sports Gambling Market

However, far more importantly, the bettors in that vast illegal Asian gambling league are also switching their bets from the local sports leagues, with all the corruption in them, to European, African and North American leagues and sports. They are betting on all measures of events from the big, prestigious Champions League all the way down to tiny games in second division women's football in the Netherlands.

Companies that only ten years ago were operating only in Asia are now working around the world. One small indicator of the power of this market — Running Ball is a gambling monitoring company based in Switzerland. This means that it employs tens of thousands of people to go to various sports events and report "live" on the action. They do this because there is frequently a time-delay in broadcasting a big sporting event. Theoretically, a bettor could set up a real-life scam as in fictional account in the 1973 film *The Sting*, where the bettors could place bets on the result or a specific action in a sports event that has already happened, but has not been recognized by the market.

For example, if there is a delay in information in the market of a minute of the reporting of a particular football match. A bettor with more timely information could bet on the scoring of the next goal or the awarding of a penalty. It is by no means the only such company. In 2013, *RunningBall* sent gambling monitors to over 30 thousand football matches in seventy different countries along with coverage of a dozen other sports such as snooker, beach volleyball and rugby league. Again, they are not just reporting on the big English Premier League, or La Liga or Serie A games.

In July 2008, in Copenhagen, Denmark the annual Tivoli Cup took place. The Tivoli Cup is a youth tournament for teams across Denmark aged eleven to nineteen. It is a big tournament, but most matches are played in parks and watched by a couple of dozen people, mostly parents. That year some of the team coaches found four Chinese gambling monitors — not working for Running Ball, but another company — reporting on the games back to the gambling market. Thus the illegal gambling market in Asia is so powerful that it is worthwhile to monitor games of Danish teenagers playing matches in a public park.

## The Globalisation of Fixing

One of the unforeseen effects of this globalisation of gambling is the spread of corruption to rest of the sports world. The Asian-based corruptors are also not stupid and they are trying to do to other leagues what they so successfully did in their own leagues — corrupt them. The fixers are travelling around the world and forming alliances with local corruptors and criminals. It is an ideal marriage. The Asian criminals get access to the teams and players; the local corruptors get access to the lucrative Asian gambling market. There are a variety of sources that show they have been fixing games in a range of different countries.

Two examples: in 2013, Europol, the pan-European police agency, announced that they suspected over six-hundred matches, ranging from Champions League matches to national team games around the world had been fixed; and the Zimbabwe Football Association released a report in 2011 showing that a group of Asian match-fixers had essentially run the national team for three years and fixed many of their games with the help of some of their senior officials, players and even some of the journalists who covered the matches, as this excerpt from the testimony of one of their team managers illustrates:

During our first match, we were paid our money [by the corruptor] at half-time when we were actually losing 0-2. We were told to concede another two goals in the second half. We were, by then, US$1,000 each richer. After the game, we were paid US$1,000 each, to the players, and US$1,400 to the technical team each. This was irresistible due to the financial meltdown in Zimbabwe by then (Testimony of Ernest 'Maphepha' Sibanda, ZIFA investigating committee report, 2011).

The range of countries that have had fixing scandals in sports linked to the Asian fixers in recent years is a long one. Here is an incomplete list: El Salvador, Guatemala, Canada, Greece, Belgium, Switzerland, Germany, Austria, Croatia, Slovakia, Macedonia, Malta, Italy, Hungary and Finland. Figure 19.1 is a chart that shows an outline of the structure of the international network of the fixers.

Possibly the best case that indicates the functioning and scale of this network of corruption between Asian sport gamblers and European criminals is the Italian prosecutor's investigation (a quote from their report began this chapter). The same Asian gang that established a fixing network across Europe linked up with a group of Balkan criminals who had connections to players and club officials in the Italian league. For any sports fan, the report makes for chilling reading as it shows that the corruptors have now crossed the line and are forming alliances with club officials and teams owners.

As we saw in Chapter 17, this merging of arrangements and gambling fixes by internal and external corruptors is one of the stages of a "collapsed" league. Currently, more than half of the Italian professional soccer teams in the top

Figure 19.1: A Globalised Corruption Network

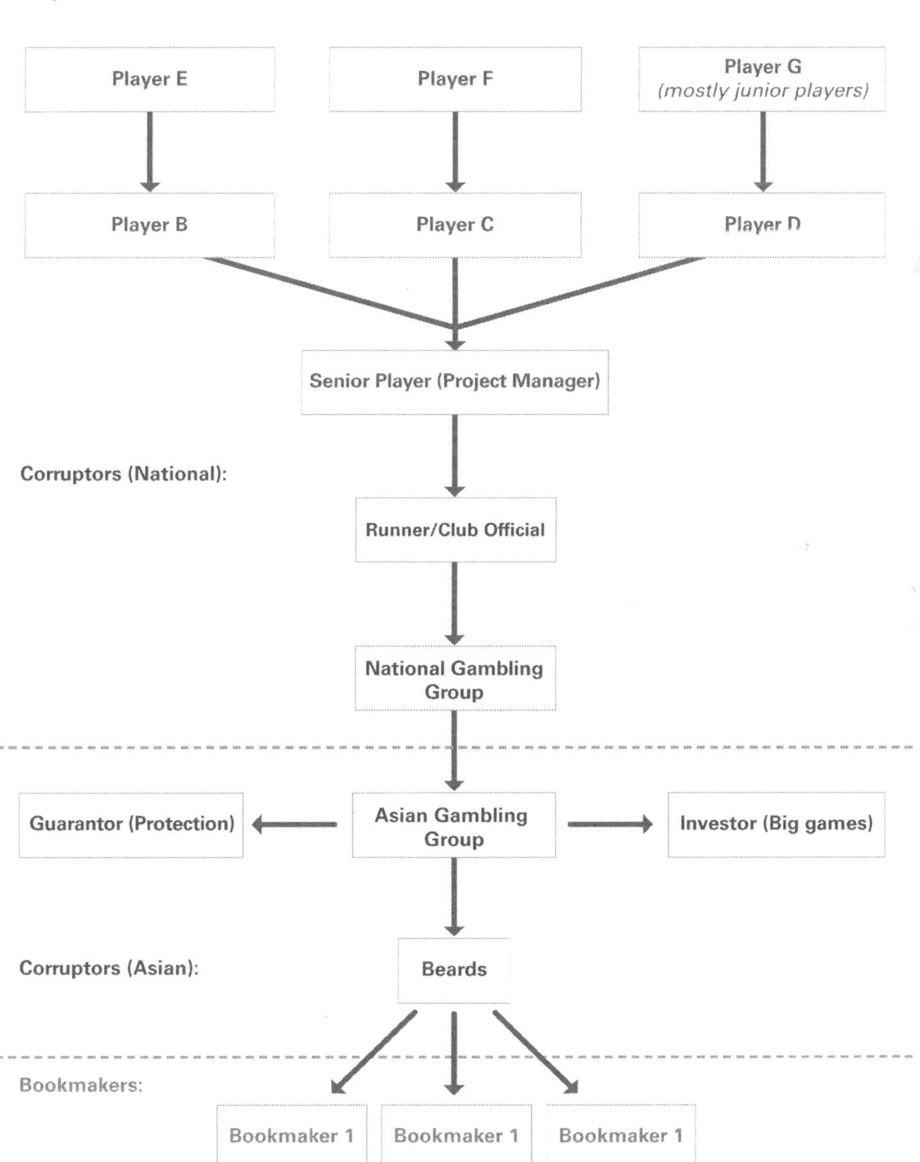

two divisions are under police investigation. However, it is not only in Italy that this pattern is seen:

**Hill:** *[why is there fixing?]*

**Sapina:** *Sometimes it is the clubs who are friends with each other. They may want to help each other. Sometimes it is the president who arranges with the other president. Or sometimes it is the boss of the club. The bosses then bet on the results. It happens a lot in lower divisions.*
*(Milan Sapina, Corruptor, May 2007.)*

Milan Sapina was one of the most successful gambling corruptors in sport. Along with his brother, Ante Sapina, he helped fix dozens of football matches in nine different countries. He was eventually arrested by the German organised crime task force and confessed to this activity. However, the Sapina brothers were able to do this work for two reasons. First, they formed alliances with Asian corruptors. In figure 19.1, they would have been "the national gambling group".

Secondly, they were able to make connections with local football owners who had made fixing part of their business strategy. Essentially, the model for many of these club owners was to win thirty games a season, then deliberately lose eight to ten games. The owners would then gamble on these loses and make more money on the gambling market from losing games, then they could by winning the other matches.

This fixing on the part of the owners is part of the reason for the widespread coercion reported in *The Black Book* of FIFPro, the international federation of players' unions. The owners are, if they cannot secure the players' willing cooperation, coercing them into cooperation with the fixes because of the large amounts of money at stake.

If you have read this far in the book, you might be quite depressed. The book has been full of stories and analysis of corrupt leagues, players, coaches, club owners and league officials. Every level of the sport seems to have been at one time or another corrupted — from the British teams of the 1950s to entire leagues in current-day sport. This chapter even began with the tragic death of a young man caught in the web of shame and dishonour that exposed corruption may bring. However, in the next chapter you will — finally! — read some good news. Widespread sports corruption is neither inevitable nor irreversible. There are a number of relatively easy ways to combat it and the next chapter shows some of these methods.

## Chapter Review

- This chapter examined the globalisation of the sports gambling market that was leading to match corruption around the world.
- As the Asian sports leagues were losing credibility with the public; the fans and punters were turning their attention to other leagues.
- These leagues were also being targeted by fixers who could make money on corrupting these sports, in a manner that would have been impossible a few years ago.

# CHAPTER TWENTY
# HOW WE CAN WIN

*One of these days the sport will be dragged out of the mire of corruption, but the grand inquisitor will not find all the guilty in the dressing-rooms. He'll have to haul his dragnet through the offices and boardrooms. He'll have to trap those clubs which deliberately flout every letter of the law in their efforts to right some of the wrongs players suffer under the heavy hand of big-time Soccer. The example from the top, where intrigue and corruption can be sheltered by officialdom, is not so difficult to follow, and for the youngsters entering the game the temptation to do as is done unto them is very strong.*

*Trevor Ford,* I Lead the Attack, *51.*

One of the great defences against sports fixing is that everyone agrees that it is corruption. We saw in the first chapters that as a rare, almost unique, universal deviancy, fixing does not allow any of the normal defences of the conmen and the crooked. There is no possibility of the traditional money-launderers' excuse that "everyone is doing it". All countries in the world play football. They all play by the same laws. The sport is organised by a consistent governance structure regardless of country. Fixing is regarded as corruption in all of these cultures.

Another great strength is that few people like fixing, even many of the corruptors who are organizing the corruption. As we saw at the beginning of Chapter 5 — "To Fix or Not to Fix?" — if many of the internal corruptors could win honestly they would. If the game is won honestly, the corruptor does not have to spend additional money or resources to ensure a victory through fixing. If the game is lost honestly, the corruptor loses none of these resources. However, if a fixed game is lost — the fix does not succeed — the corruptor loses both the game and the money spent in attempting the fix. The least desirable outcome is for a fix to be discovered as then the corruptor may lose the game, the money involved in the fix *and* face possible sanctions. Much of the time it takes extra effort to arrange a fix.

## Predictive Powers

Another powerful defence is that there are fingerprints of corruption in the statistics of sports events. These statistics do not even have to be particularly arcane. For example, much of the time just by knowing the time of the season and the strength of the team we can figure out *who* is organizing the corruption. So for example, if the fix is occurring towards the end of the season, it is more likely to be an arrangement fix: conversely, if the fix is occurring is towards the beginning of the season, it is more likely to be a gambling fix. This is all material that we covered in Chapter 3 — "Arrangements vs. Gambling" — but just knowing this basic fact of *when* the fix is occurring we can predict with some accuracy what type of fix it is and thus we can figure out the following details:

1) By having a definition of what types of fixes are going on we can predict, in general, who is organizing them: arrangements are team management and gambling are external corruptors.

2) By knowing the strength of the team or opponent (symmetry of the fix) we can predict who will be the corruptee: players or referees.
3) By knowing the patterns of significant events in the games — red cards, penalties and timing and number of goals we can potentially figure out which corruptee played an active role in the corruption.

Given these basic predictive patterns, are there ways for a league administrator, or another interested party, to stop matches from being fixed? In this next section, I outline a number of ways of reducing the rate of fixing in leagues.

## Tournament incentives

*i) Structure:* The first and most cost effective way of disrupting fixed matches is in the tournament design. During the London Olympic badminton tournament of 2012, there were a number of fixed matches. The matches were corrupted because it was to the advantage of the players to lose their final games in a round-robin stage of the tournament, for in the next round the draw would give them easier opponents. Consequently, a number of players engaged in a ridiculous competition where both sets of players tried harder than their opponents to lose the match.

This is the logical outcome of the same kind of tournament incentive that the American academics Justin Trogdon and Beck Taylor analysed in their study of the National Basketball Association (NBA) basketball. They were able to demonstrate that after a certain point in the season, it was in a losing team's interests to lose as badly as possible for they would be rewarded with a higher draft pick for the next season. A league administrator would work carefully to ensure that this type of incentive was not present.

For example, the South Korean football league after its many fixing scandals, is now imitating the Scottish league system of half-a-season of regular play, and then half-a-season of playoffs that decides relegation and promotion. In this fashion, each match has far more worth for each team which reduces the likelihood of corruption.

*ii) Eliminate Disparity of Desire:* As the economists Stefan Szymanski and Ian Preston show in their work on cricket, some fixing arises from one team being more motivated to win a game than the other. The value of matches increases after a threshold point in a season for the corruptor as they either try to win a tournament incentive or avoid relegation. However, for middle-ranking teams, the value of the final matches usually declines, so the risk of their selling their matches increases.

A league administrator who wants to fight corruption would ensure that there is a tournament incentive that continues to give games for possible corruptees as a high a value as possible right to the end of the season. In other words, each position in the league would be rewarded with a certain monetary value. At the moment, in most leagues, the tournament incentives are given to the top four or five teams — the actual championship and or promotion, places in pan-European tournaments etc. — or the lowest three or four teams — relegation.

The middle teams simply have no financial incentive to distinguish themselves between sixth or fifteenth place. However, if the league were set up so that there was a financial incentive for each position of some value x, the cost of fixing could be assumed to rise by at least x. So if a team by agreeing to sell its game dropped from tenth to twelfth in the league, and if each position in the league received $1,000, the cost of fixing by the team administrators would rise by $2,000. For example, the Premier League in England and Wales distributes a quarter of their broadcasting revenue in this way.

These payments add to the cost of the fix for the corruptor. As we saw in Chapter 5, all things being equal the team officials and athletes will not want to fix. If you can increase the cost of a game — by giving it symbolic meaning or a sponsorship — it adds to the cost for the corruptor. For example, small regional teams in one section of a country, may have a trophy given to them as being "King of the North" (or some other such title) even if they are unable to compete with teams from other regions.

*iii) Reduce the number of games:* the police reports on fixing by the Indian and Pakistani national cricket teams specifically mentioned the sheer number of matches being played by the squads. While most of the squad were honest, a group of selected players did corrupt various matches because they simply saw no value in winning these games. Thus, at times, the number of games should be reduced.

## Sporting Judicial System

*i) Increase the cost of the sanctions:* If league and national association officials wish to disrupt match-fixing, they should ensure that the sanctions arising from match-fixing are not only high, but also enforced. In the rational decision to fix a match the higher both the potential chance of detection and enforcement and of potential sanctions, the lower the risk of match-fixing. So honest officials in announcing their campaign to break up possible corrupt trust relations amongst team administrators could announce a "one-strike-you-are-out" policy. In such a scenario, any acceptance of a corrupt deal would automatically mean expulsion from the sport and possible imprisonment.

In Chapter 17, we examined the case of the British leagues in the 1950s and 60s and found them to be full of corruption, arguably almost at the level of a contemporary Asian league. The British political and judicial authorities — changed a number of things that helped reduce sporting corruption: the abolition of the maximum wage and the introduction of legal gambling. However, there was one strong inducement that the sporting authorities also undertook, and that was the heavy and very public sanctioning of three prominent players who were caught fixing during this time. This was the case of Tony Kay, David "Bronco" Layne and Peter Swan in the early 1960s. Swan was in particular, a difficult case. He had been a regular player for the England national team, but went to prison for a number of months and then was banned from the game. We can reasonably deduce that the example of a top-athlete being forced out of the sport must have played a role in reducing in future corruption.

*ii) Protection of Whistle-blowers:* Throughout the book we have seen that most people who detect corruption in sport are punished rather than rewarded. From the Chinese referee — Gong Jianping who died in a labour camp — to the Serbian player —Dragiša Pejović , who was banned from the sport — the first people to speak openly about the existence of corruption rarely do well. To ensure that corruption is both rooted out and is seen to be fought against, these whistle-blowers should be well-protected.

## Corruptor prevention

*i) Increase the advertising cost of the fix:* It is also possible to raise the "advertising cost" of a fix. In Chapter 6 "Certainty, Favour Banks and Guarantors", we saw that reputation and trust were key mechanisms in driving corrupt transactions. Rafael La Porta and his fellow authors argued in an academic journal article of the need to increase trust among public officials to prevent corrupt transactions.

I would argue that in preventing match-fixing the exact opposite approach should be favoured. Rather than increasing trust among officials, honest administrators should focus on decreasing trust among potential corruptors. One possible method of decreasing trust is for administrators to announce a very public campaign of entrapment: league/association officials and selected club officials would approach potential corruptees and propose fixing matches. If the corruptee did not immediately report the approach to league administrators he would face a penalty of some kind. A corruptee would have no way, at first, of distinguishing between "an honest" approach to fix a match and "a dishonest" approach. Eventually, corruptors may find ways of signalling their honest corruption, but we can assume that these signals would add to the price of fixing the match.

*ii) Monitor the gambling market:* A number of leagues have already put into place systems or companies to watch the price of odds on the sports events under the jurisdiction to give warning of any potential fixing. As discussed in Chapter 9 "Calling the Fix", it by no means is a definitive answer as to whether matches have been fixed; however, it is an excellent first step.

*iii) Restrict Access to potential corruptees:* This can be done in two ways. First, simple access to events should be tightly monitored. No corruptors should be allowed access to the team hotel, training camp or stadium. The Integrity Unit of the International Cricket Council [ICC] now also monitors the mobile phone use of some of the players to ensure that they are not in communication with corruptors. This is similar to the strategies implemented by the organizers of the French Open tennis tournament, where mobile phones are jammed around the stadium to prevent betting information passing out of the stadium.

We also know, from the predictive patterns mentioned earlier in this chapter, when arrangement fixes are likely to occur and who are likely to be the corruptees. Honest league administrators would change the referees at the last moment for possible symmetrical fixes.

## Player preparation

*i) Increase the price of the fix for the corruptors:* Some of the methods described above raise the "price threshold" of team officials, but what about other potential corruptees — players and referees? The Singaporean government has an excellent way of stopping corruption — they pay government officials very good salaries. In Chapter 11, in examining the motivation of players in accepting gambling corruptors' bribes, we found that non-payment of salary is a key motivation for many players to fix matches.

An honest league official would ensure that players and referees are paid both well and on-time. This would increase the cost of the fix for any potential corruptors. It should be part of the administration all professional sports leagues to ensure that all the teams before the seasons begin to place their salaries in an independent bank account that automatically pays the players.

*ii) Establish an independent, anonymous hotline:* In most sports leagues it is currently very difficult to be an honest player, if you are approached by a corruptor. As we saw in Chapter 8 "Pitching the Fix", most long-term corruptors are very good as isolating the athletes and making them think (sometimes with good reason) that their club officials are also involved in corruption. By establishing a telephone "hotline" where a player can make a report to an independent agency in an anonymous fashion, it gives the athletes a way to report corruption safely.

This method is adopted by both the Danish Football Union and the New York City Police Department. Both of these institutions face a problem in that if a player or policeman report corruption, they may risk repercussions from their workmates. The New York Police Department issues each person who uses their hotline a non-transferable number which if there is an investigation the police officer is able to quote at an appropriate time to show that they reported the corruption, but without risking any premature abuse from their fellow professionals (SO24-25). If such a hotline is established there must be a regulation mandating that all corrupt approaches have to be reported. As the Association of Tennis Professionals (ATP) report into corruption and fixing in professional tennis said,

Nobody likes the idea of having to tell tales about his colleagues but stern measures are necessary to stamp out corruption and we repeat the advice we have already given in an earlier report that there should be an obligation on a player to report any corrupt approach to another player of which he becomes aware. (ATP Report, June 2005, 40)

The ATP eventually undertook this measure and I strongly recommend other sports following their lead and making reporting of all corrupt approaches as mandatory.

*iii) Establish an Education Program for Potential Corruptees:* Few top athletes need to be taught how or why they should win competitions. It is in their nature to win. When building an education program for them it is more important to show the possible consequences of their actions. In Chapter 9 "Calling the Fix", we saw the American corruptor, Michael Franzese speak of the "slavery" of the athletes who work for corruptors. Few athletes or referees know of the change in the relationship with the corruptors after they have agreed to work with them. The Condon Report into cricket match-fixing speaks of this issue:

The corrupt approach was often subtle, ambiguous and patient. The relationship would sometimes start innocently with admiration of players being used as the reason for invitations to mix socially. Corruptors have masqueraded as journalists or other professionals to gain access to players. Gifts without obligation would follow and eventually the true motivation for the relationship would emerge (Condon Report 2001, 20).

Education of athletes should focus not on morality but on consequences of entering a relationship with a corruptor and the genuine possibility of heavy punishments if caught.

iii) Establish a benefit and education program for former players — In Chapter 12 "Jumping Into Fixing", we saw that one of the key variables for starting fixing was age. The older a player, the more likely they were to start fixing. This factor was because they could see the end of their playing careers approaching and wanted to make as much money as possible while they could. It is a realistic assessment of most sports leagues — however, an honest league/association administrator would try to counteract that be establishing an effective benefits scheme and post-career education program.

The greater the benefits (pensions, medical insurance) for an athlete after they retired, the less likely they would be tempted by corruption.

An ideal program would pay, for example, 10 pounds (or whatever the local currency would be) into the benefits of a player in his first season for every game that the played; then 20 pounds in his second season, rising each year to 50 pounds a game in his fifth season. Thus a senior player would have a far larger number of benefits than a junior player. However, if one of the players was caught fixing they would immediately lose their benefits. Not only would they lose their benefits, the money would be given to the player who turned in the potential corruption to the hotline. Thus each senior player (the most likely to fix) has a strong disincentive both to risk their benefit package for corruption and to trust anyone who approached them to fix a match, as they may be interested in setting them up to steal their benefits. This kind of inherent distrust among potential corruptees makes the possibility of corruption much more difficult.

## An International Anti-Corruption Agency

Throughout the book, we have seen the data indicates that, at times, some sports officials are themselves corrupt. The best way to avoid any potential problems with this form of institutional corruption is for the sports institutions to establish an independent, anti-corruption agency. There is model for such an organization — the World Anti-Doping Agency (WADA) that was established to combat the problem of doping in sports in 2001. An ideal

International Anti-Corruption Agency would have both an intelligence unit to gather information about potential corruptors and their approaches, but also a certification unit that would ensure that all sports organizations who wanted to receive their approval would have to enact key anti-corruption measures, some of which are outlined above.

A reader may be thinking, with some reason, at this point, "Well, all these ideas are very good on paper. But in the real world who is going to pay for them?" There is a very simple answer — the sports gambling industry. This industry makes enormous profits off sports. It has both a commercial interest and a moral duty in ensuring that these sports are well-protected. There should be a very minimal integrity charge on all gambling companies that want to make bets on sports leagues. This integrity charge should not be more than 1% of each bet placed, but even that figure out of the tens-of-billions that are bet each year on sport is more than enough to establish many of the programs outlined above.

There is much that we can do. We can establish integrity units in each national sport association across Europe. We can establish an International Anti-corruption Agency, funded in part by the gambling industry but separate from them, which can collect information and help launch investigations. An Anti-corruption Agency that would have the same purpose and structure as the World Anti-doping Agency. We can establish proper training and teaching of young players — as they come into the game they can learn the sad truth that if they sell games to these fixers, they become in effect their slaves.

We can establish proper pensions and educational benefits for the players. We can establish anti-corruption hotlines for players and referees to report corrupt approaches. There are literally dozens of easy, doable and effective ways of stopping the wide-scale corruption. If we do not do any of these things the future for sport in North America and Europe is very clear — it will become like much of Asian sport already is — a comic soap opera known for its buffoonery and fixing, but not for its athletic achievements.

This would be a tragedy for sport has now become the vessel for many of the hopes and dreams of our societies. It is the way we often teach values and ideals to our young people. Done properly, sport has that rare capacity to make us realize that we can become bigger than who we truly are – so for all those reasons, we should protect, we can protect sport and we must protect sport.

# ACKNOWLEDGEMENTS

The great British scientist J.B.S. Haldane once wrote that there are four stages in the acceptance of a new idea:

- This is worthless nonsense
- This is an interesting, but perverse, point of view
- This is true, but quite unimportant
- I always said so.

Much of these thanks are given to the people who supported the research when it was going through the first stage: before the sports world had fully woken up to the dangers of globalised corruption.

A big debt of gratitude goes to the people at Oxford: particularly, my two supervisors Professors Anthony Heath and Diego Gambetta. Others at the department who gave valuable support and good advice were Professors Heather Hamill, Peter Hill, Federico Varese, Matthew Bond, Jay Gershuny, Michael Biggs, Pär Gustafsson, Steve Fisher, Anna Zimdars, Samir K. Sinha, Carmel Hannan, Rob Ford, Didier Ruedin and Edmund Chattoe.

At my spiritual home of Green College much thanks must go to Gill Edwards, Lucie Cluver, Jamie Salo, Sean David, Emma Link, Anders Krarup, Paddy Coulter, Allison Gilmore, Jackie Davis, Dominic Bown and Michael Elkaim. Others whose kindness and intellectual guidance are very much appreciated are Professors Katherine Isbester, Michael Drolet, Gerry Bodeker, Keith Frayn, Derek Jewell, Uwe Ackerman, Colin Bundy, Sir John Hanson, Peter Bourne and Sir Richard Doll. Finally, but never last, my advisor, friend and guide at the College was Dr. Andrew Markus. Our walks and his gentle counselling will not be forgotten.

This book could not have been written without an extraordinary team of fact-checkers and researchers who were inspired by the subject and were diligent to the point of obsessiveness: any mistakes in the text are my fault. This wonderful team comprises Marc Carinci, Bryce Dymond, Adriano Lamberti, Vicky Grygar and Steven Powell – whose mutual love of football and the Arsenal has been sustained over numerous pints.

In the book world, my agent and friend is Chris Bucci always ready with a sage piece of advice; along with Film and TV agent Rene Zimmerman and media stalwarts Ruta Liormonas and Sharon Klein. Big thanks also to Christoph Biermann, Florent Massot, Matyas Esterhazy, Glenn Ringtved, Won Chai Lee, Frans van den Muijsenberg who have fought long and hard for integrity in sport to be featured in publishing.

A big thank you to Joe McGinniss for his kindness in giving permission to use excerpts from his superb book The Miracle of Castel di Sangro. It makes one wonder what Italian football would be like today, if they had listened to him.

Play the Game and its dynamic and charismatic leader Jens Sejer Andersen have been strong supporters since the beginning of this research.

Thank you as well to the British Council who were kind enough to give me a Chevening Scholarship that financed some of my studies at the university.

In Germany, Professor Johann Lambsdorff always provided helpful advice on statistical matters.

The sports gambling world was a mystery to me when I began my work and the list of people to thank is long and deep. It must start with Patrick Jay, Tjeerd Veenstra, Andre-Noel Chaker, Joe Saumarez-Smith, Alistair Flutter, Matthew Benham, Andrew "Bert" Black, Mark Davies, Robin Marks (Betfair), Graham Sharpe (William Hill), Göran Wessberg, Stephen Allmer, Wolfgang

Feldner, the SportsRadar team, and, of course, the king of the Asian part of this world - Scorpion Lam.

In the world of police and sports officials many contacts have to keep our relationship quiet. However, some of the people who can be thanked publicly are David Howman, Richard Pound, Richard McLaren, David Larkin, Richard Ings, Catherine Ordway and the FIFPro executives – Tony Higgins and Raymond Beaard.

In the public policy world, there are few better at fighting to preserve sport than the Council of Europe's Stanislas Frossard and the unstoppable Irish politician Cecilia Keaveney.

As always a big shout out to the band of brothers who comprise the loose-knit group of investigative journalists and researchers around the world, who share stories and knowledge motivated only by a desire to keep sport clean. It is a long list but must include Jan Hauspie, Douglas De Coninck, Peter Verlinden, Chris Wade, Cristian Villalta, Risto Rumnpunen, Ari Virtanen, Ezequiel Fernández Moores, Ouriel Daskal, Laura Robinson, Michael Petrou, Bruce Livesey, Alexandros Sotiropoulos, Alan Guettel, David Nayman, Dick Miller, Brian Tuohy, Ben Rycroft, Stephen Brunt, Bob McCown, Shaka Hislop, Mark Misérus, Jens Weinreich and Andrew Jennings.

The translators were many and good. Their kindness is deeply appreciated. Thanks to Kees t'Hooft, Stefan De Wachter, Tiina Ristikari, Stefania Battistelli, Graziano "Primo" Lolli, Andrea Patacconi, Julika Erfurt, Thomas Gerken, Franziska Telschow, Söhnke Vosgerau, Natasha Gorina, Ekaterina Korobtseva, Ekaterina Kravchenko, Svetlana Guzeev, Eugene Demchenko, Alisa Voznaya, Maria Semenova and Emre Ozcan.

In Canada, Anthony Blundell, Tad Homer-Dixon, James Orbinski, Noel Lomer and the staff at the Georgetown pub who quietly tolerate the eccentric in the corner tapping away on his computer.

Finally, the irrepressible Dr. Tom Dawson whose advice on the sports world was wide, varied and included, at one point, stripping off in middle of the Churchill Hospital parking lot to help me prepare for a boxing bout.

# GLOSSARY

*Asian handicap:* An odds setting method used by Asian bookmakers on football matches. The odds compilers set the odds by predicting which team will win and by how much. If a strong team is expected to beat a weak team by 3 goals, and the weak team wins, draws or loses by less than 3 goals, it is counted as a "win" for the weak team or for the bettor who picks the weak team.

*Beards:* They disguise that they are placing the bets for other people, either professional gamblers or fixers. Also known as "mules" or "runners" in betting circles.

*Betting line:* The odds on each game.

*CPI:* Corruption Perceptions Index. Constructed by Professor Johann Graf Lambsdorff, it is the first and most widely used tool for comparing rates of perceived corruption in different countries.

*Early Warning Systems (EWS):* These systems are specifically established to monitor odds of all the games to see if there is any unusual activity or too much movement in the line.

*Lay-off:* When a bookie has taken too many bets on one result of an event, they (the bookie) will try to "lay off" the money with other bookies to balance his books.

*Odds compilers:* An "odds compiler" is the person who sets "the betting line" for the bookmakers.

## FOOTBALL RULES AND TERMS

*Free kick:* A stationary kick taken from outside the defending team's penalty area. A free kick is awarded to an attacking side when the defending side has committed a foul outside their penalty area. Defenders must remain 10 metres from the ball until it is kicked.

*Own goal:* When a player scores, by mistake, on his own goal.

*Penalty:* A free shot taken 12 yards or 11 metres from goal. Given to an attacking side when the defending side has committed a foul — handling the ball or tripping an opponent — in the "penalty area" around the goal. A penalty kick is considered an excellent chance for the attacking side to score.

*Red card:* A referee will signal to a player that he must leave the field with a red card. A player is usually sent off after two particularly bad fouls or for violent play. The ejected player cannot be replaced and his team must continue play one player down.

## ORGANIZATIONS

*AFC:* Asian Football Confederation. An umbrella organization of Asian national football associations. It is one of the chapters of FIFA. Located in Kuala Lumpur, Malaysia.

*ATP:* Association of Tennis Professionals. An umbrella organization of men's tennis. Located in London, UK.

*FIFA:* Fédération International de Futbal Associations. The world organization that runs the World Cup and officially recognizes national football associations. Located in Zurich, Switzerland.

*FAM:* Football Association of Malaysia. The national federation that runs football in Malaysia.

*National Football Association or Federation:* The organization that runs football within one specific country. For example, the English Football Association controls all football played in England from the professional leagues down to children's games.

*FAS:* Football Association of Singapore. The national federation that runs football in Singapore.

*UEFA:* Union of European Football Associations. The umbrella organization of European Football Associations that runs the Champions League, European Championship and UEFA Cup. Located in Nyon, Switzerland.

# ENDNOTES

## CHAPTER 1 - WHY STUDY MATCH-FIXING

### PAGES 1-3:

*Football as big business*
See Sugden and Tomlinson 1998, 1: Hughes 2007: Blatter interview, 2008.

*"SO — Sports Official"*
See page 18, for an explanation of the interview codes.

*"5% of all people who have ever lived"*
See Midwinter 2007, i.

*Gerry Sutcliffe M.P.*
Quoted in Hamil, et al., 2000, 264.

*Barça Museum*
See Kuper 1994, 85.

*Sepp Blatter*
Quoted in Sugden and Tomlinson 2002, 138.

*1994 World Cup*
See Yallop 1999, i.

*Mimic warfare*
See Orwell, 1945.

*"There have been actual wars fought over the sport..."*
See Kapuscinski, 1969; Giulianotti 1999, 13.

*"Women beaten to death"*
Kirkup, Merick 2003; Witte et al. 2000; Police and Crime Standards Directorate 2006. These studies show that the admissions to hospitals increases during sports tournaments, as some women are beaten by their partners if their teams lose.

*Corruption Studies*
In 1978, Susan Rose-Ackerman laid out many of the fundamental ideas for this field in her book *Corruption: A Study in Political Economy*. However, the literature lay relatively dormant throughout the 1980s. This is not to ignore the work that was written in that time — see, for example, the superb works of Alatas 1990, Klitgaard 1989, Noonan 1984 and the work of Neo-institutional Economists like Coase, North, Olson and Williamson from the 1960s onwards. It is simply in comparison with the amount of research produced after 1996. See Andvig, 2000 and Williamson, 2000 for a very good analysis of the subject.

The speech is cited in numerous scholarly articles and books, see for example Wei, 2000; or Levy and Kpundeh, 2004.

*Discussion of the CPI*
See Lambsdorff 2007, Chapter 1.

"A large growth in the literature"
Andvig 2000, 7. from theoretical approaches (see for example, Heywood 1997; Elliott 1997) to historical examinations (Wei Li 1999) to large-scale surveys (see Hunt and Laszlo, 2005).

*"Corruption exists and has existed in all societies"*
For examples from ancient Greece, the Brahamin Kingdom of Chandragupta and the writings of Abdul Rahman ibn Khaldun; see Klitgaard, 1989, 7.

*"One size fits all model of corruption"*
See Rose-Ackerman 1999, 197.

*Studies of gifts*
See Lévi-Strauss, 1950 and Mauss, 1954 ed.

## PAGES 4-7:

*Academic studies among Nepalese rickshaw-wallahs, etc...*
See Kondos, 1987; Gupta, 1995; Ruud, 1998; Sissener, 2000.

*"Great disease of government"*
See Noonan 1984, 700.

*"Hidden benefits"*
See Merton 1967, 71-79.

*Rent-seek in the official economy*
See Thum and Choi, 2000; Also, Leff, 1964, Nye, 1967 and Anechiarico, Frank, and James B. Jacobs, *The Pursuit of Absolute Integrity: How Corruption Control Makes Government Ineffective*, Chicago: University of Chicago Press, 1996.

*Service actually flows from the corruption*
See Goldsmith, 1999: also Theobald 1990, 116-19.

*Globalisation of sport*
See Foer 2004; Giulianotti, 1999; Smit 2006; Jennings 2006.

*"More than those represented in the United Nations..."*
Blatter, Feb 08: Yallop 1999, i.

*"For more on 'deviancy'"*
See for example, Foucault's radio broadcast, *La loi de la pudeur* in *Politics, Philosophy, Culture* 1988, 271-285. For a more extensive exploration of these ideas in *Discipline and Punish* 1977.

Note: also that what is regarded as "deviant" in sport can also change. In the Olympic movement, before 1992, amateurism and the importance of all athletes *not* receiving money from the sport was regarded as a paramount importance. Now the subject is almost never discussed.

## PAGES 8-12:

*Imperial Roman Emperors match-fixing*
Suetonius 1914 (ed.), vol. 24.

*Byzantine Chariot Racing*
The chariot racing fan clubs in Constantinople became effectively units of organised crime akin to the Argentine fan club Burra Bravas, mobs for hire that took part in external political and religious violence (Cameron 1976).

*"Religious statues outside the stadiums"*
See Pausanias, 5.24.9ff.

## CHAPTER 2 — HOW TO STUDY MATCH-FIXING

### PAGES 1-3:

*Map of Corruption*
Gambetta, 2002 — For similar models of corrupt actors see Klitgaard's model of a principal-agent-client relationship (1989) or Lambsdorff (2007, 35).

*Deceptive Mimicry*
See Gambetta, 2005 & 2009.

### PAGES 4-6:

*"A complete disaster"*
Interview with R1, SO1

*History of the Malaysian-Singapore League*
Seneviratne 2000, 104-108; Williams 1998, 111-115; Mony 1998; also see the transcripts of the trials of match-fixing players and referees in Singapore (Abbas vs. Singapore PP; Rajmanickam vs. Singapore PP; Manat vs. Singapore PP; Kanan et al. vs. Singapore PP; Maran vs. Singapore PP). Also interviews with a wide-range of sports officials and law enforcement authorities in both countries.

*"the most professional organised investigation..."*
See Williams, 116.

*"Neglected art..."*
See Cressey 1967, 101-112: Maguire 2000.

*Interview subjects*
I write purportedly because some of the interview subjects told me of their work with the corruptors.

*Odds compiler*
The person who calculates the odds that the gambling "book" is made on.

### PAGES 9-12:

*Qualitative interviewing*
See Maguire, 2000; Atkinson, 1998; Merton et al., 1990; Varese 2001, 11-12.

*Types of interviewing*
Sayer, 1992; Morse, 1994; Atkinson, 1998; Denzin, 1989; Parry and Mauthner, 2004.

*Work on the Russian Mafiya*
See Varese 2001, 12.

Please see the acknowledgement section for the entire list of translators and languages.

See Weinstein's discussion of the system's inception and uses at http://tamsys.sourceforge.net

*Construction of databases*
The reader should note that data was not always available for all variables in every game in the database. If the information for the variable was not known, it was excluded the matches from the specific statistical calculations based on that variable. This means that the N sample varies for different tests. For example, in Chapters 4 and 15, the number and timing of goals scored in different types of fixed matches is compared to the control group of honestly played

matches. The variable of goals and their timing is available for *all* of the matches — resulting in an N sample of 237. However, in other parts of the where other variables were examined, such as number of penalties awarded, red cards, own goals or the identity of the corruptor — accurate data was not always known for every match, this means that the N sample was reduced in some of the figures and tables.

## CHAPTER 3 — ARRANGEMENTS VS. GAMBLING

### PAGES 1-3:

*Grobbelaar Case*
See Grobbelaar v. News Group Newspapers Ltd. and Another. UK House of Lords, 2002. See also David Thomas, *Foul Play: The Inside Story of the Biggest Corruption Trial in British Sporting History.* London: Bantam, 2003 — for an excellent summation of the various trials and the issues surrounding them.

*Difficulty following...*
Interviews with a number of lawyers and police officers with experience in the case.

*"Shadowy figures"*
See Mcdonnell, 1999.

*Argentine vs. British methods of cheating*
For a further discussion of this type of cultural bias, see Taylor 355-356, in Dunning et al, 1971.

### PAGES 4-7:

*Other academic definitions of fixing.*

For example, in *Cheating in Contests* (2003), the British academics Ian Preston and Stefan Szymanski mention three types of match-fixing: "internal competitive structure," "gambling" and a third, indeterminate form labelled "because one side needs to win."

Richard Giulianotti, in his book, the *Football: A Sociology of the Global Game,* argues that the essential difference in match-fixing types is one of motivation (1999, 100).

The definition that I apply is closest to that made by Simon Inglis (1985, vii).

*For more on "Tournament incentive..."*
See Preston and Szymanski, 2003.

*Different types of corporate crime*
See Clinard and Quinney (1973) (cited in Geis 1992, 39): Clinard, Marshall B., and Yeager, Peter C. *Corporate Crime.* New York: Free Press, 1980: Croall 2001, 86: also the discussion of the Iacocca and Pinto case in Slapper and Tombs, 119.

*Algeria vs. West Germany fix*
See Glanville 1997, 256.

*Third division fix*
See McLean, 1980

*Links between Real Madrid and General Franco's fascist regime in Spain*
See Ball, 2002.

*Dynamo Moscow and the Soviet KGB fixes*
See Wilson 2006, 233-234.

*Prostitutes, holidays, cars or shopping trips*
See Glanville 1991, 86-112.

*Favour banks*
For a more detailed discussion, see Chapter 6, "Certainty, Favour Banks and Guarantors."

*Strategies of Corruptors*
Interviews with COR 1, 2

*Short Term vs. Long Term Corruption Strategies*
A good example of short-term profit making was when a Chinese corruptor bought the ownership of a Finnish team and then arranged for his newly bought squad to lose one of their first matches 8-0. Presumably, this netted the corruptor a large amount of money — both for the loss, and the high amount of goals — but the fix was so obvious that eventually a police investigation was initiated (J16, 22, LE15, SO41: and Staff Writer, *Reuters*, August 4, 2005).

### PAGES 8-10:

*Map of Corruption*
See Gambetta, 2002.

*Deceptive mimicry*
See Gambetta, 2005.

## CHAPTER 4 — THRESHOLDS, POWER AND TIMING

### PAGES 6-14:

*Alliances of countries*
See Keohane 1984, 31-64, 85-109.

*Arrangement fixes in Italy*
See Petrini 2000, 109.

*Hypothesis testing*
Table 4.3: This average is in the range of goals scored per game for the 2nd Control Group of Contemporary European Leagues — 2.13-2.98.

*Non-parametric numbers*
I also tested the numbers using a standard linear regression — with the assumption of a normal distribution curve. The results were also positive.

## CHAPTER 5 — TO FIX OR NOT TO FIX?

### PAGES 1-3:

*Olympique de Marseille Fixing*
See Eydelie, 2006; Bernès, 1995.

*Jurisdictions of high and low corruption*
See Kugler et al. 2004, 16.

*"Decision trees"*
See Merkhofer, 1987 as well as Gladwin, 1989.

*the decision [to fix] is taken*
Interviews with COR 4-5.

*Utility of crime*
Becker 1968, Vol. 76, 169-217.

PAGES 4-6:

*On just one team in Russian football being sanctioned for match-fixing*
See O'Flynn, 2004

*EPL and The Championship differences in revenue*
See Hughes, 2007.

*"Disparity in desire..."*
Preston and Szymanski, 2003.

PAGES 7-9:

*For more on Luciano Moggi*
See Burke, 2006.

Jon Elster continues this line of argument in *Sour Grapes: Studies in the Subversion of Rationality* (1983) and *Alchemies of the Mind: Rationality and the Emotions* (1999). Merton also, in his writings on the latent functionalism of corruption, gives a similar caution asking researchers to "preclude the substitution of naïve moral judgments for sociological analysis" (1967, 70).

*"Honest actors like 'suckers'..."*
See Heckathorn et al. 2001, 274-77.

*An explanation of some of the moral arguments for corruption*
See Lambsdorff et al. 2005, 78.

PAGES 10-15:

*Incentive payments*
See also Saad vs. Singapore PP, Subordinate Court, 1995

*Fixing Culture and Olympique de Marseille*
Bernès would also write later in a chapter entitled '*The System of the Win*,' "before the players even walk on the pitch, the game is won or lost (41-42)." See also, Broute, 1995

*Successful gamblers calculating odds*
See Bernstein, 1996, 2007

*"Certainty for gamblers"*
was confirmed in interviews with gamblers: B1-4; see also, Peter Bernstein 1996, 207; for a more general discussion of rationality and gambling see also Giddens 2006; Munting 1996.

## CHAPTER 6 — CERTAINTY, FAVOUR BANKS AND GUARANTORS

PAGES 1-3:

*After de Carvalho was unable to deliver the correct result in many fixes*
See Rizek & Oyama, 2005.

*After Hoyzer was unable to deliver the correct result in many fixes*
See Kerner, 2005

PAGES 4-6:

*More important for corrupt people to trust each other*
See also Molm's article 2001, 268 and her description of Lévi-Strauss,

"exchange under risk and uncertainty not only *requires* trust, but *promotes* trust."

## PAGES 7-9:

*"each national sports federation had at least one medal..."*
Interview with SO4.

*"Self-reinforcing network"*
Eric M. Uslaner, 2005 *Trust and Corruption*, when he points out that in similar corrupt political systems, individuals can leave but the system continues unchanged.

*"It can seem very complex..."*
The Portuguese book *Golpe de Estadio* ('The Stadium Coup') also alleges that a similar process — also called the 'Sistema' — is prevalent in Portuguese football. Both the general comments in the McGinniss book and the Golpe de Estadio allegations have been supported by judicial investigations.

*Sumo wrestling*
Sumo wrestling is built around stables of wrestlers who compete against each other in a series of tournaments. During one of these tournaments if a wrestler can win 8 bouts in a row, he achieves the highly coveted rank of kachi-koshi. Duggan and Levitt showed that match-fixing occurred when a wrestling stable (S1) would allow the wrestler from another stable (S2) to win the eighth bout in a series.

## PAGES 10-12:

*Reputations of Moggi and Rubinov*
See Rose-Ackerman, 1999, 99-102

Transcripts of Moggi's conversations
http://bit.ly/198Vvaz (October 16, 2013)

*On the guarantor*
It is not clear if the "Chechnyan" is a member of organised crime or simply someone with whom Vanya Rubinov has done business with before.

*On corrupt contracts not being legally enforceable*
See Lambsdorff 2007, 190

*On Sedat Peker's match fixing*
Kilinç, 2006.

*Oil industry and other corrupt deals*
See Bray, 2005 as well as Della Porta and Vannucci, 1999. Also see Footnote 11 — There are other examples from the Ukrainian, Croatian, Russian and Italian leagues.

*Using agents to gain access to corruptees*
See Glanville, 1991; or the confession of Jean Elst in Appendix 2; Van Laeken 1997, 170-190: COR2.

*Notes on agents*
Other names and euphemisms for these agents are "middlemen," "go-betweens," "runners" or "intermediaries" (see Lambsdorff 2007, 145-147), "consultants." "commercial agents," "joint venture partners," "fixers," "facilitators," "coyotes" (Mexico), "tramitadores" (El Salvador) or "despachantes" (Brazil) (Bray 2005, 116).

*Horse selling in Sicily*
See Gambetta, 1993, 15-16.

## CHAPTER 7 — FIVE STEPS TO SUCCESS

### PAGES 1-3

*Note on the Chicago White Sox scandal*
The John Sayles' film Eight Men Out, 1988, about the White Sox fix is a very good exploration of all the stages of putting together a fix. The film shows the fix being set up complete with the five stages of corruption, the signalling between the players and the corruptors, and the problems of fixing the betting market.

*Academic network theorists*
See the work of Baker and Faulkner, 1993; Granovetter, 1985 as well as Lin, 2001 cited throughout the chapter.

*Turkish Fixing Scandal*
See Yasin Tuncer, "Sali Hakan şikeyi 90'dan çıkardı!" *Zaman, Spor,* (Istanbul) April 12, 2005. My thanks to Chris Wade and Emre Ozlan for their translations and insights into Turkish football.

### PAGES 4 -7:

*Shooting in relation to Turkish fix*
See staff writers, Turkish Daily News, Star Gazete, (Istanbul), *Zaman, Spor,* CNN-Turkey: Hürriyetim 2005.

*On corruptors establishing themselves in bars or clubs to get direct contact access to players*
See Prosecutor's Report, Staatsanwaltshcaft Berlin, June 2005. Also interviews with COR1, 4.

*On Chinese gambling syndicates*
See Van den Abeele, 2006: Mardulier, 2011.

*Runners being contacted by potential corruptors*
See Kannan, et al. vs. Singapore PP, Singapore Law Report, 1995, 3, SLR; and Kurusamy testimony, in Ong, et al. vs. Singapore PP, Subordinate Court transcripts, 1994. Also interview with LE10.

*Actors in a corrupt deal*
Should note there is also the "truster" — the audience who is affected by the corrupt deal.

### PAGES 8-10:

*A successful cluster or a coalition of clusters*
See Gambetta 1988, Chapter 7, 11. See also Lin 2001, Chapter 5 and Burt (2001), and his discussion of brokerage network where markets are seen as "a network of separate groups" and Baker and Faulkner's description of "action sets" in illegal networks in price-fixing in the heavy electrical industry of the United States, 1993, 843.

*Betrayal of team-mates*
For a discussion of the internal group norms on sports teams which make informing outsiders about any transgressions inside the team prohibited: see Cloward and Lloyd 1998; Young 1971; Benedict 1998; and Skolnick 2005. Also see Albert Cohen's term "delinquent sub-cultural norms," protect insiders from having their delinquent actions revealed to anyone outside the group.

*"Decentralized network"*
See Baker and Faulkner 1993, 830-867

Limited network to stop information exchange.

P3's views were supported in interviews with a number of other former players: P6-7, SO9.

## CHAPTER 8 — PITCHING THE FIX

### PAGES 1-3:

*Business strategies of erotic dancers*
See Thompson and Harred, 1992; Skipper and McCaghy 1970; Salutin 1971; and Boles and Garbin 1974, Bruckert, et al., 2003, 48-51. In contrast there is the "counterfeit intimacy" approach, in which case, see Enck and Preston, 1988.

### PAGES 4-6:

*For more on Art Hicks*
See Whelan 1992, 137.

*Robert Hoyzer*
See Kerner, 2005.
Also interviews with Hoyzer and Milan Sapina.

*Michael Franzese*
See Mortensen 1991.

### PAGES 7-12:

*Play made up of dialogue between corruptors and corruptees in Prague*
See Zachovalova, 2007 and Czech Daily Monitor 2006.

*Describing bribes in covert talk:*
Zachovalova, 2007.

*Corruptors using neutral terms*
See, in particular, Sykes and Matza, 1957, 664.

*[the corruptors] would call it coffee money.*
Interview SO1.

*We will let people know that you took the money.*
Interview with LE5.

## CHAPTER 9 — CALLING THE FIX

### PAGES 1-3:

*English cricket and match-fixing in 1806*
See Pycroft 1922, chapter 4.

*On Beldham's attitude change*
See Pycroft 1922, 138.

*"you were in their arms for life"*
Interview with P6.

*For more on Franzese*
See interview with him from February 1999 and September 2011.

*that the players deliver the result.*
Interview with COR 1.

### PAGES 4-7:

*"The successful gambling corruptor has to avoid all these problems, and the challenges can be as difficult as fixing the actual game"*
See Konick, 2006.

*On fixing now being more difficult with the advent of early warning systems*
Interviews with Blatter: B23, SportRadar.

*Privately admit.*
Interviews with B14-18, 32.

*Drunken players story.*
Interview with B15.

*"Playing the middle..."*
Konick 2006, 40-60; also B5.

*Michael Konick as a "mule" in Las Vegas*
Essentially, these bookies steal the research and calculations of the professional gamblers for their own personal benefit. Strategies used by beard to place bets for others, Konick 2006, 18-110.

*Personal benefit.*
Interview with B6-8, 20.

*Beards placing bets.*
Interview with COR 1, 3-5, B6-8, 20.

*"muscle" can take over their network.*
Interview with COR 2, 4.

*Easier to fix the gambling market for big matches.*
Interview with COR1, 3-4; B14.

*Fixing the 'other' team.*
Interview with COR1-2.

*Placing bets late.*
Interview with COR 1.

### PAGES 10-14:

*For more information on "long term" as opposed to "one shot" games*
See Dasgupta 2000.

*Ways in which corruptors conceal paying players with a winning lottery ticket*
See, for example, Fernandez, 1993.

Note
Conversely, some interview subjects alleged that the payments of the players were augmented by putting their rewards as bets on the gambling market. This had a two-fold advantage, it increased the payout for the players, and it more readily guaranteed their cooperation with the fix.

*If a fix should go through a runner or an agent*
See, for example, Grobbelaar's discussion of "safe lock ups" at Selfridges in Thomas 2003.

*For places where payment takes place*
See Manap vs. Singapore PLP, 1996; Kurusamy vs. Singapore PLP, 1997; Malaysian Police Confession: no. 3.

## CHAPTER 10 — JUMPED OR PUSHED?

### PAGES 1-3:

*Tales of intimidation.*
For a compilation of similar types of stories see the *Daily Mail*, March 30, 1999, 77 "One player died in a mysterious accident and another found a cobra in his car. This is life in the twisted country of fixers and gambling

syndicates."
Also interviews with J 4 – 6.

*U. S. college basketball players being coerced*
See Whelan 1992, 139

## PAGES 4-7:

*Violence not being used as a tool of coercion*
See Tuncer 2005 as well as Kilinic 2005
Also interviews with COR 1, 3-4, LE 1-5.

*Enforcing player's continued involvement*
See Whelan, 1992, 139

*Gambling corruptor threatening a Liverpool player*
See Staff Writer, *The Daily Dispatch*, July 6, 1917

*Al Capone's dry cleaning racketeering*
See Landesco 1929, 156-160

*U. S. Army procurement contracts in South Korea*
See Klitgaard 1989, 134-55

## PAGES 8-10:

*Replacing laundry operators in Capone's dry cleaning scam*
See Landesco 1929, 156-60

*Sepp Blatter quote on footballers*
See staff writer, BBC, 2007

# CHAPTER 11 — TRUSTING ALL THE WRONG PEOPLE

## PAGES 1-3:

*Trust in Societies*
See Eric Uslaner 2005, 78.

*For more on the porn industry*
See the sex industry magazine *Adult Video News*, also Frederick S. Lane III, *Obscene Profits: The Entrepreneurs of Pornography in the Cyber Age*, Routledge, London, 2000 and Frank Rich, "Naked Capitalists", *New York Times Magazine*, May 20, 2001. For a sceptical view see, Dan Ackman, "How Big Is Porn?" *Forbes*, May 25, 2001.

*Asian Gambling Industry*
See Booth 2000, 378-379. Booth writes that Asian gambling profits are in the billions of dollars. In Hong Kong, alone, the legal gambling industries have been highly influential: "Complete universities, schools, hospitals and even Ocean Park, Asia's biggest seaquarium, have all been funded entirely from racing profits" (378-379).

*"$450 billion U.S. a year..."*
See Holliday 2006. Note this estimate also includes casinos, bingo halls and national lotteries, as well as sports betting. See also, Martin Booth, *The Dragon Syndicates: The Global Phenomenon of the Triads*, Bantam Books, London, 2000, 378-379.

*Asian steel industry*
See Liew, 2006.

*"$90 billion..."*
See WLA, 2009.

*"$500 million..."*
See Montague, 2011.
*"$1 trillion..."*
See work by Forrest 2012.

*War on Drugs*
Lupsha, 1986.

*Adidas comparison*
Buschman, 2011.

*Structure of Asian Sports Gambling Industry*
Interviews with B 1 – 4, 6 - 9, COR 1 – 2.

## PAGES 4-7:

*For more on the Sicilian mafia*
See Gambetta 1993, 230-234.

*Protection systems in Asian triads*
See Lintner 2002, 7-14; Posner, 1988.

*Range of bets*
Interviews with LE4, B 1 – 12. For a view of the formal side of the gambling market see: www.betfair.co.uk

*Change in technology and structure*
Interviews with LE3, B 1, 2, 4 – 12.

*Las Vegas*
See Konick 2006, 18-100.

*Asian bookmakers vs. European bookmakers*
According to professional gamblers, the British and American corporations are bookmakers only and therefore do not like to deal with consistently successful long-term bettors. Whereas Asian bookmaking syndicates are often gambling as well, so they will take the bets of their successful punter and then replicate their bets with other bookmakers (B1-4).

## PAGES 8-10:

*Betrayal is an imminent threat.*
Interviews with P2, 7: and Malaysian Police Confession, No. 5, 6.

*Trust in the enforcement*
Dasgupta 2000, 1.

*Reputational hostage taking*
See Rose-Ackerman 1999, 102-103.

*Informal gambling markets honouring pay-outs.*
Interviews with B 1 – 10, SO 6, 9, LE 1 – 4.

## PAGE 12:

*Long-term relationship*
See Good 1988, 3. In particular Good's discussion of the work of Pruitt and Kimmel. See also Axelrod and their finding that the long-term vs. short-term relationship as the key to understanding strategy games in the prisoner's dilemma experiment.

## CHAPTER 12 — JUMPING INTO FIXING

### PAGES 1-3:

The neo-Marxist School of Criminology does not seem to help either when examining this question. For its proponents, like Young or Taylor, (Young 2002; Taylor, et al., 1994) criminal deviancy can, at times, be explained by "social exclusion" or a variation on Merton's theory of disadvantaged working class youth. But again, professional football players, although mostly from the working class, are simply not excluded from society.

*"...arrangement type of fixing"*
See FIFPro 2012, 1-20.

*The most cited article in American sociology*
See Cole, 1975.

Many men, women and children adulate them: MIT and Manufacturing Foundation surveys, cited by Kuper 2005.

Both the Singapore and English Football Associations view potentially corrupt players as directly comparable to white-collar criminals. In an internal document (unpublished, 2003) circulated by their disciplinary committee they specifically compare potential match-fixing players who share information with corruptors as "analogous" to stock market insider trading (Zainal, Mohamed, Ali, Mohamed and Lomri, Ali — Disciplinary Hearing. no1-3/2003, 6. Disciplinary Committee, Football Association of Singapore 2003).

### PAGES 4-8:

*Database source*
For a full list and examples from this database see Appendix 6.

*Life history method of interviewing*
For a fuller discussion of this method see Atkinson,1998; Denzin, 1989; or the classic, *The Polish Peasant* by Thomas and Znaniecki, 1918.

*Anomie and Strain Theories*
For a good summation of this area, see Adler and Laufer, 1995.

*Ethnic grouping of players*
Interviews with SO 1 – 6.

*Sharecroppers as players*
SO1; SO5.

*Dominant sociological puzzles of the field*
See Katz, 1988 or Hoffman, 2002; Biblical mention see, for example, Proverbs 7, 7-27

### PAGES 9 -14:

*More details on Figure 12.1*
Seneviratne 2000, 110-116. The ages of four of the players that are unknown have been excluded, and this figure does not include the Malaysian confessions that may have been included in Seneviratne's work.

*Statistical source of Football League Fourth Division*
Football Association of England and Wales Annual 1961-62, 42.

*"The average professional football player, generally, starts his paid employment in the years between 19 and 22."*
Interview with SO1 and SO5; Football Association Annual 1962.

*Dick Hobbs quote Katz has other — American — criminals expressing similar views*
See Katz 1988, 215.

*On physical capital*
Pierre Bourdieu's ideas are explored by Wainwright and Turner when they write that physical capital (shape, gait, posture, etc) were products of our social environment so that upper-class women will, for example, have different bodies and practice different sports than lower-class women (Wainwright and Turner 2006). See also Wheeler, et al. 1991, for a discussion of similar themes.

*Making money now*
Interviews with P 6, 8, 10.

## CHAPTER 13 — WHY SOME BUT NOT OTHERS?

### PAGES 1-3:

*It is difficult to do justice to the entire range of discussion that Sutherland's original ideas have generated*
See also Sykes and Matza, 1966; and Kornhauser, 1978 but in brief, these authors are arguing that criminal behaviour does not only arise from a lack of economic or social opportunities (Merton and Agnew), but rather from a plethora of criminal opportunities. Sutherland originally wrote of the nine explanatory factors for deviancy, the key ones for analyzing match-fixing in professional football are the second and third:

*On criminal behaviour*
Criminal behaviour is learned in interaction with other persons in a process of communication. The principal part of the learning of criminal behaviour occurs within intimate personal groups. See also Cressey, 1960; Matsueda, 1988; Reinarman and Fagan, 1988 as well as Waring et al. 1995, 207-225.

### PAGES 4-6:

*Senior players teaching younger players to fix*
Interviews with LE2, P2-3, J8, SO7.

*Note on role of international players being heavily represented in the database*
There may be sample bias as the database is mostly composed of widely-publicised cases. International players would, in general, receive more press attention then ordinary players.

*Goalkeepers' role in fixing*
See Gregg, 2002; St. John, and Lawton 2006; Tuncer, 2006.

*Rajendran Kurusamy testimony*
See Singapore PP vs. Maran et al., 1997

*lower divisions and lesser leagues*
See Sharpe 1997, 84.

### PAGES 7-9:

*Number of international players in a league*
See Football Association, 1962.

*Indian bookmakers and cricket fixing*
See Cronje 2002 as well as Craddock, 2004.

*Player who loved a bet*
Interviews with P 6, 7, SO 9 and J 4.

*"Publicly-professed morality"*
In Malaysia, there were several players, who at least when caught, quoted Biblical or Islamic scripture (see, for example, Staff Writer, *Malay Mail,* February 23, March 7, 1994).

### PAGES 10-13:

*"Reputation as a completely straight person…"*
Gabbert 1964, x.

*Charitable institutions*
Lambsdorff 2005, 138.

## CHAPTER 14 — SINS OF OMISSION

### PAGES 1-3:

*For legal cases involving match-fixing*
See, for example, (UK) Grobbelaar vs. News Group Newspapers Ltd. and Another, 2002 (Singapore) Public Prosecutor vs. Manap bin Hamat & Anor, 1997.

*Genoa vs. Venice Fix*
Dellacasa, 2005; Hawkey, 2005; Preziosi, 2005.

*Juventus vs. Bologna Fix*
Petrini 1999, 110-122.

*Canada vs. North Korea Fix*
McKeown, 1989; Da Costa, 1995 and Interview with P15.

### PAGES 4-7:

*Two types of corruption*
See also Morton, 1993; Skolnick, 2005. Lambsdorff, 2007 and others write of types or kinds of corruption: "clientalist, grand, market, monopolistic, patrimonial and petty" or the corrupt networks rising from "party, clans, gangs and entrepreneurial." However, what I am writing of is the *mechanisms* of specific acts of corruption. For more see Aquinas 1920, 71-89.

*Honest players do not know what is going on*
Interviews with P6 - 7, 13, COR1, SO10.

*Two types of fixing*
Supdt 2000, 2 — finds a similar pattern in match-fixing cricketers; Pallo 1985, chapters 1-3; Ibid, 5-20.

*Difficulty of judging referees' performances*
Interviews with R1 – 3, SO 24.

*Edílson Pereira de Carvalho Case*
See Rizek, 2005.

*The Hansie Cronje affair*
See King, 2002 as well as the section on "publicly professed morality" in this book, Chapter 13.

*British players in the 1960s*
Borissow et al. 1960, ii.

*"Foot off" underperforming*
See interview with CO1, P6-8 as well as Petrini, 1999

### PAGES 8-10:

*Finnish player*
See staff writer, Ilta-Sansomet 2005.

*Corrupt English goalkeeper*
See Gabbert 1963, ii as well as Clough 2003, 69.
*Liverpool vs. Manchester United fix*
See staff writer, Daily Dispatch 1917.

## CHAPTER 15 — SINS OF COMMISSION

### PAGES 1-3:

*For more on Soviet chess and Japanese Sumo wrestling fixes*
See Moul, 2006 and Levitt, 2005 respectively.

### PAGES 4-7:

*1966 European Champion Clubs' Cup Semi-Final*
See Glanville 1991, 110-112
Football Against the Enemy
See Kuper 1994, 37.

### PAGES 9-11:

*On informants*
See, for example, Kuper 1994, 34.

## CHAPTER 16 — A CRITICALLY CORRUPT LEAGUE

### PAGES 1-4:

*Yang Zuwu protesting Chinese Super League (CSL)*
See interview with SO10; China.org.cn by Shao Da, October 31, 2004; China Super League website; Blatter, 2008.

*China's struggles for football credibility*
See interview with SO10; see also Watts 2004; Gidney 2007.

### PAGES 5-8:

*Demise of Malaysian-Singaporean football*
See interviews with SO7; R1; SO1; J4; J5; J8; P2; COR1; and SO13.

*Bookies being one step ahead at all times*
See P1-8; SO1-4; see also Fernandez 1993.

*Links between corruptors and sports officials*
Interviews with SO13, COR1 - 2.

*Early-to-mid 1990s in Malaysia and Singapore*
During this time both newspapers in Singapore and Malaysia ran frequent articles about the match-fixing investigations that were going on in their respective countries. Two such examples are: Chong, Elena. "Trial begins with dispute over statement: Match-fixing of S-League games," *Singapore Straits Times*, September 9, 1997: and Fernandez,

Johnson, "How do you pin down a racket? Officials are into it too." *The Malay Mail.* Kuala Lumpur, July 29, 1993.

*For more on public crime*
Or in criminological terms, Thomas Gabor's 1994 book *Everybody Does It* which argues that "most, if not all of us break laws, formal rules, and other social conventions at some point" (cited by Weisburd et al. 2001, 148).

*Widespread fixing and corruption in Malaysian football*
There was a similar case allegedly in the Zimbabwean Football Association in 2011, when according to a report written by the ZFA many of the officials, players and journalists covering the matches had been on the pay of a group of Asian match-fixers.

### PAGES 9-12:

*Senior police officers getting mixed up in corruption*
See J3-5, 8-9

*"Critical mass"*
See Marwell and Oliver (1993) for a more detailed discussion of the term, "critical mass." Although, it should be noted that they were using it in connection with crowds and collective actions.

*"Grand corruption"*
See Andvig 2000, 18-20.

*On cognitive dissonance*
Festinger 1962, 2 (see also footnote 19) — used the example of the person who believes that smoking causes lung cancer, yet continues to smoke.

*Interview on football associations being "so corrupt they do not know they are being corrupt"*
See Sugden and Tomlinson 2003, 155.

## CHAPTER 17 — WHY SOME LEAGUES BUT NOT OTHERS?

### PAGES 1-3:

The Corruption Perceptions Index (CPI)
Published by the international non-governmental not-for-profit organisation Transparency International which was founded in Berlin in 1993. For more information on the Corruptions Perception Index please see Chapter 1 or Lambsdorff 2007, 20-6 and CPI 2012 — www.transparency.org.

*Assumptions that Malaysia and Singapore still have match-fixing.*
Interviews with SO 1 – 4, 8, 9, 11: J 2 – 4, LE 1 – 5, B 6, 7: P 6 - 9.

*For more on Stanley Matthews*
See Bartholomew 2005, Chapter 1.

*Scottish Fix*
See St. John and Lawton 2006, 62-65.

### PAGE 4-7:

*Illegal gambling*
See Preston and Szymanski, 2003. Also — Michael Franzese, the former capo of a New York Mafia family, estimated that illegal sports gambling contributed over half of the revenue of American organised crime as per Mortensen, 1991.

*Conditions in Singapore sports gambling*
See Moore, 1999. Also interviews with SO 8, 11; COR1 - 2.

*Conditions in UK sports gambling*
See Vamplew 1988 as well as Inglis 1985, 20-30.

*Prohibition in the United States*
See Lupsha, 1986.

*Latent functionalism*
See Merton 1968, 71-76.

### PAGES 7 -11:

*White City and labour strike*
See Imlach 2005, 55. Also interviews with Harry Gregg and Tommy Banks, September 2005, May 2008, June 2013.

*"Relative deprivation"*
See Runciman, 1967; Merton, 1950; Yngwe, et al. 2003; also Van Rijckeghem and Weder, 2001 on income and relative deprivation.

## CHAPTER 18 — THE DEATH OF A LEAGUE

### PAGES 1-3:

*Chinese football*
See Gittings 2002; Staff Writer, *Shanghai Star*, 2002.

*"Institutional public dilemma"*
See Inglis 1985, vi-viii.

*The game as a product*
See Szymanski and Kuypers 1999, 7.

*"Loneliness of the honest policeman..."*
See Whyte 1940, 132-137.

*Journalists banned for exposing corruption*
See Inglis 1985, 202.

### PAGES 4-7:

*More on Chinese football*
See interview J24; Gittings 2002; and Staff Writers www.chinasuperleague.com, 2002.

*More on the Luciano Moggi case*
Burke, 2006 as well as staff writer, La Stampa, 2006.

*UEFA and integrity officers*
Please See Oberli, 2010 as well as SO25 and SO32.

*Limacher story*
See Oberli, 2010; SO29-31.

*Pejović story*
FIFPro, 2012. — After a long battle Pejović was able to return to the sport.

### PAGES 8-10:

*Bellini Case*
See O7; see also Hall Hero, *Scapegoat, Martyr*, 1999.

*Havelange Case*
See Yallop 1999, 73, 210.

*China and the Freedom House*
China has a ranking of 84 with 100 being the worst rank possible. Vietnam is at 77. For comparison the United States,

Canada and the United Kingdom have rankings of 16, 17 and 19 respectively; while North Korea has a rank of 97 (Report of Press Freedoms, Freedom House, New York, 2007. Available at www.freedomhouse.org

*The alternative market effect*
Interviews with SO1-4, 10: Blatter, 2008; and JE 3,40.

*Arsenal vs. Manchester United*
Interview with J7 and 40: and ESPN media, January 2008.

*Collapse of leagues*
Interviews with SO1-4, 15.

## CHAPTER 19 — THE DEATH OF A SPORT

### PAGES 1-3:

*Suicide of South Korean player*
See Orlowitz, 2012.

*Other deaths related to match-fixing*
See Ibid and Hill 2010, i.

*Series of police and judicial investigation*
Rovaniemi, 2011; Salvini, 2012; ZIFA and Greek Anti-Corruption Agency Report. Interviews with LE1, 10, 12 and 15.

*Chinese soccer scandal*
See Minter, 2011.

*Other soccer scandals in Asia*
See Hill, 2010.

*Cabinet Minister's estimate of extent of fixing*
See Williams, 115. Interviews also with SO12 and LE4.

### PAGES 4-7:

*Vietnam and SEA Games*
See Hill, 2010.

*Extent of corruption in some Asian sports*
See Nunns, 2012 as well as Levitt, et al., 2002.

*Asian fans turning to international sports*
See Hill, 2010.
*Range of sports possible to bet on*
See www.betfair.co.uk — accessed September 28, 2013.
Interviews with B2-12.

*Running ball and gambling monitors*
Visit www.rball.com — September 28, 2013.

*Tivoli Cup and gambling monitors*
Interviews with B 2 -12 and SO 24, 25.

*Europol investigation*
See http://tinyurl.com/ps24m34 (September 28, 2013).

*Zimbabwean match-fixing report*
ZIFA report, 2011.

*Match-fixing extent*
See Salvini, 2011.

*Business strategies of corruptors and team owners*
Interviews with COR 7 - 8.

*FIFPro Report*
http://tinyurl.com/pp797d2 September 28, 2013.

## CHAPTER 20 — HOW WE CAN WIN

### PAGES 1-3:

*Money launderer's excuse*
See Mazur, 2009.

*Number of fixed badminton matches*
See Fitzgerald, 2012 as well as video at www.telegraph.co.uk/sport/olympics.badminton/not-the-first-time-China-have-tried-to-manipulate-results-html. (available October 1st, 2013)

*Tournament incentives for fixing in the NBA*
See Trogdon et al, 2006.

*"Disparity of desire"*
See Preston and Szymanski, 2003.

### PAGES 4 -10:

*Merit payments in Premier League*
Visit http://tinyurl.com/kwvpmvv September 28, 2013.

*Fixing in cricket*
See Supdt, 2000; Condon, 2001.

*Kay, Layne and Swan Case*
See Swan, 2006.

*Cricket fixing*
See Condon 2001.

*New York Police Department reports on their anti-corruption measures*
Visit: http://www.nyc.gov/html/ccpc/html/reports/reports.shtml
Interviews LE 10, O 8.

*Tennis Fixing*
Association of Tennis Professionals — ATP 2005.

*Payment of high salaries to stop corruption*
The long serving president of Singapore Lee Kwan Yu is famous for espousing this view: See also the academics Van Rijckeghem and Weder, 2001.

## ACKNOWLEDGEMENTS

*Four stages of acceptance of a new idea*
See J.B.S. Haldane, Journal of Genetics #58, 1963, 464.

# BIBLIOGRAPHY

## BOOKS

Aburish, Said K. *Pay-Off: Wheeling and Dealing in the Arab World*. London: Andre Deutsch, 1985.

Adams, Tony. *Tony Adams Addicted: His Open and Inspiring Autobiography*. London: Collins Willow, 1998.

Adler, F and Laufer, W.S. (eds). *The Legacy of Anomie Theory: Advances in Criminological Theory. Advances in Criminological Theory*. Ed. F and Laufer Adler, W.S.(eds). Vol. 6. New Brunswick, New Jersey: Transaction Publishers, 1995.

Akers, Ronald. *Social Learning and Social Structure: A General Theory of Crime and Deviance*. Boston: Northeastern University Press, 1998.

Alabarces, Pablo, ed. *Futbologías: Fútbol, Identidad Y Violencia En América Latina*. Buenos Aires: CLASCSO — Consejo Latinoamericano de Ciencias Sociales, 2003.

Alatas, Syed Hussein. *Corruption: Its Nature, Causes and Functions*. Aldershot: Avebury, 1990.

Anderson, Annelise Graebner. *The Business of Organised Crime: A Cosa Nostra Family*. Stanford, California: Hoover Institution Press, Stanford University, 1979.

Andvig, Jens C. *Issues of Corruption: A Policy-Oriented Survey of Research*. Chr. Michelsen Institute (CMI) and Norwegian Institute of International Affairs (NUPI), Oslo, 2000.

Anonymous. *Man of Respect: The True Story of a Mafia Assassin*. Trans. Avril Bardoni. London: Pan, 1991.

Aquinas, Thomas. *Summa Theologica of St. Thomas Aquinas*. Trans. Fathers of the English Dominican Province. Second and Revised ed. London: Online edition, 1920. Available at www.newadvent.org/summa.

Arlacchi, Pino. *Mafia Business: The Mafia Ethic and the Spirit of Capitalism*. Trans. Martin Ryle. London: The Imprint of New Left Books, 1986.

Arthur, Max. *The Manchester United Aircrash: 25th Anniversary Tribute to the Busby Babes*. Aquarius Design and Print, 1982.

Asinof, Eliot. *Eight Men Out: The Black Sox and the 1919 World Series*. New York: Henry Holt, 1987.

Askwith, Richard. *Feet in the Clouds: A Tale of Fell-Running and Obsession.* London: Aurum Press, 2004.

Atkinson, Robert. *The Life Story Interview. Qualitative Research Methods.* Ed. John Van Maanen. London: Sage, 1998.

Auger, Michel. *The Biker Who Shot Me: Recollections of a Crime Reporter.* Trans. Jean-Paul Murray. Toronto: McClelland & Stewart, 2001.

Ball, Phil. Morbo: *The Story of Spanish Football.* London: WSC Books, 2001.

— White Storm: 1*00 Years of Real Madrid.* Edinburgh and London: Mainstream, 2002.

Banfield, C.E. *The Moral Basis of a Backward Society.* New York. The Free Press, 1958.

Banks, Simon. *Going Down: Football in Crisis, How the Game Went from Boom to Bust.* Edinburgh and London: Mainstream Publishing, 2002.

Barker, Thomas and Roebuck, Julian. *An Empirical Typology of Police Corruption: A Study in Organizational Deviance.* Springfield, Illinois: Charles C Thomas, 1973.

Bartholomew, James. *The Welfare State We're In.* London: Politico, 2005.

Barzel, Yoram. *Economic Analysis of Property Rights.* Cambridge: Cambridge University Press, 1989.

Beha, Oliviero and Chiodi, Roberto. *Mundialgate.* Rome: Avagliana Editore, 2005.

Bellos, Alex. F*utebol: The Brazilian Way of Life.* London: Bloomsbury, 2002.

Benedict, Jeffrey R. *Athletes and Acquaintance Rape.* Ed. C. Terry Hendrix. London: SAGE Publications Ltd., 1998.

Berger, Ronald J., Free, Marvin D. and Searles, Patricia. *Crime, Justice and Society.* Boulder, Colorado: Lynne Rienner Inc, 2005.

Berne, Eric. *Games People Play: The Psychology of Human Relationships.* London: The Quality Book Club, 1964.

Bernès, Jean-Pierre with Bernard Pascuito. *Je Dis Tout: Les Secrets De l'OM sous Tapie.* Paris: Albin Michel, 1995.

Bernstein, Peter L. *Against the Gods: The Remarkable Story of Risk.* New York: John Wiley & Sons, 1996.

Berri, David J., Schmidt, Martin B., Brook, Stacey. *The Wages of Wins: Taking Measure of the Many Myths in Modern Sport.* Stanford, California: Stanford University Press, 2006.

Blok, Anton. *The Mafia of a Sicilian Village 1860-1960: A Study of Violent Peasant Entrepreneurs.* Pavilion Series. Ed. F.G. Bailey. Oxford: Basil Blackwell, 1974.

Boli, Basile with Claude Askalovitch. *Black Boli*. Paris: Bernard Brasset, 1994.

Boock, Richard and Fleming, Stephen. *Balance of Power*. Auckland: Hodder Moa Beckett, 2004.

Booth, Martin. *The Dragon Syndicates: The Global Phenomenon of the Triads*. London: Bantam Books, 2000.

Bose, Mihir. *Manchester Unlimited the Rise and Rise of the World's Premier Football Club*. London: Orion Business Books, 1999.

Brown, Adam (ed). *Fanatics! Power, Identity, and Fandom in Football*. 1st ed. London: Routledge, 1998.

Burke, Roger Hopkins. *An Introduction to Criminological Theory*. Cullompton, Devon: Willan Publishing, 2005.

Burns, Jimmy. *Barça A People's Passion*. London: Bloomsbury, 2009.

Cameron, A. *Circus Factions: Blues and Greens at Rome and Byzantium*. Oxford: Clarendon Press, 1976.

Clarke, Michael. *Business Crime: Its Nature and Control*. Cambridge: Polity Press, 1990.

Clinard, Marshall B., and Yeager, Peter C. *Corporate Crime*. New York: Free Press, 1980.

Clough, Brian with John Sadler. *Cloughie: Walking on Water — My Life*. London: Headline Book Publishing, 2003.

Cloward, Richard A. and Ohlin, Lloyd. *Delinquency and Opportunity: A Theory of Delinquent Gangs*. London: Routledge, 1998.

Coakley, Jay and Dunning, Eric, (eds), *Handbook of Sports Studies*. London: Sage Publishing, 2000.

Connor, Jeff. T*he Lost Babes: Manchester United and the Forgotten Victims of Munich*. London: HarperSport, 2006.

Cook, Karen Schweers and Levi, Margaret. *The Limits of Rationality*. Chicago: University of Chicago Press, 1990.

Corrupt Practices Investigation Bureau. *Swift and Sure Action: Four Decades of Anti-Corruption Work*. Singapore: CPIB (self-published), 2000

Cosgrave, James F. (ed). *The Sociology of Risk and Gambling Reader*. Abingdon, Oxon: Routledge, 2006.

Cressey, Donald R. Theft of the Nation: *The Structure and Operations of Organised Crime in America*. New York: HarperCollins, 1969.

Crick, Michael and Smith, David. *Manchester United: The Betrayal of a Legend*. London: Pan Books, 1990.

Croall, Hazel. *Understanding White Collar Crime*. Buckingham, UK: Open University Press, 2001.

Crouch, Colin. *Social Change in Western*

*Europe*. Oxford: Oxford University Press, 1999.

de Coninck, Douglas. *Gokziek: Ons Voetbal in Handen Van de Chinese Gokmaffia*. Antwerp: Lampedaire, 2009.

de Sardan, Jean-Pierre Olivier. *Anthropology and Development: Understanding Contemporary Social Change*. London: Zed Books, 2005.

Della Porta, Donatella and Vannucci, Alberto. *Corrupt Exchanges: Actors, Resources, and Mechanisms of Political Corruption*. New York: Walter Gruyter, 1999.

Dempsey, Paul and Reilly, Kevan. *Big Money, Beautiful Game: Saving Soccer from Itself*. London: Nicholas Brealey Publishing, 1998.

Denzin, Norman. *Interpretive Biography*. Newbury Park: Sage, 1989.

Derber, C. *The Wilding of America: How Greed and Violence Are Eroding Our Nation's Character*. New York: St. Martin's, 1996.

Desailly, Marcel with Philippe Broussard. *Capitaine*. Paris: Stock, 2002.

Dobson, Stephen and Goddard, John. *The Economics of Football*. Cambridge: Cambridge University Press, 2001.

Dodd, Christopher. *The Story of World Rowing*. London: Stanley Paul, 1992.

Dowding, Keith. *Power: Concepts in Social Sciences*. Ed. Frank Parkin. Buckingham: Open University Press, 1996.

Dubro, James. *Dragons of Crime*. Toronto: McClelland and Stewart, 1992.

Dubro, James, and Rowland, Robin. *Undercover: Cases of the RCMP's Most Secret Operative*. Toronto: McClelland and Stewart, 1992.

— *King of the Mob*. Markham, Ontario, Canada: Penguin, 1987.

Dunning, Eric. *The Sociology of Sport*. New Sociology Library. Ed. Norbert Elias. London: Frank Cass and Company, 1971.

Durkheim, Émile. *Suicide: A Study in Sociology*. Trans. George Simpson John A. Spaulding. London: Routledge & Kegan Paul, 1952.

— *The Elementary Forms of Religious Life*. Trans. Karen. E. Fields. New York, London: Free Press, 1995.

Dyer, William. *Team Building: Issues and Alternatives*. Reading, Mass. Addison-Wesley, 1977.

Eichenwald, Kurt. *The Informant*. New York: Random House, 2000.

Elleray, David. *The Man in the Middle*. London: Time Warner, 2004.

Elliott, Kimberly Ann, (ed). *Corruption and the Global Economy*. Washington:

Institute for International Economics, 1997.

Elster, Jon. *Ulysses and the Sirens: Studies in Rationality and Irrationality*. Cambridge: Cambridge University Press, 1985.

— *Sour Grapes: Studies in the Subversion of Rationality*. Cambridge: Cambridge University Press, 1985.

— *Nuts and Bolts for the Social Sciences*. Cambridge: Cambridge University Press, 1989.

Eydelie, Jean-Jacques and Biet, Michel. *Je Ne Joue Plus! Un Footballeur Brise L'Omerta*. Paris: L'Archipel, 2006.

Falcone, Giovanni with Padovani, Marcelle. *Men of Honour: Truth About the Mafia*. Trans. Edward Farrelly. London: Warner, 1992.

Ferguson, Alex with Hugh McIlvanney. *Managing My Life: My Autobiography*. London: Coronet Books, 2000.

Ferris, Ken. *Football Fanatic: A Record Breaking Journey through English Football*. London: Mainstream, 2000.

Festinger, Leon. *A Theory of Cognitive Dissonance*. Stanford, California: Stanford University Press, 1957.

Fiorentini, Gianluca and Peltzman, Sam. *The Economics of Organised Crime*. Cambridge: Cambridge University Press, 1997.

Foer, Franklin. *How Soccer Explains the World: An Unlikely Theory of Globalization*. New York: HarperCollins, 2004.

Follain, John. *A Dishonoured Society*. London: Little, Brown, 1995.

Follorou, Jacques and Nouzille, Vincent. *Les Parrains Corses: Leur Histoire, Leurs Réseaux, Leurs Protections*. Paris: J'ai Lu — Librairie Artheme Fayard, 2004.

Foot, John. *Calcio: A History of Italian Football*. London: Fourth Estate, 2006.

Ford, Trevor. *I Lead the Attack*. London: Stanley Paul, 1957.

Foucault, Michel. *Discipline and Punish: The Birth of the Prison*. Trans. Alan Sheridan. London: Allen Lane, 1977.

Freeman, Simon. *Own Goal! How Egotism and Greed Are Destroying Football*. London: Orion, 2000.

Friedman, Robert I. *Red Mafiya: How the Russian Mob Has Invaded America*. Boston: Little Brown, 2000.

Gabor, Thomas. *Everybody Does It!: Crime by the Public*. Toronto: University of Toronto Press, 1994.

Galeano, Eduardo. *Soccer in Sun and Shadow*. Trans. Mark Fried. English ed. London: Verso, 1999.

Gambetta, Diego. *Were They Pushed or Did They Jump? Individual Decision Mechanisms in Education. Studies in Rationality and Social Change.* Cambridge: Cambridge University Press, 1987.

— *The Sicilian Mafia. The Business of Private Protection.* Harvard: Harvard University Press, 1996.

— *Trust: Making and Breaking Cooperative Relations.* Oxford: Basil Blackwell, 1988.

— *Making Sense of Suicide Missions.* Oxford: Oxford University Press, 2006.

— *Crimes and Signs. Cracking the Codes of the Underworld.* Princeton: Princeton University Press, forthcoming.

Giulianotti, Richard. *Football: A Sociology of the Global Game.* Cambridge: Polity Press, 1999.

Gladwell, Malcolm. *The Tipping Point: How Little Things Can Make a Big Difference.* Boston: Little, Brown and Company, 2002.

Gladwin, Christina H. *Ethnographic Decision Tree Modelling. Qualitative Research Methods Series. Vol. 19.* London: Sage, 1989.

Glanville, Brian. *Champions of Europe: The History, Romance and Intrigue of the European Cup.* Enfield: Guinness Publishing, 1991.

— *The Story of the World Cup.* London: Faber and Faber, 1997.

Goldstock, Ronald, Marcus, Martin, Thacher, Thomas D. II and Jacobs, James B. *Corruption and Racketeering in the New York City Construction Industry: Final Report to Governor Mario M. Cuomo from the New York State Organised Crime Task Force. Construction Industry Project.* Ed. Thomas D. II Thacher. New York: New York University Press, 1990.

Goldthorpe, John H. *On Sociology: Numbers, Narratives, and the Integration of Research and Theory.* Oxford: Oxford University Press, 2000.

Gottfredson, Michael R. and Hirschi, Travis. *A General Theory of Crime.* Stanford: Stanford University Press, 1990.

Gregg, Harry, and Anderson, Roger. *Harry's Game: The Autobiography.* London: Mainstream, 2002.

Guest, Alex and Fynn, Lynton. *For Love or Money: Manchester United and England — the Business of Winning.* London: Boxtree, 1998.

Halladay, Eric. *Rowing in England: A Social History: The Amateur Debate. International Studies in the History of Sport.* Ed. J.A. Mangan. Manchester: Manchester University Press, 1990.

Hamil, Sean, Michie, Jonathan, Oughton, Christine and Warby, Steven (eds).

*Football in the Digital Age: Whose Game Is It Anyway?* London: Mainstream, 2000.

Handelman, Stephen. *Comrade Criminal: The Theft of the Second Russian Revolution.* Michael Joseph: London, 1994.

Hardaker, Alan with Butler, Byron. *Hardaker of the League.* London: Pelham Books, 1977.

Hargreaves, John. *Sport, Power and Culture: A Social and Historical Analysis of Popular Sports in Britain.* Cambridge: Polity Press, 1991.

Harriss, John, Hunter, Janet, and Lewis, Colin (eds). *The New Institutional Economics and Third World Development.* London: Routledge, 1995.

Hedstrom, Peter and Swedberg, Richard, (eds). *Social Mechanisms: An Analytical Approach to Social Theory.* Cambridge: Cambridge University Press, 1998.

Henry, Stuart and Einstadter, Werner (eds). *The Criminology Theory Reader.* New York: New York University Press, 1998.

Heywood, Paul, ed. *Political Corruption: Problems and Perspectives.* Oxford: Blackwell Publishers, 1997.

Hill, Declan. *The Fix: Soccer and Organised Crime.* 2nd edition, Toronto: McClelland & Stewart, 2010.

Hill, Jeff. *Sport, Leisure and Culture in Twentieth-Century Britain.* Basingstoke: Palgrave, 2002.

Hill, Peter B.E. *The Japanese Mafia: Yakuza, Law, and the State.* Oxford: Oxford University Press, 2003.

Hobbs, Dick. *Bad Business: Professional Crime in Modern Britain.* Oxford: Oxford University Press, 2003.

Hobsbawn, E.J. *Bandits.* London: Penguin, 1969.

Horoszowski, Pawel. *Economic Special-Opportunity Conduct and Crime.* Lexington, Massachusetts: Lexington Books, 1980.

Huntington, Samuel P. *Political Order in Changing Societies.* New Haven, Connecticut: Yale University Press, 1968.

Hutchison, T.W. *The Significance and Basic Postulates of Economic Theory.* London: MacMillan and Co., Ltd, 1938.

— *Knowledge and Ignorance in Economics.* Oxford: Basil Blackwell, 1977.

Imlach, Gary. *My Father and Other Working-Class Heroes.* London: Yellow Jersey, 2005.

Inglis, Simon. *Soccer in the Dock: A History of British Football Scandals, 1900-1965.* London: Willow Books, 1985.

Jackson, Bruce. *A Thief's Primer.* London: Collier-Macmillan Ltd., 1969.

Jackson, Jon. *On Edge: Backroom Dealing, Cocktail Scheming, Triple Axels, and How Top Skaters Get Screwed.* New York: Thunder's Mouth Press, 2005.

Jacoby, Joseph E. (ed). *Classics of Criminology.* Long Grove, Illinois: Waveland, 2004.

Jacoby, Neil H., Nehemkis, Peter and Eells, Richard. *Bribery and Extortion in World Business: A Study of Corporate Political Payments Abroad. Studies of the Modern Corporation.* Ed. Columbia University Graduate School of Business. New York: MacMillan Publishing Co, 1977.

Jankowski, Martin Sanchez. *Islands in the Street: Gangs and American Urban Society.* Berkeley: University of California Press, 1992.

Jennings, Andrew. *Foul! The Secret World of FIFA: Bribes, Vote Rigging and Ticket Scandals.* London: Harper Sport, 2006.

Jennings, Andrew and Simson, Vyv. *The Lords of the Rings: Power, Money and Drugs in the Modern Olympics.* London: Simon & Schuster, 1992.

Johnson, Graham. *Football and Gangsters.* London: Mainstream, 2006.

Johnson, Tim and Sprake, Stuart. *Careless Hands: The Forgotten Truth of Gary Sprake.* Stroud: Tempus Publishing, 2006.

Kapuściński, Richard. *The Soccer War.* Trans, William Brand. London: Granta Books (in association with Penguin), 1990.

Katz, Jack. *Seductions of Crime: Moral and Sensual Attractions in Doing Evil.* New York: Basic Books, 1988.

Kelly, Robert J. *The Upperworld and the Underworld: Case Studies of Racketeering and Business Infiltrations in the United States.* Criminal Justice and Public Safety. Ed. Philip John Stead. New York: Kluwer Academic/Plenum Publishers, 1999.

Keohane, Robert O. *After Hegemony: Cooperation and Discord in the World Political Economy.* Princeton: Princeton University Press, 1984.

King, Roy D. and Wincup, Emma, (eds). *Doing Research on Crime and Justice.* Oxford: Oxford University Press, 2000.

Klitgaard, Robert. *Controlling Corruption.* Berkeley: University of California Press. 1989.

Konick, Michael. *Smart Money: How the World's Best Sports Bettors Beat the Bookies out of Millions.* New York: Simon & Schuster, 2006.

Kornhauser, Ruth. *Social Structures of Delinquency.* Chicago: University of Chicago Press, 1978.

Krugman, Paul R. *The Age of Diminished*

*Expectations: U.S. economic policy in the 1990s*. Cambridge, Mass. MIT Press, 1996.

Kuper, Simon. *Football Against the Enemy*. London: Orion, 1994.

Lambsdorff, Johann Graf. *The Institutional Economics of Corruption and Reform: Theory, Evidence and Policy*. Cambridge: Cambridge University Press, 2007.

Lambsdorff, Johann Graf, Taube, Markus and Schramm, Matthias. *The New Institutional Economics of Corruption. Frontiers of Political Economy*. London: Routledge, 2005.

Landesco, John. *Organised Crime in Chicago: Part III of the Illinois Crime Survey 1929*. [1968 ed]. Chicago: The University of Chicago Press, 1968.

Lane, Frederick S. III. *Obscene Profits: The Entrepreneurs of Pornography in the Cyber Age*. London: Routledge, 2000.

Lane, Frederic Chapin. *Venice: A Maritime Republic*. Baltimore, London: John Hopkins University Press, 1973.

Lanfranchi, Pierre, Eisenberg, Christiane, Mason, Tony and Wahl, Alfred. *100 Years of Football: The FIFA Centennial Book*. London: Weidenfeld & Nicolson, 2004.

Lansley, Peter. *Running with Wolves*. Newport: Thomas Publications, 2004.

Lasch, Christopher. *The Culture of Narcissism: American Life in an Age of Diminishing Expectations*. New York: Norton, 1979.

Lecasble, Valérie and Routier, Airy, *Le flambeur: La vraie vie de Bernard Tapie*. Paris: Bernard Grasset, 1994.

Leith, Alex. *Over the Moon, Brian: Language of Football*. London: Boxtree, 1998.

Levin, James and Fox, James. *Overkill*. New York: Dell Publishing, 1994.

Levine, Donald and Goddard, Michael. *Undercover*. London: Grafton Books, 1991.

Lévi-Strauss, Claude. *Sociologie et anthropologie*. Paris: Presses des universitaires de France, 1950.

Levy, Brian and Kpundeh, Sahr (eds). *Building State Capacity in Africa: New Approaches, Emerging Lessons*. Washington: World Bank Institute, 2004.

Likert, Rensis. *New Patterns of Management*. New York. McGraw-Hill, 1961.

Lin, Nan. *Social Capital: A Theory of Social Structure and Action*. Cambridge: Cambridge University Press, 2002.

Lintner, Bertil. *Blood Brothers: Crime Business & Politics in Asia*. Sydney: Allen & Unwin, 2002.

Lovell, Stephen, Ledeneva, Alena and Rogacheskii, Andrei. *Bribery and Blat in Russia: Negotiating Reciprocity from the Middle Ages to the 1990s*. Studies in Russian and Eastern History and Society. Ed. R.W Davies. London: MacMillan Press Ltd., 2000.

Lowe, Mick. *Conspiracy of Brothers: A True Story of Murder, Bikers and the Law.* Toronto: Macmillan Canada, 1989.

Maguire, Mike; Morgan, Rod, and Reiner, Robert, (eds). *The Oxford Handbook of Criminology*. Oxford: Oxford University Press, 2002.

Mainstream Publishing Staff (eds). *Power, Corruption and Pies: Twelve Years of the Best Football Writing from When Saturday Comes*. Edinburgh: Mainstream, 1999.

Mangan, J.A. (ed). *Militarism, Sport, Europe: War Without Weapons*. The European Sports History Review. Vol. 5. London: Frank Cass, 2003.

Maradona, Diego: Arcucci, Daniel and Cherquis Bialo, Ernesto. *Yo Soy El Diego de la Gente*. La Habana, Cuba: Instituto Cubano del Libro, 2001.

Mars, Gerald. *Cheats at Work — An Anthropology of Workplace Crime*. London: Unwin, 1982.

Marwell, Gerald and Oliver, Pamela. *The Critical Mass in Collective Action*. Cambridge: Cambridge University Press, 1993.

Mason, Richard and Holt, Tony. *Sport in Britain 1945-2000. Making Contemporary Britain*. Ed. Anthony Seldon. 2000 ed. London: Blackwell, 2000.

Mauss, Marcel. *The Gift: Forms and Functions of Exchange in Archaic Societies*. London: Cohen & West, 1954.

McGinniss, Joe. *The Miracle of Castel Di Sangro*. London: Little, Brown and Company, 1999.

McIlvanney, Hugh. *McIlvanney on Football*. London: Mainstream, 1994.

McLean, Iain. *Public Choice: An Introduction*. Oxford: Blackwell, 1994.

McLean, Iain and Urken, Arnold B. (eds). *Classics of Social Choice*. Ann Arbor: The University of Michigan Press, 1995.

McLintock, Frank and Bagchi, Rob. *True Grit: The Frank McLintock Autobiography*. London: Headline Publishing, 2005.

Merkhofer, Miley W. *Decision Science and Social Risk Management: A Comparative Evaluation of Cost-Benefit Analysis, Decision Analysis, and Other Formal Decision-Aiding Approaches*. Technology, Risk, and Society. Boston: D. Reidel, 1987.

Merton, Robert K. *Social Theory and Social Structure*. New York: The Free Press, 1967.

Merton, Robert K., Fiske, Marjorie, and Kendall, Patricia L. *The Focused Interview: A Manual of Problems and Procedures*. New York: The Free Press, 1990.

Midwinter, Eric, *From Parish to Planet*. London: Know the Score Books, 2007.

Millman, Chad. *The Odds: One Season, Three Gamblers and the Death of Their Las Vegas*. Cambridge, Massachusetts: DaCapo Press, 2001.

Moldea, Dan. *Interference: How Organised Crime Influences Professional Football*. New York: William Morrow, 1989.

Moore, David Cresa. *The Politics of Deference: A Study of the Mid-Nineteenth Century English Political System*. Hassocks; New York: Harvester; Barnes & Noble, 1976.

Moore, Douglas and Dorai, Joe. *That's the Goal! How to Win at Football*. Singapore: Landmark Books, 1999.

Morrison, Ian. *The World Cup: A Complete Record*. London: Breedon Books Sport, 1990.

Mortensen, Chris. *Playing for Keeps: How One Man Kept the Mob from Sinking Its Hooks into Pro Football*. New York: Simon & Schuster, 1991.

Morton, James. *Bent Coppers: Survey of Police Corruption*. London: Little, Brown and Company, 1993.

Munting, Roger. *An Economic and Social History of Gambling in Britain and the USA*. Manchester: Manchester University Press, 1996.

Murphy, Patrick, Williams, John and Dunning, Eric. *Football on Trial: Spectator Violence and Development in the Football World*. London: Routledge, 1990.

Nauright, John and Schimmel, Kimberly S. *The Political Economy of Sport*. International Political Economy Series. Ed. Timothy Shaw. New York: Palgrave, Macmillan, 2005.

Noonan, John T. *Bribes*. New York: Macmillan, 1984.

Nordlinger, Eric A. *The Working-Class Tories; Authority, Deference and Stable Democracy*. London: MacGibbon & Kee, 1967.

North, Douglas and Thomas, Robert Paul. *The Rise of the Western World*. Cambridge, Mass. Cambridge University Press, 1973.

Nozick, R. *Anarchy, State and Utopia*. Oxford: Basil Blackwell, 1974.

O'Leary, David. *Leeds United on Trial: The Inside Story of an Astonishing Year*. London: Little, Brown, 2002.

Oliver, Alan. *The Geordie Messiah: Keegan Years*. Edinburgh: Mainstream, 1997.

Olson Jr., Mancur. *The Logic of Collective*

*Action: Public Goods and the Theory of Groups*. Harvard Economic Studies. Cambridge, Massachusetts: Harvard University Press, 1971.

Pallo, Jackie. *You Grunt, I'll Groan: The Inside Story of Wrestling*. London: Macdonald Queen Anne, 1985.

Park, Stanley. *FIFA 192: The True Story Behind the Legend of the Brunei Darussalam National Football Team*. Boca Raton, Florida, USA: Universal Publisher, 2004.

Pausanias. *Description of Greece*. Trans. W.H.S. Jones. Internet Ancient History Source. London: Harvard University Press and William Heinemann Ltd., 1918.

Peraldi, Michel and Samson, Michel. *Gouverner Marseille: Enquête Sur Les Mondes Politiques Marseillais*. Paris: La Decouverte/Poche, 2005.

Petrini, Carlo. *Nel Fango Del Dio Pallone*. Trans. Andrea Patroconi. Milan, Italy: Kaos Edizione, 2000.

Phongpaichit, Pasuk, Priyarangsan, Sungsidh and Treerat, Nualnoi. *Guns, Girls, Gambling, Ganja: Thailand's Illegal Economy and Public Policy*. Chiang Mai: Silkworm, 1998.

Pontell, Henry (ed). *Social Deviance: Readings in Theory and Research*. Upper Saddle River, New Jersey: Pearson — Prentice-Hall, 2005.

Popper, Karl W. and Notturno, M.A. (ed). *The Myth of the Framework*. London: Routledge, 1994.

Posner, Gerald. *Warlords of Crime: The New Mafia*. New York: McGraw Hill, 1989.

Pound, Richard. *Inside the Olympics: A Behind-the-Scenes Look at the Politics, the Scandals and the Glory of the Games*. London, Wiley, 2004.

Powell, Walter W. and DiMaggio, Paul J. (eds). *The New Institutionalism in Organizational Analysis*. Chicago: University of Chicago Press, 1991.

Punch, Maurice. *Dirty Business: Exploring Corporate Misconduct — Analysis and Cases*. London: Sage, 1999.

Putnam, Robert D. B*owling Alone: The Collapse and Revival of American Community*. New York: Simon & Schuster, 2000.

Pycroft, James. *The Cricket Field*. London: St. James' Press Co. Ltd, 1922 (originally published in 1851).

Quirk, James and Foot, Rodney D. *Hard Ball: The Abuse of Power in Pro-Team Sports*. Princeton, New Jersey: Princeton University Press, 1999.

Rae, Simon. *It's Not Cricket: A History of Skulduggery, from Sharp Practice and Downright Cheating in the Noble Game*. Paperback ed. London: Faber and Faber, 2002.

Rauch, James E. and Casella, Alessandra. *Networks and Markets.* New York: Russell Sage Foundation, 2001.

Reuter, Peter. *Disorganised Crime: The Economics of the Visible Hand.* Cambridge, Massachusetts: MIT Press, 1983.

Ritzer, George and Smart, Barry, (eds). *Handbook of Social Theory.* London: Sage, 2003.

Roethlisberger, F.J. and Dickson, William J. *Management and the Worker: An Account of a Research Program Conducted by the Western Electric Company, Hawthorne Works, Chicago.* Cambridge, Mass. Harvard University Press, 1947.

Rose-Ackerman, Susan. *Corruption: A Study in Political Economy.* New York: Academic Press, 1978.

— *Corruption and Government: Causes, Consequences and Reform.* Cambridge: Cambridge University Press, 1999.

Ruggiero, Vincenzo; South, Nigel and Taylor, Ian. *The New European Criminology: Crime and Social Order in Europe.* London: Routledge, 1998.

Runciman, W.G. *Relative Deprivation and Social Justice: A Study of Attitudes to Social Inequality in Twentieth-Century England.* Reports of the Institute of Community Studies. London: Routledge and Kegan Paul, 1967.

Russo, Gus. *The Outfit: The Role of Chicago's Underworld in the Shaping of Modern America.* London: Bloomsbury, 2004.

Sanders, Teela. *Sex Work: A Risky Business.* Portland, Oregon: Willan Publishing, 2005.

Saviano, Roberto. *Gomorrah.* Trans. Virginia Jewiss. London: MacMillan, 2007.

Sayer, A. *Method in Social Science: A Realist Approach.* London: Routledge, 1992.

Schelling, T. *The Strategy of Conflict.* Cambridge, Mass: Harvard University Press, 1960.

— *Choice and Consequence.* Cambridge, Mass: Harvard University Press, 1984.

Schlegel, Kip and Weisburd, David. *White Collar Crime Reconsidered.* Boston: Northeastern University Press, 1992.

Seneviratne, Percy. *History of Football in Malaysia.* Kuala Lumpur: PNS, 2000.

Sharpe, Graham. *Coups and Cons.* London: Aesculus Press, 1991.

— *The Essential Gambler.* London: Robert Hale, 1995.

— *Gambling on Goals: A Century of Football Betting.* Edinburgh: Mainstream, 1997.

— *The Book of Bizarre Football: Freaky Forwards, Strange Strikers, Dodgy*

*Defenders and Other Soccer Sensations*. London: Robson Books, 2000.

— *Free the Manchester United One: The Inside Story of Football's Greatest Scam*. London: Robson Books Ltd, 2003.

Shover, Neal. *Aging Criminals*. Sociological Observations, 17. Beverley Hills: Sage Publications, 1985.

Slapper, Gary and Tombs, Steve. *Corporate Crime*. Longman Criminology Series. Ed. Tim Newburn. Harlow, Essex: Longman, 1999.

Sleap, Mike. *Social Issues in Sport*. London: Macmillan Press, 1998.

Smit, Barbara. *Pitch Invasion, Three Stripes, Two Brothers, One Feud: Adidas, Puma and the Making of Modern Sport*. London: Penguin, 2007.

Sprott, W.J.H. *Human Groups*. London: Pelican, 1966.

St. John, Ian and Lawton, James. *The Saint: My Autobiography*. London: Hodder & Stoughton, 2006.

Stille, Alexander. *Excellent Cadavers: The Mafia and the Death of the First Italian Republic*. London: Jonathan Cape, 1996.

Stoller, Robert J. and Levine, I.S. *Coming Attractions*. Binghamton: Vail-Ballou Press, 1993.

Stott, Richard. *Dogs and Lampposts*. London: Metro Publishing, 2002.

Suetonius, Gaius Tranquillus. *The Lives of the Twelve Caesars*. Trans. J.C. Rolfe. Ed. Bill Thayer: Loeb Classic, 1914.

Sugden, John. *Scum Airways: Inside Football's Underground Economy*. Edinburgh: Mainstream, 2003.

Sugden, John and Bairner, Alan. *Sport, Sectarianism and Society in a Divided Ireland. Sport, Politics and Culture*. Leicester: Leicester University Press, 1993.

Sugden, John, and Tomlinson, Alan. *Hosts and Champions: Soccer Cultures, National Identities and the USA World Cup*. Popular Cultural Studies; 4. Aldershot: Arena, 1994.

— *FIFA and the Contest for World Football: Who Rules the People's Game?* Cambridge: Polity Press, 1998.

— *Great Balls of Fire: How Big Money Is Hijacking World Football*. Edinburgh: Mainstream, 1999.

— *Power Games: A Critical Sociology of Sport*. London: Routledge, 2002.

— *Badfellas: FIFA Family at War*. London: Mainstream Sport Publishing, 2003.

Sutherland, Edwin H. *The Principles of Criminology*. 4th ed. Chicago: J.B. Lippincott Co, 1947.

Swan, Peter with Nick Johnson. *Peter Swan: Setting the Record Straight.* Stroud, Gloucestershire: Stadia, 2006.

Szymanski, Stefan and Kuypers, Tim. *Winners and Losers: The Business Strategy of Football.* Harmondsworth, Middlesex, England: Penguin Books, 1999.

Taylor, Chris. *The Beautiful Game: A Journey through Latin American Football.* London: Phoenix Books, 1998.

Theobald, Robin. *Corruption, Development and Underdevelopment.* London: The MacMillan Press, 1990.

Thomas, David. *Foul Play: The Inside Story of the Biggest Corruption Trial in British Sporting History.* London: Bantam, 2003.

Thomas, Donald. *An Underworld at War: Spivs, Deserters, Racketeers & Civilians in the Second World War.* London: John Murray, 2003.

Thomas, William Isaac and Znaniecki, Florian. *The Polish Peasant in Europe and America.* 1918.

Udehn, L. T*he Limits of Public Choice: A Sociological Critique of the Economic Theory of Politics.* London: Routledge, 1996.

Vamplew, Wray. *Pay Up and Play the Game: Professional Sport in Britain, 1875-1914.* Cambridge: Cambridge University Press, 1988.

Van Brunschot, Erin Gibbs. *Gambling in Context: The Socio-Cultural Domain Literature Overview and Annotated Bibliography.* Calgary, Alberta, Canada: The Alberta Gaming Research Institute, 2000.

Van Laeken, Frank. *Blunderboek Van Het Belgisch Voetball.* Brussels: Icarus, 1997.

Varese, Federico. T*he Russian Mafia: Private Protection in a New Market Economy.* Oxford: Oxford University Press, 2001.

Venkatesh, Sudhir Alladi. A*merican Project: The Rise and Fall of a Modern Ghetto.* Cambridge, Massachusetts: Harvard University Press, 2002.

Volkov, Vadim. *Violent Entrepreneurs: The Use of Force in the Making of Russian Capitalism.* Ithaca: Cornell University Press, 2002.

Walton, Paul, Taylor, Ian and Young, Jock. *The New Criminology: For a Social Theory of Deviance.* London: Routledge and Paul Kegan, 1994.

Warner, Robin, and University of Bristol. *Bungs, Bribes and Bad Language: Some Strategies of Portuguese and Spanish Conspiratorial Talk.* Bristol: Department of Hispanic Portuguese and Latin American Studies University of Bristol, 1996.

Weber, Max. *The Protestant Ethic and the Spirit of Capitalism: The Relationship between Religion and the Economic and Social Life in Modern Culture.* Trans. Talcott Parsons. New York: Charles Scribner's Sons, 1958.

Weisburd, David, Waring, Elin and Chayet, Ellen. *White-Collar Crime and Criminal Careers.* Blumstein, Alfred and Farrington, David. Ed. Cambridge Studies in Criminology. Cambridge: Cambridge University Press, 2001.

Westcott, Chris. *Joker in the Pack: The Ernie Hunt Story.* Stroud, Gloucestershire: Tempus Publishing, 2004.

Wheeler, Stanton, Mann, Kenneth and Sarat, Austin. *Sitting in Judgement: The Sentencing of White-Collar Criminals.* New Haven: Yale University Press, 1988.

Whelan, David C. *Organised Crime, Sports Gambling, and Role Conflict: Victimization and Point-Shaving in College Basketball.* New York: City University, Unpublished PhD thesis, 1992.

Whyte, William Foote. *Street Corner Society: The Social Structure of an Italian Slum.* Chicago: The University of Chicago Press, 1993.

Wigglesworth, Neil. *The Social History of English Rowing.* London: Frank Cass, 1992.

Williams, Russ. *Football Babylon.* London: Virgin, 1996.

— *Football Babylon 2.* London: Virgin, 1998.

Wilson, Jonathan. *Behind the Curtain: Travels in Eastern European Football.* London: Orion Publishing, 2006.

Winlow, Simon. *Badfellas: Crime, Tradition and New Masculinities.* Oxford: Berg, 2001.

Wolf, Daniel R. T*he Rebels: A Brotherhood of Outlaw Bikers.* Toronto: University of Toronto Press, 1991.

Yallop, David. *How They Stole the Game.* London: Poetic Publishing, 1999.

## BOOK SECTIONS

Anderson, Annelise Graebner. "Organised Crime, Mafia and Governments." In *The Economics of Organised Crime* ed. Gianluca Fiorentini and Sam Peltzman. Cambridge: Cambridge University Press, 1995.

Biggs, Michael. "Dying Without Killing: Self-immolations 1963-2002." In *Making Sense of Suicide Missions,* ed. Diego Gambetta, 173-208 and 320-324. Oxford: Oxford University Press, 2005.

Bray, John. "The Use of Intermediaries." In *The New Institutional Economics of Corruption* ed. Johann Graf Lambsdorff, Markus Taube, and Matthias Schramm, 112-37. London: Routledge, 2005.

Burt, Ronald. "The Social Capital of Structural Holes." In *New Directions in Economic Sociology* ed. Mauro F. Guillen, Randall Collins, Paula England, and Marshall Meyer. New York: Russell Sage, 2001.

Cole, Stephen. "The Growth of Scientific Knowledge." In the *Idea of Social Structure*, ed. Lewis A. Coser. New York: Harcourt Brace Jovanovich, 1975.

Conan-Doyle, Arthur. "The Silver Blaze." In *The Adventures of Sherlock Holmes*. London: Wordsworth Classics, 1996.

Dasgupta, Partha. "Trust as a Commodity." In *Trust: Making and Breaking Cooperative Relations*, ed. Diego Gambetta, 49-72. Original edition, 1988. Electronic edition. Oxford: Department of Sociology, University of Oxford, 2000.

Elliott, Delbert S. "The Assumption That Theories Can Be Combined with Increased Explanatory Power: Theoretical Integrations." In *Theoretical Methods in Criminology* ed. Robert F Meier. Beverly Hills, California: Sage, 1985.

Foucault, Michel and Kritzman, Lawrence D. "Sexual Morality and the Law." In *Politics, Philosophy, Culture: Interviews and other writings 1977-1984*. Trans. Alan Sheridan. London: Routledge, 1988.

Gambetta, Diego. "Mafia: The Price of Distrust." In *Trust: Making and Breaking Cooperative Relations* ed. Diego Gambetta,158-75. Electronic Edition Oxford: Department of Sociology, University of Oxford, 2000.

— "Corruption: An Analytical Map." In *Political Corruption of Transition: A Sceptic's Handbook*, ed. S. Kotkin and A. Sajo. Budapest: Central European University Press, 2002.

— "Deceptive Mimicry in Humans." In *Perspective on Imitation: From Cognitive Neuro-Science to Social Science*, ed. S. Hurley and N. Chater, vol. 2, 221-241 Cambridge: MIT Press, 2005.

— "Two Types of Corruption and the Self-fulfilling Nature of the Beliefs about Corruption." In *The Corruption Monster: Ethik, Politik und Korruption*. ed. M. Kreutner, 137-44 Wien: Czermin Verlag, 2006.

Geis, Gilbert. "White-Collar Crime: What Is It?" In *White-Collar Crime Reconsidered* ed. Kip Schlegel and David Weisburd, 31-52. Boston: Northeastern University Press, 1992.

Giddens, Anthony. "Fate, Risk and Security." In *The Sociology of Risk and Gambling Reader* ed. James F. Cosgrave. Abingdon: Routledge, 2006.

Good, David. "Individuals, Interpersonal Relations and Trust." In *Trust: Making and Breaking Cooperative Relations* ed. Diego Gambetta, 31-48. Electronic Edition Oxford: Department of Sociology, University of Oxford, 2000.

Heckathorn, Douglas D. "Sociological Rational Choice." In *Handbook of Social Theory* ed. Barry Smart and George Ritzer. Paperback (2003) ed. London: Sage, 2001.

Hobbs, Dick. "Going Down the Local: The Local Context of Organised Crime." In *Reflections on Organised Crime: Patterns and Control* ed. Michael Levi. Oxford: Blackwell Publishers for the Howard League, 1998.

— "Researching Serious Crime." In *Doing Research on Crime and Justice* ed. Emma Wincup and Roy D. King vol. 1, 447. Oxford: Oxford University Press, 2000.

Levi, Michael. "Perspectives on 'Organised Crime': An Overview." In *Reflections on Organised Crime: Patterns and Control* ed. Michael Levi. Oxford: Blackwell Publishers for The Howard League, 1998.

— "The Organization of Serious Crimes." In *The Oxford Handbook of Criminology* ed. Rod Morgan, Mike Maguire, and Robert Reiner. 3rd edition, vol. 1, 1227. Oxford: Oxford University Press, 2002.

Lupsha, Peter A. "American Values and Organised Crime: Suckers and Wiseguys." In *The American Self: Myth, Ideology, and Popular Culture* ed. Sam B. Girgus, 144-54. Albuquerque: University of New Mexico, 1981.

— "Organised Crime in the United States." In *Organised Crime: A Global Perspective* ed. Robert J. Kelly, 32-57. Totowa, New Jersey: Rowman & Littlefield, 1986.

Maguire, Mike with Michael Levi. "Violent Crime." In *The Oxford Handbook of Criminology* Rod Morgan, Mike Maguire, and Robert Reiner. 3rd edition, vol. 1, Oxford: Oxford University Press, 2002.

Merton, Robert. "Social Structure and Anomie." In Pontell, Henry (ed). *Social Deviance: Readings in Theory and Research*. Upper Saddle River, New Jersey: Pearson — Prentice-Hall, 2005: 37-44.

Merton, Robert and A. Rossi. "Contributions to the Theory of Reference Group Behavior." In *Studies in the Scope and Method of "the American Soldier"* ed. Robert Merton & Paul Lazersfeld, 40-105. New York: The Free Press, 1950.

Molm, Linda D. "Theories of Social Exchange and Exchange Networks." In *Handbook of Social Theory* ed. George Ritzer and Barry Smart. London: Sage, 2001.

Morse, J.M. "Designing Funded Qualitative Research." *Handbook of*

*Qualitative Research*. Ed. Denzin, N.K., and Lincoln, Y.S. Thousand Oaks, CA: Sage, 1994.

Passas, Nikos. "Continuities in the Anomie Tradition." In *The Legacy of Anomie Theory* ed. Freda Laufer and William Adler. Vol. 6. Advances in Criminological Theory, 91-112. New Brunswick, New Jersey: Transaction Books, 1995.

Rawlinson, Patricia. "Mafia, Media and Myth: Representations of Russian Organised Crime." In *Reflections on Organised Crime: Patterns and Control* ed. Michael Levi. Oxford: Blackwell Publishers for the Howard League, 1998.

— "Mafia, Methodology and "Alien" Culture." In *Doing Research on Crime and Justice*, ed. Emma Wincup and Roy D. King, 441. Oxford: Oxford University Press, 2000.

Reiss, Albert J. Jr. "Co-Offenders Influences on Criminal Careers." In *Criminal Careers and Career Criminals* ed. Alfred Blumsteing. Washington D.C.: National Academy Press, 1986.

Reuter, P. and Diego Gambetta. "Conspiracy among the Many: The Mafia in Legitimate Industries." In *The Economics of Organised Crime*, ed. Gianluca Fiorentini and Sam Peltzman, 116-39. Cambridge: Cambridge University Press, 1995.

Rock, Paul. "Sociological Theories of Crime." In *The Oxford Handbook of Criminology* Rod Morgan, Mike Maguire, and Robert Reiner. 3rd edition, vol. 1. Oxford: Oxford University Press, 2002.

Schlegel, Kip and David Weisburd. "White-Collar Crime: The Parallax View." In *White-Collar Crime Reconsidered* ed. Kip Schlegel and David Weisburd, 3-30. Boston: Northeastern University Press, 1992.

Sharpe, Karen. "Sad, Bad, and (Sometimes) Dangerous to Know: Street Corner Research with Prostitutes, Punters, and the Police." In *Doing Research on Crime and Justice* ed. Roy D. King and Emma Wincup. Oxford: Oxford University Press, 2000.

Sissener, Tone. "Anthropological Perspectives on Corruption." In Andvig, Jens C. *Issues of Corruption: A Policy-Oriented Survey of Research*. Chr. Michelsen Institute (CMI) and Norwegian Institute of International Affairs (NUPI), Oslo, 2000.

Skolnick, Jerome H. "Corruption and the Blue Code of Silence." In *Policing Corruption: International Perspectives* ed. Rick Sarre, Dilip K. Das, and H.J. Albrecht, 301-16. International Police Executive Symposia. Oxford: Lexington Publishers, 2005.

Sutcliffe, M.P., Gerry. "Why Football Needs an Independent Regulator."

In *Football in the Digital Age* ed. Jonathan Michie, Sean Hamil, Christine Oughton and Steven Warby. London: Mainstream, 2001.

Taylor, Ian. "Football Mad." In *The Sociology of Sport* ed. E. Dunning. London: Frank Cass, 1970.

Tilly, C. "War Making and State Making as Organised Crime." In *Bringing the State Back In*, ed. D. Rueschemeyer and T. Skocpol. Cambridge. Cambridge University Press, 1985.

Uslaner, Eric M. "Trust and Corruption." In *The New Institutional Economics of Corruption*, ed. Johann G. Lambsdorff, Markus Taube, and Matthias Schramm. Routledge Frontiers of Political Economy. London: Routledge, 2005.

Waring, Elin, David Weisburd, and Ellen Chayet. "White-Collar Crime and Anomie." In *The Legacy of Anomie Theory*, ed. Freda Laufer and William Adler. Vol. 6. Advances in Criminological Theory, 207-25. New Brunswick, New Jersey: Transaction Publishers, 1995.

Warren, Mark E. "The Nature and Logic of Bad Social Capital." In *Oxford Handbook of Social Capital*, ed. Dario Castiglione and Jan Van Deth, 135. Oxford: Oxford University Press, 2004.

Young, Jock. "Crime and Social Exclusion." In *The Oxford Handbook of Criminology*, ed. Mike Maguire, Rod Morgan, and Robert Reiner, 457-90. Oxford: Oxford University Press, 2002.

## JOURNAL AND MAGAZINE ARTICLES

Åberg Yngwe, M., Fritzell, J., Lundberg, O., Diderichsen, F. and Burström, B. "Exploring Relative Deprivation: Is Social Comparison a Mechanism in the Relations between Income and Health?" *Social Science and Medicine*. Vol. 57 (2003): 1463-73.

Ackman, Dan. "How Big Is Porn?" *Forbes*, May 25, 2001. Available at: www.forbes.com/2001/05/25/0524porn.html

Agnew, R. "Foundation for a General Strain Theory." *Criminology*. 30.1 (1992): 47-87.

Akers, Ronald, Lee, Gang and Borg, Marian. "Social Learning and Structural Factors in Adolescent Substance Use." *Western Criminology Review* 5.1 (2004): 17-34.

Alexander, Barbara. "The Rational Racketeer: Pasta Protection in Depression Era Chicago." *Journal of Law and Economics* 40.1 (1997): 175-202.

Anonymous. "Sports Corruption." *Sports Law Bulletin* 1.2 (1998): 15.

Baker, Wayne E. and Faulkner, Robert R. "The Social Organization of

Conspiracy: Illegal Networks in the Heavy Electrical Industry." *American Sociological Review* Vol. 58 no. 6 (1993): 837-60.

Banfield, C.E. "Corruption as a Feature of Governmental Organisation." *Journal of Law and Economics* 18.3 (1975): 587-605.

Bebchuk, Lucian Arye and Grinstein, Yaniv. "The Growth of Executive Pay." *Oxford Review of Economic Policy* 21 (2005): 283-303.

Becker, Howard. "Whose Side Are We On?" *Social Problems* (1967): 239.

Becker, Howard. "Crime and Punishment: an Economic Approach" *Journal of Political Economy* (1968), Vol. 76, 169-217.

Bikhchandani, Sushil, Hirshleifer, David and Welch, Ivo. "A Theory of Fads, Fashion, Custom and Cultural Change as Informational Cascades." *The Journal of Political Economy*. Vol. 100.5 (1992): 992-1026.

Blair, Dale James. "Did the Dons Play Dead." *Australian SSH*. June 30, 1999. 3-15.

Boles, J. and Garbin, A.P. "The Strip Club and Customer-Stripper Patterns of Interaction." *Sociology and Social Research*. Vol. 58 (1984): 136-44.

Bond, Matthew. "Social Influences on Corporate Political Donations in Britain." *The British Journal of Sociology*. Vol. 55, 1 (2004): 55-77.

Bond, Matthew. "Elite Social Relations and Corporate Political Donations in Britain." *Political Studies*. Vol. 55, 1 (2007): 59-85.

Choi, Jay Pil and Thum, Marcel. "Corruption and the Shadow Economy." *CESifo Working Paper Series* no. 633. January 2002. Available at SSRN: http://ssrn.com/abstract=297602

Constabulary, Hampshire. "Closing the Gap in Policing Organised Crime." (2002).

Crawford, Garry and Gosling, Victoria K. "The Myth of the Puck Bunny: Female Fans and Men's Ice Hockey." *Sociology: A Journal of the British Sociological Association*. Vol. 38.3 (2004): 477-94.

Cressey, Donald. "Epidemiology and Individual Conduct: A Case from Criminology." *The Pacific Sociological Review* 3.2 (1960): 47-58.

Cressey, Donald. "Methodological Problems in the Study of Organised Crime." *Annals of the American Academy of Political Science* 374 (1967): 101-12.

De Souza, Roberto Pereira. "Joao Havelange: O Poderoso Chefao." *Playboy Brazil*, Vol. XX, no 226, May 1994, 124-141.

Duke, V. "Perestroika in Progress? The Case of Spectator Sports in

Czechoslovakia." *British Journal of Sociology*, 41 (1990): 41: 145-56.

Enck, G. E. and Preston, J.D. "Counterfeit Intimacy: A Dramaturgical Analysis of an Erotic Performance." *Deviant Behavior* vol. 9.4 (1988): 369-81.

Englander, Steven and Gurney, Andrew. OECD Productivity Growth: Medium-Term Trends. *OECD Economic Studies*. no.22, Spring 1994.

Goldsmith, Arthur A. "Slapping the grasping hand: Correlates of political corruption in emerging markets." *American Journal of Economics and Sociology*. Vol. 58.4 (1999): 866-883.

Granovetter, M. "The Strength of Weak Ties." *American Journal of Sociology*. Vol. 78.6 (1973): 1360-80.

— "Threshold Models of Collective Behavior." *American Journal of Sociology*. Vol. 83, no. 6 (1978): 1420-43.

— "Economic Action and Social Structure: The Problem of Embeddedness:" *American Journal of Sociology*. Vol. 91.3 (1985): 481-510.

Gupta, Akhil. "Blurred Boundaries: the discourse of corruption, the culture of politics, and the imagined state." *American Ethnologist*. Vol. 22.2 (1995): 375-402.

Hechter, Michael and Kanazawa, Satoshi. "Sociological Rational Choice Theory." *Annual Review of Sociology*. Vol. 23: (1997) 191-214.

Heywood, Paul. "Political Corruption, Problems and Perspectives." *Political Studies*. Vol. 45.3 (1997): 417-35.

Hoffman, John. "A Contextual Analysis of Differential Association, Social Control, and Strain Theories of Delinquency". *Social Forces*. 81.3 (March, 2002): 753-785.

Holliday, Simon. "Risky Business." *Foreign Policy*. March/April 2006. Available at http://www.foreignpolicy.com/story/cms.php?story_id=3406

Hunt, Jennifer and Laszlo, Sonia. "Bribery: Who Pays, Who Refuses, What Are the Payoffs?" *National Bureau of Economic Research*. http://www.nber.org/papers/W11635.Working paper 11635 (2005): 1-46.

Kirkup, W. and Merrick, D.W., "A matter of life and death: population mortality and football results," *Journal of Epidemiology and Community Health*, Jan 2003, 57, 429-432.

Kondos, Alex. "The Question of 'Corruption' in Nepal." *Mankind*. Vol. 17, no. 1. 1987.

Kugler, M. et al. "Organised Crime, Corruption and Punishment." Feb 2003, CEPR discussion paper, no 3806.

Lambsdorff, Johann Graf. "Exporters' Ethics: Some Diverging Evidence." *International Journal of Comparative Criminology* 1.2 (2001): 27-44.

— "Making Corrupt Deals: Contracting in the Shadow of the Law." *Journal of Economic Behaviour and Organization* 48.2002 (2002): 221-41.

— "How Confidence Facilitates Illegal Transactions: An Empirical Approach." *The American Journal of Economics and Sociology*. Vol. 61.4 (2002): 829-53.

La Porta, Rafael; Lopez-de-Silanes, Florencio; Shleifer, Andrei and Vishny, Robert. "Trust in Large Organizations." *The American Economic Review*. Vol. 87.2 (May 1997): 333-338.

Leff, Nathaniel. "Economic development through bureaucratic corruption." *American Behavioral Scientist*. Vol. 8, no. 3, (1964): 8-14.

Levi, Michael. "Reflections on Organised Crime: Patterns and Control." *The Howard Journal of Criminal Justice*. Vol. 37.4 (1998): All.

Levitt, Steven D. and Duggan, M. "Winning Isn't Everything: Corruption in Sumo Wrestling." *American Economic Review*. Vol. 92.5 (2002): 594-605.

Levitt, Steven D. "How Do Markets Function? An Empirical Analysis of Gambling on the National Football League." *National Bureau of Economics Working paper* available at http://www.nber.org/papers/w9422 (2002).

Li, Wei, "A Tale of Two Reforms." *RAND Journal of Economics*. Vol. 30, no. 1., Spring 1999, 120-136.

Liebling, Alison. "Whose Side Are We On?" *British Journal of Criminology*. Vol. 41 (2001): 472-84.

Lile, Emma. "Professional Pedestrianism in South Wales During the Nineteenth Century." *The Sports Historian* (became *Sport in History* in 2003), no. 2 (2000): 94-105.

Lundahl, M. "Inside the Predatory State." *Political Economy*. Vol. 24.1 (1997): 31-50.

Lupsha, Peter A. "Transnational Organised Crime Versus the Nation-State." T*ransnational Organised Crime*. Vol. 2, 1, (1996): 21-48.

Matsueda, R. L., and Anderson, Kathleen. "The Dynamics of Delinquent Peers and Delinquent Behavior." *Criminology* 36.2 (1988): 269-308.

McLean, Iain. "A non-zero-sum game of football." *British Journal of Political Science* 10 (1980): 253-9.

Middleton, Russell, "Brother-Sister and Father-Daughter Marriage in Ancient Egypt," *American Sociological Review*, Vol. 27, no. 5 (Oct., 1962), 603-611.

Murphy, K.M., Shleifer, A and Vishny, R.W. "Why Is Rent-Seeking So Costly to Growth?" *The American Economic Review Papers and Proceedings*. Vol. 82.2 (1993): 409-14.

Nti, Kofi O. "Comparative Statistics of Contests and Rent-Seeking Games." *International Economic Review*. Vol. 38.1 (1997): 43-59.

Nye, J.S. "Corruption and Political Development." *American Political Science Review*. Vol. 61.2 (1967): 417-427.

Orwell, George. "The Sporting Spirit." Originally, December 1945. Available at: http://www.george-orwell.org/The_Sporting_Spirit/0.html

Parry, Odette and Mauthner, Natasha S. "Whose Data Are They Anyway: Practical, Legal and Ethical Issues in Archiving Qualitative Research Data." *Sociology: Journal of the British Sociological Association*. Vol. 38.1 (2004): 139-52.

Paton, David, Williams, Leighten Vaughan, and Fraser, Stuart. "Regulating Insider Trading in Betting Markets." *Bulletin of Economic Research*. Vol. 51.3 (1999): 237.

Police and Crime Standards Directorate. "Lessons Learned from the Domestic Violence Enforcement Campaigns 2006." *British Home Office*, October 2006. Available at: http://www.homeoffice.gov.uk/documents/Domestic-Violence-10731.pdf

Preston, Ian and Szymanski, Stefan. "Cheating in Contests." *Oxford Review of Economic Policy*. Vol. 19:4 (2003). 612-24.

Reinarman, Craig and Fagan, Jeffrey. "Social Organization and Differential Association: A Research Note from a Longitudinal Study of Violent Juvenile Offenders." *Crime & Delinquency*. Vol. 34.3 (1988): 307-27.

Rich, Frank. "Naked Capitalists", *New York Times Magazine*, (May 20, 2001): available at: http://query.nytimes.com/gst/fullpage.tml.?res 9D04E0DD173AF933A15756COA967C8B63

Riordan, Jim. "Playing to New Rules: Soviet Sport and Perestroika." *Soviet Studies*. Vol. 42.1 (January 1990) (1990): 133-45.

Rizek, André and Oyama, Thais. "A Máfia Do Apito." *Veja* 28 September, 2005: 72-80.

Ruud, Arild Engleson, "Corruption as everyday practice. Rules and rule-bending in local Indian society." *SUM: Working Paper 4*: 1998: Oslo, Centre for Development and the Environment.

Salop, Steven. "Raising Rivals' Costs." *American Economic Review*. Vol. 73.2 (1983): 267-71.

Salutin, M. "Stripper Morality." *Transitions*. Vol. 8 (1971): 12-22.

Schelling, Thomas. "What is the Business of Organised Crime?" *Journal of Public Law*. Vol. 20.1 (1971).

Shelley, Louise. "Mafia and the Italian State: The Historical Roots of the Current Crisis." *Sociological Forum*. Vol. 9.4 Special Issue "Multiculturalism and Diversity" (1994): 661-72.

Shleifer, A. and Vishny, R.W. "Corruption." *The Quarterly Journal of Economics* (1993): 599-617.

Skipper, James K. and McCaghy, Charles. "Stripteasers: The Anatomy and Career Contingencies of a Deviant Occupation." *Social Problems*. Vol. 17 (1970): 391-405.

Sparkes, Andrew. "Narratives of Self as an Occasion of Conspiracy." *Sociology of Sport Online*, Vol. 1.1 (1998).

Staff Writer, "Brise de Mer", Grand Banditisme, Milieu du Football Politique et la Mort de Dominique Rutily", *L'investigateur*, (Paris), 2003. www.investigateur.info/affaires/corse/articles/rutily.html

— Report on Press Freedoms, Freedom House, New York, 2007. Available at http:://www.freedomhouse.org.

Sugden, John and Tomlinson, Alan. "Digging the Dirt and Staying Clean: Retrieving the Investigative Tradition for a Critical Sociology of Sport." *International Sociology of Sport Review*, Vol. 34 (1999): 385.

Sykes, G. and Matza, D. "Techniques of Neutralization." *American Sociological Review*. Vol. 22 (1957): 664-70.

Tabb, William K. "Wage Stagnation, Growing Insecurity, and the Future of the U.S. Working Class." *Monthly Review*. Vol. 59.2 (2007): available at http://www.monthlyreview.org/0607wkt.htm

Taylor, B. and Trogdon, J. "Losing to Win: Tournament Incentives in the National Basketball Association." *Journal of Labour Economics*. Vol. 20, 1 (2002).

Thompson, William E. and Harred, Jackie L. "Topless Dancers: Managing Stigma in a Deviant Occupation." *Deviant Behavior*. Vol. 13 (1992): 291-311.

van Rijckeghem, C. and Weder, B. "Bureaucratic Corruption and the Rate of Temptation: Do Wages in the Civil Service Affect Corruption, and by How Much?" *Journal of Development Economics*. Vol. 65.2 (2001): 307-31.

Varese, Federico and Yaish, Meir. "Altruism: The Importance of Being Asked. The Rescue of Jews in Nazi Europe." *Discussion Papers in Economic and Social History*.

University of Oxford Sociology Working Papers. No. 24 (1998).

Wainwright, Steve P. and Turner, Bryan S. "'Just Crumbling to Bits?' An Exploration of the Body, Ageing, Injury and Career in Classical Ballet Dancers." *Sociology: Journal of the British Sociological Association*. Vol. 40.2 (2006): 237-56.

Waring, Elin and Finchenauer, James O. "Challenging the Russian Mafia Mystique." *National Institute of Justice Journal*, Washington, 2001.

Wei, Shang-Jin. How Taxing is Corruption on International Investors?" *The Review of Economics and Statistics*. Vol. LXXXII, no. 1, February 2000, 1-11.

Witte, Bots, Hoes AW, et al., "Cardiovascular mortality in Dutch men during the 1996 European football championship: longitudinal population study," *British Medical Journal*. 2000, 321: 1552-4.

Wonders, Nancy A. and Michalowski, Raymond. "Bodies, Borders, and Sex Tourism in a Globalised World: A Tale of Two Cities — Amsterdam and Havana." *Social Problems*. Vol. 48.4 (2001): 545-71.

## COURT CASES

Abbas Saad vs. Singapore Public Prosecutor, Subordinate Court, May 1995.

Chan Wing Seng v. Public Prosecutor. *Singapore Law Reports* [1997]. Singapore High Court, Magistrate's Appeal 1997.

Cheong Ah Cheow v. Public Prosecutor A. Cr. J. (Chan J.). Kuala Lumpur Federal Territory Criminal Appeal 1985.

Grobbelaar v. News Group Newspapers Ltd. Judge Simon Brown. UK Court of Appeal 2001.

Grobbelaar v. News Group Newspapers Ltd. and Another. Lord Bingham of Cornhill, Lord Steyn, Lord Hobhouse of Woodborough, Lord Millett and Lord Scott of Foscote. UK House of Lords, 2002.

Kannan S/O Kunjiraman & Anor v. Public Prosecutor. Magistrate's Appeal 96/95/01-02. Singapore High Court, 1995.

Kannan S/O Kunjiraman v. Public Prosecutor. *Singapore Law Reports* 3 SLR Cheung Phei Chiet, 1995.

MasterCard International Incorporated v. Fédération Internationale de Football Association. Judge Loretta A. Preska, Amended Findings of Fact and Conclusions of Law. United States District Court Southern District of New York, 2006.

Manap Bin Hamat & Anor v. Public Prosecutor. Singapore Subordinate Court, 1997.

Mathan Jagannathan, et al. v. Public

Prosecutor, Singapore High Court, 1996.

Ong, et al. v. Public Prosecutor. Singapore Subordinate Court, 1994.

Ong Smith Bernal v. R. UK Court of Appeal, (Criminal Division) 2000.

Rajamanickam Thirujnanasammathan v. Public Prosecutor. Singapore Subordinate Courts, 1994.

Rajendran S/O Kurusamy & Ors v. Public Prosecutor. Magistrate's Appeal. Singapore High Court, Nos. 237/97/01-05, 1998.

Teo Tiang Hoe v. Public Prosecutor. Criminal Case no. 8, 1995 Rubin, J. High Court of the Republic of Singapore, 1995.

Testo Della Decisione Relativa Al Commm. Uff. N1/C Riunione Del 29 Giugno, 3-7 Luglio 2007." Prcoura Federale Della F.I.G.C. Rome: Italian Football Federation, 2006. 154. 1 vols.

United States of America v. Alimzhan Tokhtakhtunov Aka Taiwanchuk. Southern District of New York, 2002.

United States of America v. Vyacheslav Kiriovich Ivankov, United States District Court. Eastern District of New York (Brooklyn), 1997.

United States of America v. Neteller PLC. United States District Court. Southern District of New York, 2007.

Zainal, Mohamed, Mohamed Ali, and Ali Lomri, — Disciplinary Hearing. No 1-3/2003, 6. Disciplinary Committee, Football Association of Singapore 2003.

## REPORTS

Association of Tennis Professionals (ATP). *Report on Corruption Allegations in Men's Professional Tennis*. June 2005.

Bruckert, Chris, Parent, Colette and Robitaille, Pascale. "Erotic Service, Erotic Dance Establishments: Two types of marginalized labour." *Department of Criminology, University of Ottawa, Law Commission of Canada, & Status of Women*. January 2003.

Condon QPM, Sir Paul. *Report on Corruption in International Cricket.* London: International Cricket Council, 2001.

Cronje, Hansie. "*Hansie Cronje's Statement before the Edwin King Commission of Inquiry into Cricket Match-Fixing and Related Matters,* Cape Town, South Africa, June 2000." Audio and video at www.rediff.com/cricket/betting.htm.

Dowd, John M. *Report to the Commissioner, In the Matter of Peter Edward Rose, Manager Cincinnati Reds Baseball Club.* Office of the Commissioner of Baseball, May 9, 1989.

FIFPro. Black Book: Eastern Europe — *The problems professional footballers encounter: Research.* Hoofddorp, The Netherlands. January, 2012.

Hill, Declan, testimony before the Council of Europe, Strasbourg, May 2010.

Husock, Howard. *Soccer Betting in Hong Kong: A Challenge for Home Affairs.* Boston: Harvard University, John F. Kennedy School of Government Affairs, 2002.

Institut de Criminologie de Paris Département de Recherche sur les Menaces Criminelles Contemporaines. *Tapie, Courbis, Filippedu, le Belge, mafia(s), foot, argent sale et coups tordus.* Paris: Université Panthéon-Assas (Paris II), 2005.

King, Judge El. *Commission of Inquiry into Cricket Match-fixing and Related Matters, 2nd Interim Report.* Cape Town, South Africa: Republic of South Africa, 2000.

Lange, Scott R. *The Solicitation Cycle.* Gifted Memory.com. Available at www.giftedmemory.com/cycle

Liew, Kou Yew. *Asian Pharmaceutical Outlook.* Pharma Focus Asia, 2006. Available at: http://www.pharmafocusasia.com/Knowledge_bank/articles/asia_pharmaceutical_sector.htm

Malaysian Police Confessions, no 1-6.

Mony, Paul Samuel. *M League: A Brief Outline and Report 1998.* Kuala Lumpur: Football Association of Malaysia, 1998.

*Prosecutor's Report. Hoyzer Case.* Berlin: Staatsanwaltshcaft Berlin, 2005.

Qayyun, M.M. *Reports of the Judicial Commission.* Lahore, Pakistan: Pakistan Cricket Board, 1998.

Remote Gambling Association. *Report to the Trade Barriers Regulation Committee: Examination Procedure Concerning an Obstacle to Trade, Within the Meaning of Council Regulation (EC) NO 3286/94, Consisting of Measures Adopted by The United States of America Affecting Trade in Remote Gambling Services: Complaint Submitted by the Remote Gambling Association (RGA).*

Rovaniemen Toimipiste KRP. *Report on the Activities of Wilson Raj Perumal.* August 2011.

Salvini, Guido. *Tribunale Ordinario di Cremona. Ufficio del Giudice per le indagini preliminari dr. Guido Salvini. ORDINANZA DI APPLICAZIONE DELLA MISURA DELLA CUSTODIA CAUTELARE IN CARCERE,* December 2011.

Smith, Sir John. *Game at Risk.* London: English Football Association, 1997.

Staff writer. *Police Corruption in England and Wales.* Unpublished, SOCA

Assessment, Metropolitan Police. London, February 2007, 14-18.

Supdt, Sd/- M.A. Ganapathy. *Report on Cricket Match-Fixing and Related Malpractices.* New Delhi: CBI Special Crimes Branch — Central Bureau of Investigation, 2000.

Testimony of Michael Franzese before the Permanent Subcommittee on Investigations of the Committee on Governmental Affairs United States Senate: One hundred and fourth Congress, Second Session — May 15, 1996, 36-42.

United States Bureau of Labor Statistics. *Wages and Benefits: Real Wages (1964-2004).* 2004: Available at: http://www.workinglife.org

Zimbabwe Football Association Report, *Match Fixing.* August 2011.

## FILMS AND TV PROGRAMS

Docherty, Neil and McIntyre, Linden. *Mafia Power Play.* PBS Frontline. Boston. October 12, 1999.

Ford, Trevor. *Trevor Ford in Conversation with Ron Jones.* Recorded November 3, 2000. Wales Video Archives — in conjunction with the National Library of Wales, Cardiff, 2000.

Kerner, Johannes B. *Interview with Robert Hoyzer.* ZDF — Kulissen Germany. February 9, 2005.

McKeown, Bob. *The Fix Is In.* The Fifth Estate. Canadian Broadcasting Corporation, Toronto, 1989.

Meng, Wang. "Patrick on Taboo Topics: My Rise in Soccer." *The New Paper,* April 7, 2003: electronic edition.

Montague, James. *Soccer's Year Zero: How Match-Fixing Ruined The Beautiful Game.* CNN Television, August 2011.

Rocksen, Andreas and Jespersen, Soren Steen. *Dream Catchers. The Beautiful Game.* TV 2 Danish Television, Denmark-Sweden Co-production. June 2004.

Sayles, John. *Eight Men Out.* Orion Pictures Distributor, USA. 1988.

Van den Abeele, Chris, Dupain, Eric, Straemans, Wim, van de Weghe, Tom and Dechamps, Kris. *Tackling the Mafia.* Panorama. Brussels. *VRT* Belgium, 5 February, 2006.

## CONFERENCE PROCEEDINGS

Abell, Peter. "Causality, and Low Frequency Complex Events: The Role of Comparative Narratives." *ISA Conference.* Montreal, Canada, 1998.

Breen, Richard. "Formal Theory in the Social Sciences." *University of Oxford, Social Science lecture,* 2005.

Cancio, Miguel. "Sociología De La

Violencia En El Fútbol. La Defensa Del Juego Limpio: De La Ideología Proclamada Del Juego Limpio a La Practica Real, a Su Aplicación Frente a Los Hooligans De Arriba Y Abajo, a Los Hooligans Mediáticos Y De Todo Tipo, Es Decir, Frente a La Violencia Primaria Y Secundaria, a Los Abusos, Maltratos, Acosos Físicos, Verbales, Psicológicos Y Morales." La violencia en el fútbol. Universidad de Navarra: Internet edition, 2002.

Dew-Becker, Ian and Gordon, Robert J. "Where did the Productivity Growth Go? Inflation Dynamics and the Distribution of Income." *Brookings Panel on Economic Activities.* Washington D.C. 2:2005.

Fernandez, Moores Ezequiel. "The Magic in Brazil Soccer Corruption." *Play the Game: Organised Crime and Sport. Copenhagen, Denmark,* 2002.

Hill, Declan. "Organised Crime in Ice Hockey." *Play the Game. Copenhagen, Denmark*: 2002.

Sanders, Teela. "Sex Work." *University of Oxford, Department of Sociology Seminar.* January 2005.

Vassort, Patrick. "En Marge de La Coupe du Monde — Le Cloaque Mafieux du Football Mondial." *Maître de conférences — l'Université de Caen,* 2002.

## NEWSPAPER ARTICLES

For background, I used articles from newspapers and wire services in Australia, Belgium, Brazil, Bulgaria, Canada, China, Colombia, the Czech Republic, Denmark, England, Finland, France, Germany, Ghana, Ireland, Israel, Italy, Kenya, Lithuania, Malaysia, Poland, Russia, Scotland, Singapore, Slovakia, Spain, South Africa, Thailand, Turkey, the United States, and Vietnam. For brevity's sake, I have listed only the articles that were used directly, in the Notes section.

# INDEX

## A



## B

## C

## D



## E

## Q



## R

## T



## U

Printed in Germany
by Amazon Distribution
GmbH, Leipzig